Tales of Western Inspiration and Indian Karma

By

Dilip K. Datta

Tales of Western Inspiration and Indian Karma

By

Dilip K. Datta

Originals
Delhi

First Published 2005
Reprinted (With Additions) 2009

ISBN 978-81-8454-090-1

Published by
Originals
A-6, Nimri Commercial Centre,
Ashok Vihar Phase-IV, Delhi-110052
Phones: 27302453
e-mail: info@Lppindia.com
url: www.Lppindia.com

Printed at
D K Fine Art Press P Ltd.
Delhi-110052

To

Kendall, Katie and Zachery
of Geneva, Switzerland
Arjun, Aditya and Luit of Guwahati, India
Caroline of Cincinnati, Ohio
Swapnav and Akanksha of Dallas, Texas

"Avoiding all narrowness of thought or class or creed with charity towards all, let students and staff remember that education is only of value as it leads to greater service to mankind, that narrowly pursued it produces but Dead sea fruit of disappointment and embitterment."

Frederick W. Sudmersen

Table of Contents

Table of Contents

Preface

India's Northeast now consists of seven small states: Arunachal, Nagaland, Manipur, Mizoram, Tripura, Meghalaya, and Assam. The mighty Himalayan range and its subranges dominate the landscape of this region. The mighty river Brahmaputra, fed by the melting ice of the Himalayas and the monsoon rain, runs first eastward and then drops south onto this region and begins its westward journey towards the Bay of Bengal. On its westward journey Brahmaputra, which literally means the son of the Creator Brahma, determines the destiny of a narrow valley and its people. Before entering the Bay of Bengal Brahmaputra is joined by river Barak from the southern part of the region. Assam includes the Brahmaputra valley, the Barak valley, and some of the hills surrounding these valleys. The British had incorporated these regions to the British Empire only in the nineteenth century and had administered them as a single province under the name 'Assam'. Before the advent of the British, this region was never part of any empire ruled from Delhi or Calcutta. This was because Assam was ruled by the powerful Ahom monarchs from the twelfth century. For six hundred years, the Ahoms thwarted all attempts by the Delhi and Calcutta rulers to subjugate them. Failing to establish any foothold in the Brahmaputra valley, the central rulers of Delhi could never make any inroads into the neighboring hill areas. So, the rainforests of this region with its teeming wildlife, the exotic hill-tribes, and its hundreds of rivers remained undisturbed for centuries. In the early part of the nineteenth century, the Ahoms were uprooted and Assam was plundered by the Burmese. The British finally drove the Burmese out and brought the present Assam under its fold in 1826. Later, they slowly added the neighboring hill regions.

In the early part of the British rule, westerners did not have any interest in Assam excepting some adventurers who sought glory by discovering the source of the Brahmaputra river.[1] Even the rest of India regarded the Northeast as a region outside the pale of Hindu civilization. Things changed, however, when tea was discovered (some time before 1830) in the hills of Assam, and the American Baptist Mission decided to send missionaries to Assam.

---

[1] Charles Allen, in A Mountain in Tibet, gives a lively account of the early British adventurers in the Northeast region of India.

In 1835, the British government sent a brilliant young scientist, William Griffith, to explore the possibility of growing tea in the region. The American Baptist Mission sent an energetic young linguist, Nathan Brown, and his enlightened wife, Eliza Brown, to Assam. The arrival of those great souls in the region were epoch-making. In the subsequent years, life in the Northeast changed completely. Visibly, the tea industry flourished in Assam, and Christianity found a foothold in the region. But the civilization of the valley changed in more ways than was visible. The norm of a good life among the inhabitants of the region took a new shape. Griffith, the Browns, and others like them, sparked the natives with a new zeal for learning which changed the very character of the people in the Northeast. Those changes are perhaps more pronounced in the field of education than in any other area.

The stories of that transformation form the subject matter of this book. I am intimately connected with the process of that transformation because my father Phanidhar Datta was actively associated with the founding of the first private college, the first Girls' College, and, above all, in building the first university in the region. So, this is partly the story of my father as well. In addition, my ancestors were closely connected with the tea-industry. My grandfather worked in a tea plantation for twenty years and my father's elder brother for thirty-five years. Even now many of my relatives are involved with the tea-industry. My brother-in-law, Dip Phookan, rose from an assistant manager to the rank of the Superintendent of a British Company and later retired as the Managing Director of Assam Government Tea Corporation. My nephew is the area Manager of an European tea-trading company, and so on. Nevertheless, the major part of this book is based on authentic, well-documented historical accounts. I have freely borrowed materials from several of the books mentioned in the bibliography.

Another part of the book is a contemporary history about which I have direct knowledge of or have supporting evidence for. The contemporary history is based on articles or items appearing in newspapers or newsmagazines of Assam.

I have supplemented the contemporary history with a large amount of oral histories of eye-witnesses. Mention should be made of the following persons: Jogneswar Sharma, one of the founder professors of JB College, Dandeswar Gogoi, a former professor of Cotton College, Binanda Barua, a former President of the Assamese Literary Society, and my father's elder brother Nanda Datta.

In addition to oral history, I have reconstructed certain incidents based on the recollection of my aunt Aikon (Phanidhar Datta's younger sister), who left her abusive husband a few years after her marriage in the early 1930's and lived most of her 93 year long life in Jorhat. She was a close companion of my paternal grandmother and heard everything about her father (Dandiram) and her grandfather (Baluram). I have been given a good account of the life of Baluram and his last days in the tea garden by my aunt Aikon. It is from aunt Aikon that I heard the details of Baluram's association with an Englishman, his work at Sadiya, and about the book burning incident that are described in this book.

Historically, it is true that the British scientist Griffith was met by representatives of the then king of Assam Purandar Singh on the banks of river Brahmaputra near Jorhat. King Purandar also gave him food, servants and other supplies. The stories of Parboti, Khamti damsel Joni, Yong, are documented in the *Whole World Kin*. I have used Baluram to bring their stories to light without distorting the historical character or the historical events. The stories of Runga and Supohi, the Brahmin, and the wives of Mr. Silmon and Mr. Ward are based on problems and situations of the time—the connected events are historically true. Those tales are based on true accounts of conditions existing at that time. Everything about Dandiram's education, his marriage to Damayanti, his life at the tea-garden, his decision to leave the tea garden to educate Phanidhar are true accounts given by Phanidhar Datta, his brother Nanda and his sisters. The bet between Mr. Silmon and Mr. Ward is also true and was narrated by Mr. Silmon to Phanidhar Datta when the latter went to the former seeking financial assistance to pursue higher studies. Mr. Silmon had also mentioned the feelings of their wives at the time. Here, I have tried to reconstruct their possible conversations on the basis of my knowledge about the sorrows and sufferings of the European wives of tea-planters that persist to this day. They have been inserted to bring alive the troubled conditions of the time.

Of course, my main concern is 'Education', especially the education of children. Therefore, this history, these biographies and this fiction all evolve around the search for what we can or should do to educate our children. To get an answer the reader will have to go through these pages.

Dilip K. Datta

Kingston, RI, USA

Acknowledgements

My grandmother, my mother, my father's elder brother, my aunt and many others who helped me to write this book have since returned to the abode of eternal bliss. I owe their memory a debt of gratitude. Among the dead, I am indebted to my father's friends Binanda Barua, Jogneswar Sharma, and Dandeswar Gogoi for all the hours they spent with me telling me some of the stories in this book. I am also indebted to Rev. Richard G. Beers, a former missionary to Assam, and Rev. George Peck, a former President of Andover Newton Theological School and a former Principal of Eastern Theological College, Jorhat, Assam for the insight and information they gave me about the lives and works of the American missionaries in Assam.

Now to the living persons and institutions that helped my research, I would like to thank George Gillespie, who gave me copies of his publications on American missionaries in Assam; Miss Diana Yount, the librarian of Andover Newton for assisting me with the Bronson papers; the Williams College Library which houses the Nathan Brown Memorial Collection; the University of Rhode Island Library for making some of the rare books available to me through its Inter Library Loan Scheme.

I would like to thank my friend Richard Neuse, who had high school education in England and who for 47 years taught English at University of Rhode Island, for helping me to correct inaccuracies and to improve the contents of the book. My thanks to Dr. Laura Bora and Dr. Sanjib Baruah for reading the manuscript and offering valuable suggestions.

Special thanks to June Dean for typesetting the manuscript from my somewhat terrible handwriting, and to Andrea Pisani who corrected the first set of proofs.

Many thanks to Dr. Satyendra Nath Das of Lutheran Medical Center, Brooklyn, NY for providing the artistic portrayals of a young man's resolve to acquire learning and of a founding professor of JB College. My thanks are also to Sukanya Basu, a math student with artistic talent for redrawing the sketches of Sibasagar temple and Moored To A Brahmaputra Sandbank from old on the spot sketches by Nathan Brown.

I would like to thank my son Darik Datta for helping me with the scanning works and for all the technical assistance in making the manuscript ready for the publisher. I am also fortunate to get the editorial services of Atreyee Phukan, who is born in Assam and who helped me with the manuscript while working towards a doctorate degree in Comparative literature at Rutgers University. My special thanks to Atreyee Phukan whose help and enthusiasm enabled me to complete this book. Dr. Atreyee Phukan is at present teaching at Sandiego University, California.

I am also grateful to Swami Yogatamananda, the Minister at Vedanta Society of Providence for bringing to my notice the details of Swami Vivekananda's comments about his meeting with Sir Henry Cotton, a major character of this book.

Introduction

Some men are destined to deliver—deliver something good to society. They may do so by pursuing knowledge, they may do so by showing a righteous path to live, or they may do so by helping others become decent human beings. The activities of these men of destiny are marked by a deep commitment to doing good for others. They usually do so in humble ways that often energize the spirit of others and inspire others to find new meaning in life. Like monsoon clouds, these men often rise in distant places, but like rainwater, they flood the whole earth with inspiration and good karma. Some such men of destiny blessed Assam in the northeast corner of India. This book is the true story of a British scientist, some British educators, a few American missionaries, and some British tea-planters who came to Assam after the British took over the administration of Assam in 1826. They awakened the spirit of the ravaged natives of Assam and sparked them with a new zeal which changed that corner of the world for all days to come. This is also the true story of others who were later born in Assam and were destined to deliver uplifting services to its people.

Where is Assam?

Assam is a tiny state in the northeast corner of India, which is jammed against the Himalayas and linked to the rest of India by a narrow corridor between Bhutan and Bangladesh. In natural resources and minerals, Assam is undoubtedly the richest state in India. Assam supplies 55 percent of the total tea produced in the country. Assam provides 60 percent of the country's crude oil. It supplies almost 100 percent of India's plywood needs. Over and above this, a considerable amount of coal, jute, timber, and 95 percent of the world's syllemnite are produced in Assam. About Rs. 3000 crores (nearly $3 billion) worth of goods are pumped into the rest of India by Assam every year.

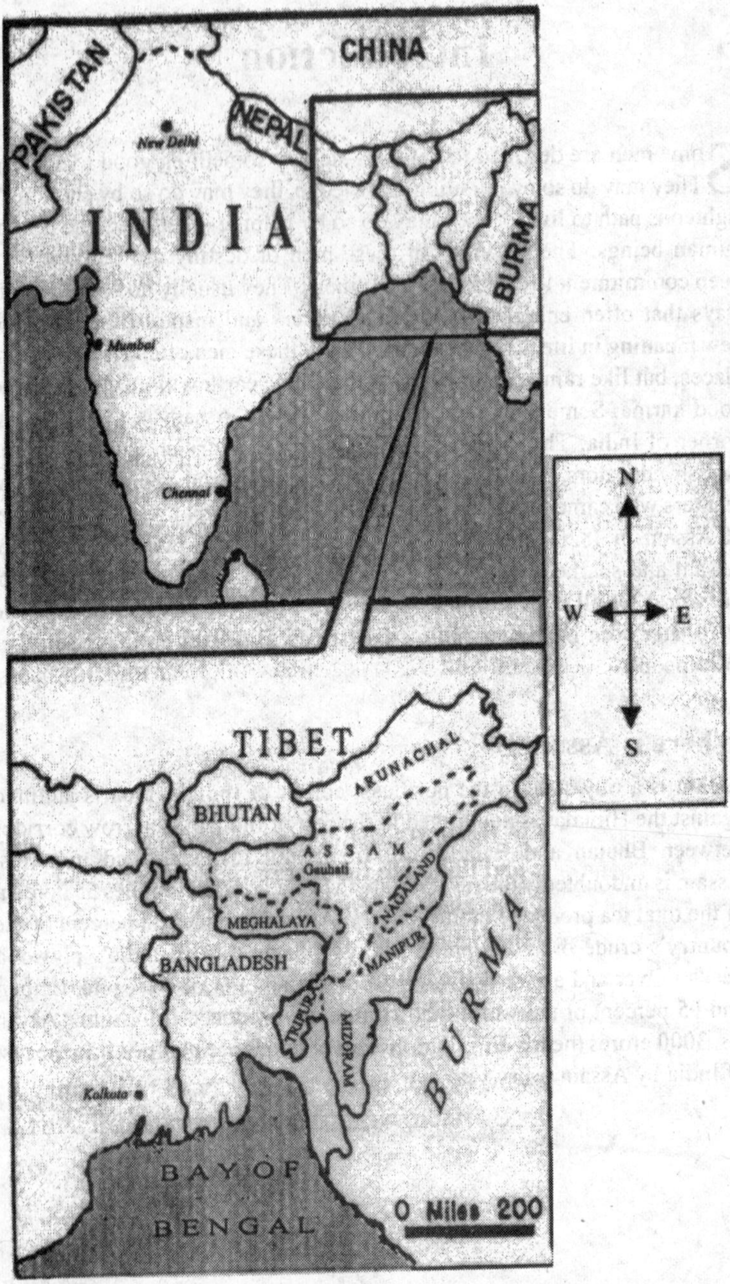

A Historical Perspective of Assam

Assam's early history has three phases. The first phase started around 1500 BC, when Assam was known as Pragjyotish. The second phase began around the fourth century AD when it was known as Kamarupa. According to the sixth century Chinese traveler Hieuen-Tsang, Kamarupa was a flourishing kingdom ruled by a powerful Hindu king, and its inhabitants were mostly Hindus. Around the twelfth century, Kamarupa was divided into small independent kingdoms before its disappearance into history. The third phase started about this time and Kamarupa entered a new era under an altogether different name.

Between 1215 AD to 1228 AD, Sukapha, a Shan, crossed the hills from Burma and entered the plains. For forty years, he moved with skill and wisdom to lay strong foundations for a powerful kingdom. Sukapha, his fellow Shans, and their descendents came to be known as Ahoms and their kingdom was known as `Asom' or `Assam'. The Ahom dynasty, founded by Sukapha, ruled Assam for the next six centuries. Under the Ahoms, Assam managed to retain its independence from the successive mediaeval empires, ruled from Delhi, until the nineteenth century. In the early part of the nineteenth century, the Ahom dynasty fell apart due to internal strife. In the second decade of that century, the Burmese conquered and plundered Assam. Assam came under British rule in 1826, when the latter defeated the Burmese. Our story has its roots in the strife-torn days of the early nineteenth century. Following is a chronology of events during that period:

1810 Chandrakanta Singh, a child, becomes king of Assam and a power struggle begins between the prime minister or Burha Gohain, and Badan Chandra, the chief administrator of the western part of the kingdom.

1816 The Burha Gohain attempts to remove Badan Chandra. Badan Chandra flees to Burma and gets help from the Burmese.

The Burmese invade Assam. The Burha Gohain commits suicide. The Burmese retain Chandrakanta as king but make Badan Chandra the Prime Minister.

1817 Badan Chandra is assassinated. The son of Burha Gohain enters Jorhat and sets Brajanath on the throne. His son Purandar Singh soon replaces Brajanath because Brajanath's physical deformities[2] make him ineligible. Chandrakanta flees from the capital.

---

2. The Ahoms had a rule that any person missing a limb from birth or later in battlefield or by accident could not be a king. Therefore many aspirants or usurpers would cut an ear or a finger of his rivals just to make them ineligible for the throne.

1818 The Burmese invade Assam again and restore Chandrakanta as the nominal ruler.

The Burmese plunder the whole kingdom.

British chase the Burmese out and take over the administration of Assam.

The British Government put Purandar Singh as the ruler of whole of Upper Assam, except Sadiya and the Matak country.

1838 The British finally deposes Purandar Singh and places his territories under the direct administration of British officers. This brings the reign of the Ahoms to an end.

Who Are the Assamese?

The Europeans coined the words 'Assam' and 'Assamese' which are both of Hindustani origin. The Moslem rulers of India applied the word 'sham' or 'shan' to the people of Tai family who ruled the Assam valley from the 12th century till the beginning of the 19th century. It is said that the Moslem rulers of Bengal used the term 'Asham ki Mulk' (the land of the shams) to describe the countries beyond their eastern frontiers. Even Mughal historians used the term Mulk-i-Asham. 'Asham' is the plural form of 'Sham'.[3]

Picking their cue from the Mughals, the early Europeans that came to India used words sounding somewhat like 'Asham' to describe the same region. Thus 'Assam' and 'Assamers' are mentioned in the 1675 Dutch book *Vervarelijke schipbreuk van 't oost-indisch jacht Ter schelling, onder het landt Bengale - en voorts in 't velt-leger van den Grooten Mogol, tot in 't koninkgrijk van Assam landwaerts opgevoert zijn* .. by van der Heijden, Frans, and Willem Kunst. The book details the experiences of Dutch sailors who came ashore in Bengal after their boat *Ter Schelling* was shipwrecked. The Dutch sailors were conscripted into the Mughal army and sent to fight against Assam. The book is based on the diary of one of the sailors, van der Heijden. A more recent version of the book is by O. de Jong with the title *Schipbreuk in Bangalen*, Lanasta, Uitgeverij, The Netherlands, 2006. The English sailor Thomas Bowrey (circa 1650 - 1713) wrote that by Mir Jumla's

3. In the Hindustani language a plural is often indicated by putting the prefix 'A' in front of a word: khabar (one news item) - akhbar (many news, a newspaper), sabab (furniture) - asbab (furnitures), mula (a courtesan) - amula (courtesans), samar (a fruit) - asmar (fruits). This is perhaps an Arabic influence.

death, "they lost the best of Nabob, the kingdom of Acham, and by consequence many other privileges." (*Anglo-Assamese Relations* 61, hereafter referred to as AAR).

William Hedges wrote about his interview with Nawab Shaista Khan at Dacca on October 29 (1682) that the Nawab was, "very busy in despatching and vesting diverse principal officers sent with all possible diligence with recruits for their army lately overthrown in Asham and Silhet, two large plentiful countries." (AAR 62).

Assam also finds mention in stories about Clara, a baby rhino captured in Assam in 1738. The baby rhino was presented to the then Director of Dutch East India Company and sent to the Netherlands.

By September 1759, the English were using the word Assam instead of `Asham' or 'Acham'. For example, Paul Richard Pearkes writes to a friend in England some time in 1759, 'I am at present on my voyage to Assam, a country that only two Europeans have visited besides myself, and where a trade may, I am certain, be carried on greatly to the advantage of the company.'

Since the Europeans did not really have many contacts with the people of Assam in those days, it is doubtful that people like Pearkes, Bowrey or Hedges got the name from the native people of Assam, who used the word 'Asom' or 'Ahom' to describe their land.

'Assam' thus means the land of the Shans as applied to the 'Ahoms', as well as to all the sub-races of the Tai family or tribes of other Mongoloid stock inhabiting the regions. Their Mongolian features marked the Assamese or the people of Assam. Even present day Assamese who claim Aryan or Dravidian descent, bear distinct Mongolian features. It is believed that mostly Dravidian tribes once occupied Assam. Many of these Dravidians came from central and south India when the Aryans coming into India from the Northwest pushed them eastward. In due course of time, these Dravidians in Assam were assimilated by various Mongolian tribes, who came from China and Western Asia. It has been suggested that certain Aryan tribes must have found their way into Assam long before the epic *Mahabharata* began to be composed. In the *Mahabharata*, we find references to powerful non-Aryan kings in Assam like Bhagadatta, Hirimba, and of Aryan kings like Bhismak. Then the *Vishnu Purana* (written circa 1725 AD) and the *Srimad Bhagavatam* also refer to other non-Aryan kings of Assam like Ban and Narakasur.

The process of Aryanization of Assam began long before the epic period, so that by the time Hieuen-Tsang came to Assam in the sixth century, Assam was ruled by a Hindu king and the people of Assam were mostly Hindus. Even the epics describe marriages of Aryan Bhima with Hirimba of Assam, Aryan Aniruddha with Usha of Assam, and Aryan Arjuna with Chitrangada of Manipur.

Thus, Rev. P.H. Moore makes the correct observations in 1886 when he says: "Take an Aryan substratum, mingle with it a Mongolian element from the north; then with this mixture a Dravidian element from the west; add to this an element whose quality and quantity are both unknown; once more mingle with this a strong element from the Shan race; allow many centuries for the process of commingling; give now a sprinkling of Burmese; keep in mind that each one of these elements is preserved in every degree of change from absolute purity to the most thorough adulteration; take into account on the one hand a fluctuating immigration not hitherto mentioned, and on the other the influence of the tribes on the hill sides that have preserved their aboriginal qualities in various degrees of purity, and you have people of the plains of Assam."[4]

In the nineteenth century, the growth of the tea industry in Assam necessitated the import of laborers from other parts of India. People from such tribes as Kols, Dangars from central India and others from Madras, Bengal and Orissa were brought to Assam. By and by these people settled in Assam and their descendents became an integral part of the Assamese community. In recent years, many Bengalis (both Hindus and Moslems), Marwaris, Sikhs, Nepalies, Biharis, and others have assimilated into the Assamese society through marriage or by accepting Assamese or a native tribal language of Assam as their own.[5]

---

[4] *The Assam Mission of The American Baptist Missionary Union: Papers and Discussions of the Jubilee Conference held in Nowgong, December 18-29, 1886,* hereafter referred to as *ABM 7*.

[5] To learn about the present day Assamese, see Sanjib Baruah, *India Against Itself: Assam and the Politics of Nationality*, University of Pennsylvania Press, Philadelphia, 1991.

William Griffith(1810 – 1844)

Drawn on stone by Edward Morton from a Daguerreotype

Courtesy: Journals of Travels in Assam

1
The British Scientist William Griffith Kindles a Spark for Knowledge

Assam was under Burmese occupation from about 1810. The Burmese committed the most atrocious barbarities and carried off into slavery 30,000 Assamese. The British finally drove the Burmese out of Assam by 1823. The British decided to administer Assam (with the exception of two tracts in Sadiya and Matak) as a British province. Its management was entrusted in November 1823 to David Scott. At his request, the administration of Upper Assam was entrusted first to Colonel Cooper and afterwards, in 1823, to Captain Newville.

When the British assumed charge of Assam, the country was in near-famine condition. The small remnant of the Assamese, who survived the Burmese carnage, were in total despair. They had not cultivated their land for years and were living virtually on whatever grew in the jungles. Their spirits were drained beyond repair. So, the only thing they could do was to heave a sigh of relief to see the end of the most brutal oppression and harassment.

During the Ahom rule, the whole male population between the ages of fifteen and fifty were liable to render service to the State. The nobles, priests and persons of high caste and their slaves were exempt from that service. The males at the service of the state were known as paiks, or foot soldiers, a term which was formerly very common in Bengal where, for instance, it was applied to the guards who surrounded the palace of the independent Muhammadan kings. The paiks were organized into small groups called 'goots'. A goot originally contained four paiks, but in the reign of Rajeswar Singh the number was reduced to three in Upper Assam. One member of each goot was obliged to be present, in rotation for such work as might be required of him, and, during his absence from home, the other members were expected to cultivate his land and keep him supplied with food. In times of peace, it was the custom to employ the paiks on public works. That is how the enormous tanks and the high embanked roads of Upper Assam came into existence. When war broke out, two members of a 'goot,' or even three, might be called on to attend at the same time.

Fortunately, the paik system always brought brothers together. Since one brother had to look after the family when the other was away serving the king, brothers depended on each other. They were held together by a deep sense of commitment to one another. Even when the British government forced them out of their bondage, the brothers remained bound to each other by strong ties. Every one of them was like prince Bharat, faithfully carrying on his duties to his brother and the duties that fell upon his shoulder because of the absent brother. The brothers put their resources together to build their lives anew and give whatever they could to bring up their children. This task, however, was not easy.

The first tale of inspiration concerns a paik named Baluram. Baluram was born in Jorhat soon after the British had acquired Assam in 1826. Baluram's father and his only surviving brother came back to their village in Jorhat (then called Bahatia village or the village of laborers). The British threw the Burmese out but introduced opium into Assam. It is believed that opium was introduced into Assam by the British troops of Captain Welsh in around 1792. The British government, under the pretext of helping the people to give up the habit of cultivating and using opium, started a monopolistic trade of opium. British traders flourished, and, in a short period of time, three-fourths of the population were opium eaters. As reported in the Mill's report of 1853, women and children alike used the drug. Many concerned officials thus felt that, "something should be done to check the immoderate use of the drug, and rescue at least the rising generation from indulgence in a luxury which destroys the constitution, enfeebles the mind, and paralyzes industry; moreover, the indulgence has been so abused as to cause the Ryot to disregard the culture of the more valuable products, and to take large advances to be repaid in opium which, owing to the uncertainty of the seasons, oftentimes entails great loss, and establishes a demoralizing system of gambling." (Mill's Report 19).

Baluram, who was born in those days of turmoil (sometime around 1824), spent his childhood in despair and hopelessness. The Assamese society of that period was completely devoid of spirit, purpose, or direction. The British brought peace but that peace could not inspire the people of Assam. Kids like Baluram became free of the bondage to serve the king but there was no role or direction for their lives. The small plot of land that they got to keep was barely enough to support the family. They had no means to acquire cash. There were no schools for their education. In addition, there were no facilities for vocational training, and, since they were not artisans, they did not inherit any traditional training in some craft. So, Baluram grew up in that environment of inactivity, uncertainty, and aimlessness. He was illiterate and untrained for any job except helping his father in the field. Their only pleasure was looking after the cows and imitating the role of Krishna, the cowboy God of Vaishnavism. Singing the pastime songs of Lord Krishna, dancing or rehearsing for the drama that they would perform in the village namghar (prayer house) was their greatest pleasure. The environment was perfect for the Vaishnab leaders to come and sow the seeds of "love for Krishna" and this they did. In each village where the paiks got to live, the Vaishnab leaders came and organized the villagers to build their lives according to Vaishnab principles. This was a blessing because it gave new meaning to their lives and a foundation upon which to build their cultural lives. But it could not get them out of poverty or protect them from exploitation by the rich, the powerful, and often by the religious leaders themselves.

The British created some higher classes of people by selecting some men from the upper caste or from the high dignitaries of the Ahom king. Those men were appointed as tax collectors or as administrators or as police officers. These higher classes showed no desire whatever to uplift the common people. This was observed by Mills as can be inferred from comments like, "They show no desire whatever to see the rising generation educated or made wiser than themselves; in fact, I believe if the higher classes could prevent the Assamese youth being educated, they would not hesitate to do so. The surpineness and indifference of the most influential men in the District, the Mouzahdars, can scarce be conceived, except by those in personal and constant intercourse with them." (Mill's report, 27).

The lack of opportunities and motivation to improve their conditions gradually led to a people with a death-like inertia. The situation is described very well by an American missionary, A.H. Danforth (1817 – 1864), who was in Assam from 1848 to 1858, "The want of an enterprising and impulsive spirit is everywhere seen, and until this monotony is broken up by drawing the attention of the natives to the advantages of commerce, and the blessings which honest industry is certain to secure, little can be hoped from the Province. I think I speak advisedly when I say that the taxes are almost the only motive that now moves the great mass of the people to put forth a single effort beyond what is required for the actual necessities of life. To find an antidote for this death-like inertia, the means for arousing the slumbering energies of a people who have the natural ability for greatly improving their own condition, developing the resources of the country and adding materially to its revenue, is a question alike interesting to the statesman and the philanthropist. Nor are we without some principle on which to operate. The self-interest of every native is a motive sufficiently strong, when the means of securing domestic comfort and wealth are laid open before him and shown to be within his reach, to awaken a spirit of enterprise and call forth his activity. That education can do much toward unfolding the bright prospects of affluence is perfectly evident both from history and the nature of the case." (Mill's report, 90 – 92).

Danforth did not stop at describing a desperate situation. He also gave some concrete suggestions to energize the Assamese. His formula was education. In the same letter, quoted above, he suggested, "Another thing which seems to me essential to the welfare of the schools, and which I have in part anticipated is, that the exact sciences should be taught in Vernacular. The great object of those studies is to excite inquiry, call out the reasoning powers, and develop and discipline the mind; such knowledge should therefore be conveyed through the most natural channels of thought, so that the whole mind may be occupied with the subject matter untrammeled by the medium. To an ignorant, stupid and bigoted people like the Assamese, abstract studies are often difficult and unattractive even when communicated in the most common language; how much more so must it be when veiled in a foreign tongue." (Mill's report, 90-92).

A spark for knowledge and an education to uplift them from their world of ignorance had to come from elsewhere. For Baluram that spark came in the form of a brilliant young scientist named William Griffith. It happened in the manner detailed below.

In 1833, the whole of Upper Assam, except Sadiya and the Matak country was turned over to Purandar Singh. By a treaty entered into with him at the time of his installation, Purandar Singh was placed on the same footing as other protected princes; the entire civil administration was left in his hands, and his territory was secured from the attacks of hostile states on condition of his paying a yearly tribute of Rs. 50,000[6] out of an estimated revenue of Rs. 1,20,000. The British Government still maintained direct political relations with the Chief of Matak and it

[6] Rs. is abbreviation for Rupees, and rupee is the Indian unit of currency.

continued to keep a garrison and a Political Officer at Sadiya. Jorhat was made the capital of the new State, and the headquarters of the Political Agent. That arrangement did not work well. Purandar Singh was not able to install an efficient system of administration. As a matter of fact, owing to mismanagement and the general system of corruption, he was unable to collect enough revenue to meet the stipulated target. As a last resort, he oppressed his subjects, which made his rule very distasteful to the bulk of the population.

In 1836, when Baluram was about 12 years old, his father took him to work for the household of the king. Soon afterwards, Captain Mathie, the British administrator in the neighboring Darrang province, sent a message that a group of Englishmen were proceeding towards Sadiya. King Purandar Singh was directed to meet the group on the sands of the Brahmaputra river and supply him with necessary food, supplies, men, and equipment. The king sent them a good amount of rice, lentils, oil, vegetables, and other foodstuff. The king also sent a few men and Baluram to wait upon the Englishman. The Englishman was William Griffith.[7] He was sent to investigate the possibility of growing tea in Assam.

William Griffith took Baluram and two other youths from Jorhat to help him. It turned out to be a matter of good fortune for Baluram to accompany a great scientist like Griffith and to watch him conduct a very scientific study of Assam. Griffith studied the flora and fauna of Assam with deep interest. Every leaf, every fruit, and every flower of a newly found tree or plant would excite Griffith. He collected them carefully, measured them, weighed them, drew beautiful pictures of them and tried to gather from the natives as much information as possible. Even though he was incessantly after plants, on occasion, he would even pick up certain kinds of fish, snakes and birds and study them. Day and night he would write in his notebook about the things he saw or collected. Once they reached Sadiya, they set up a base camp from which every morning Griffith, with one or two associates, Baluram, and few other helpers, would venture out to the Mishime, Khamti, and Singpho territories to collect tea plants or anything looking like a tea plant.

Tea was a favorite drink of the Singphos. They would pick the freshly sprung tea leaves and would dry them on a big iron pan heated by a low fire. While drying, they would roll the leaves by hand. Then they would dry them in the sun for about three days. Some of them would dry them in the sun and moisten them in the dew for three days. Then they would

---

[7] See Appendix A for details of William Griffith's life and work.

pack the tea leaves in bamboo cans and pack it tight by hammering. The result was hard teacakes. Later on they would take out these cakes, cut small pieces, boil them in water and drink the hot water.

Baluram's party went to Sadiya via Negherijan and Sadiya. All along the way Griffith drank Singpho style black tea with the natives. Baluram, however, stayed away from tea because he regarded tea to be as bad as opium. He had seen from his childhood how people in Jorhat were going downhill by taking opium. Even in his own village, he saw how both men and women were going crazy after opium.

The opium eaters would even give up their meals to take their daily dose of opium, and, if they did not get their opium they could not do anything either physical or mental. Baluram had also seen how some opium eaters became weak and disabled like very old people and died very young. Baluram's father always told him "Do whatever you want but never put opium in your mouth no matter how sick you are." Baluram's mother told him, "I think tea is as bad as opium, so don't drink tea either."

Alone and away from home, Baluram was homesick but he felt that if he followed his father's advice, he would be free of trouble. He also knew that his mother was always right. He always did whatever she told him to do. "Before you go outdoors, before you go to bed or at times of distress always remember to chant—Ram, Krishna Prabhu—several times, and remember we will always pray for your well being and wait for your safe return." Not being able to decide what was right and what was wrong, Baluram steadfastly obeyed his parents' advice. He felt the strength of his character when he was able to do so.

One day Griffith offered him a little bowl of tea. In fear, Baluram ran away. Griffith assured him that tea was not a bad thing but a medicine. Baluram remembered what his father had replied when a friend of his father was persuading him to share a little bit of opium. So, he boldly told Griffith, "I am not sick, so I do not need any medicine." An associate of Griffith supported Baluram's stand, telling Griffith that people introduced opium among the Assamese as a medicine. Realizing Baluram's apprehension, Griffith told Baluram, "Right, don't take opium, don't drink tea and never take any medicine when you have no ailment." Then, putting his hand on Baluram's shoulder, Griffith, almost with tearful eyes, told Baluram, "But my dear little friend, I am really suffering from many ailments and I really have to take a lot of medicine." Baluram looked at Griffith with piercing eyes and tried to understand the man. He suddenly realized that Griffith was not like any other man he had seen or met before. He had a different spark, a different strength and he appeared to be fearlessly fighting a battle. At that time, Baluram did not realize that a great scientist like Griffith had never before set foot on Assam's soil. Griffith's white skin or blue eyes did not matter to him anymore; they were normal to him but the personality of Griffith appeared to him to be very exceptional. Griffith continued,

> I have to take medicine so that I can live a little longer and enrich man's knowledge. These plants you see are my friends. They are your friends too. We live on the same planet, we need them very much. We must know them well. I want to find out about all the trees and plants in this beautiful Brahmaputra valley and these gorgeous mountains. Then I want to pass that knowledge to the rest of the world. That is called science. We must always advance scientific knowledge a step further. That's why I have come here in spite of my ill health, and that is why I have to take medicine. I have to drink tea. I am not like Captain Bruce; he destroyed many tea plants to make some money. Of course, the East India Company is also after money. I have not come here for money but for science. Opium, tea, and money are bad things—men get addicted to them. Science and education are good things. You must teach your people that opium, tea, and money—no, never, we don't need them. Science and education—yes, we always need them, we must sacrifice everything for them.

All of a sudden Baluram felt deep respect for Griffith and felt that Griffith was like his father. He felt secure that Griffith, like his father, wished him well. Griffith worked for the betterment of everybody around him just like Baluram's father always worked for the betterment of his village and his community. Baluram's loneliness and homesickness disappeared and he felt very much at home with Griffith.

After travelling along the banks of Dihing river through the Matak kingdom, Griffith's party reached as far as Tingrai and Makum. Then they went to Rungagara where Griffith had special conference with the Matak chief. The Matak Chief, Bor Senapati, as he was called, was a very independent and a very respectable man. Bor Senapati took special care of Griffith and his plants. As desired by Griffith, the chief even built a special house for Griffith's plant collection.

The Slate-house

In February, 1836, Griffith's party reached Sadiya. In Sadiya, Baluram met two other white families who were the families of the American missionaries Nathan Brown and Oliver Cutter. Baluram thought those white men, like Griffith, also would be interested in plants, flowers, animals, birds, and fishes. They were, but in a different way. They would point to something and would try to get the name of the object from a native tongue and then they would repeat it to themselves till they could say it almost like natives. At times they would closely look at the lips, the movement of the tongue when a native was speaking, and would even sketch the pictures of the mouth or position of the lips.

Baluram soon realized that Brown, Cutter, and their wives were interested in learning the Assamese, the Khamti and the Singpho languages for they would recite the native words day and night. Further, they would not roam around in the forest like Griffith. Instead, they started building their own houses in Sadiya. To build their houses they used native people and built their houses very much like an Assamese house. Of all the things about Brown and Cutter Baluram was most surprised that while building their houses, and in their day to day life, they (Brown, Cutter and their wives) would join hands with the laborers. Whether digging a trench, whether cutting a tree, cutting bamboo, they were always joining hands with the laborers and sharing the work—this was something very strange because Baluram never saw an Assamese gentry work with the servants.

The Assamese gentry regarded it below their dignity to do anything that a paik would do. Their only job was to order and get everything done by the paiks, whom they often treated like slaves. In this regard, Brown and Cutter were even different from Griffith, who liked to be waited upon by his servants. His food had to be served, his clothes had to be cleaned and kept ready, his bed had to be made and even the water for his bath had to be brought by the servants and that too on time and the way he wanted. With Brown and Cutter nothing was like that. They had servants but the servants were like friends who helped them in their work and they shared all the work with the servants. The Assamese men of power and prestige regarded digging, plowing, cutting wood or carrying burdens as degrading employment. The high dignitaries of Assam would never dream of eating or drinking with their servants. So, it was shockingly surprising for Baluram to see Brown and Cutter, whom he knew to be superior to any native nobleman, join hands with the laborers and participate in the so called "degrading work". He even saw how Nathan Brown himself made an axe to cut wood.

To make an axe, Nathan Brown collected a few pieces of iron and softened them in fire. The softened metal was beaten out and ground into something that would cut down trees. Of course, there were plenty of trees and bamboo to build houses. Brown himself would go into the woods and cut down trees and make posts. The natives transported those posts by hand to the building spot. Brown constructed houses very much like the natives but made some improvements based on his experience in Burma. The supporting posts were firmly planted five or six feet deep, and stood several feet high above ground A bamboo floor is mounted on the posts and reed walls were tied. Nathan Brown grew up near the lime-kilns of Vermont and his observations there helped him to plaster the reed walls with a composition of which mud was the principal ingredient. Lime for whitewash was the next necessity. Brown taught the natives how to make a kiln and burn lime.

While the two Sahibs were busy constructing houses, their wives were busy teaching some native kids how to read and write. In the beginning, the boys and girls used to be apprehensive; they would come near the white ladies but would maintain a distance even though their curious eyes and feet used to follow the ladies wherever the ladies went.

After the houses were completed, they called one house the "Slate-house". In that house, Mrs. Brown would come and ring a bell every morning and the children would come running with their slates and clay chalks. The children were of all ages. The slate-house was ready in June, and by then the rainy weather set on. Griffith had no choice but to stay indoors. He stopped going out to the forests. Instead, he spent his time studying and organizing the plants he had collected. He was busy writing and sketching. So, there was very little work for Baluram. Therefore, Griffith willingly agreed when Baluram asked permission to go join Mrs. Brown's slate-house. Mrs. Brown was very happy to find one more willing youth for her school. In the beginning kids were not very willing to attend the Slate-house. Later on, the kids started liking the two ladies, Mrs. Brown and Mrs. Cutter, and started following their instructions.

To the youths who were willing to do something in life and who had the vision to realize that it was only through education that they could find meaning in life, Mrs. Brown's slate-house brought new hope and promise.

One day, a young Buddhist priest, sixteen or eighteen years of age, came to Mrs. Brown of his own accord, and offered to lay aside his sacred garments if she would teach him English. Mrs. Brown agreed and even promised to provide him with full support. The next day he set aside his garments and became a student. (It is known that he was later baptized as Elijah Hutchinson and he later became a schoolteacher at the mission. People from the far off town of Windsor, Vermont (USA), sent the money necessary to support him.) Another day, a girl named Louburi came to Mrs. Brown and begged her for a home. She said she was held slave and she had run away from her cruel master. Mrs. Brown took Louburi also under her charge. Slowly but surely, in that manner Mrs. Brown's slate-house became full. The children and the youths all started to read and write happily, and a new era dawned in Assam's world of education. By the time fall came and Griffith was ready to start his quest in the jungles, Baluram had learned both the English and the Assamese alphabets and was able to read Assamese quite well. He also came to know that Brown and Cutter were missionaries who had come to teach a new religion and a new religious book to the Assamese people.

Ronga and Supahi

In October, 1836, Griffith's party left Sadiya and spent some time looking around the Brahmakunda area. After that they went to the Mishmi kingdom. They did not find many tea plants in the Mishmi land. In the Mishimi village Jingsha (at a distance of two days march from Brahmakunda), they met an Assamese slave named Ronga.

Ronga was about twenty years old. He was a slave taken by the Mishmies but they treated him well. Of course, he had to work very hard the whole day. Baluram told Ronga about the Brown families, their slate-house, and how they were giving shelter to runaway slaves like Louburi. Baluram told Ronga how he could flee and go there. Ronga was not willing to do so.

Ronga told Baluram that he was a groom in waiting for a girl named Supahi. It was the custom among many tribes in that area that if a young man proposed to marry a girl, and her parents were willing, then he had to go and work in the household of her parents for about a year and perform certain tasks. After that, if the parents were satisfied that he would be able to manage a household with their daughter, and the girl accepted him, the two would be united. Ronga was working towards that goal with Supahi's parents. All that remained for Ronga to do was to supply two pigs and a certain amount of salt, after which he would be able to marry Supahi and live freely like a Mishmi in that village. Ronga did not want to run away leaving his sweetheart Supahi behind. He also informed Baluram that only a few days earlier he had caught two wild pigs and all he needed then was some salt. So, Ronga requested Baluram to help him get some salt from Griffith.

Salt was a rare commodity in the Mishmi villages. One day while

Griffith was applying salt to some boiled chicken, a Mishmi chief cursed his own fate saying, "See how unfortunate we are—the Sahib lavishly puts salt on boiled skins but we can't even get a drop of salt." Then many Mishmi also begged of Griffith, "Sahib, if you show us where we can find salt, then we will serve you as your slave all our lives, we will show you around all over the Mishmi land—just tell us where we can find salt." That's why Griffith was not surprised when Baluram told him about Ronga and the salt. Thanks to Griffith, Ronga was able to get all the salt he needed to win Supahi's hand in marriage. Ronga and Supahi were married while Griffith and Baluram were in Jingsha village.

Supahi's mother was also Assamese and she knew Ronga since his childhood. The infant Ronga and some of his relatives were hiding in a forest on the bank of the river Brahmaputra and near Jorhat when the Burmese were plundering Assam. They were able to arrange a boat to flee Jorhat. Supahi's grandparents lost their lives before they could reach the boat. Supahi's parents and Ronga's relatives were able to flee and settle in Sadiya. They could not find peace there either because even though Sadiya was part of the Ahom kingdom, it became a happy hunting ground for the Singpho, Khamti, Mishimi[8&9] and other tribes of the surrounding area when the Ahom kings became weakened. The tribes would frequently raid Sadiya, kill those who put up a fight, capture others and carry women and children away as slaves. Such a raid by the Khamtis orphaned Ronga. He was later sold to a Mishimi chief. Supahi's father had lost his life in a Mishimi raid. She and her mother were taken away from Sadiya and brought to Jingsha village, where a Mishimi man took her mother as his wife.

From Jingsha, Griffith's party could not go much farther into Mishmi country because of internal fights between two chiefs and invasion by the Lamas. It so happened that two chiefs of the Mizho and Digaru tribes had a feud that had its roots in a marriage settlement. The Mizho chief took help from the Lamas and killed about twenty men of the Digaru tribe to settle the score. However, fear and uneasiness prevailed for some time and nobody was willing to offer assistance to Griffith. Griffith also did not see much point in going deeper because he did not see tea plants in the Mishmi countries.

Griffith also realized that marriage settlements are serious business in those areas. So, he paid a visit to Ronga's in-laws and gave the old man

[8] See glossary to learn about these tribes in the northeast region

[9] See Glossary for information about these tribes.

some more salt. "Take this but don't disturb the young couple. I don't like to see troubles here. Leave them alone." Blessing the young couple, Griffith returned to Rungagarha to inspect the tea seedlings that he had marked there a year earlier. Unfortunately, Major Bruce got there before him and he had made them completely barren. In any case, Griffith was able to draw the following conclusion about tea plants, which proved very useful to the tea industry that spread in Assam in the following century. "My conviction is that the tea will not flourish in open sunshine; at any rate, subjection to this should be gradual. Further, the cutting the main stem is detrimental, not only inducing long shoots, but most probably weakening the flavor of the leaves. It appears to me to be highly desirable, that an intelligent superintendent should reside on the spot, and that he should at least be a good practical gardener, with some knowledge of the science also."

After spending a couple of months in Rungagarah, Griffith decided to proceed to Rangoon following the route by which the Burmese had invaded Assam. Baluram was given the choice to either go back to Jorhat and report to King Purandar Singh, or to accompany Griffith's party for a few more months. Baluram was having so much fun working for Griffith and watching him do all the things he had never seen anybody else do before that he decided to stay with Griffith's party. He chose to hike through the mountains and the jungles with the strange white man who sparked him to seek a new meaning in life and a new pursuit for knowledge.

From Sadiya they came to Namrup through many villages under Singpho and Khamti control. In every village they came through, they saw many Assamese slaves. Baluram advised every Assamese slave he met to run away and seek shelter at the slate-house in Sadiya. However, Griffith noticed that the Singphos and the Khamtis were taking to opium with a passion. He commented that in a few years those two tribes would be so weakened that the Assamese slaves would become not only free but also masters over them.

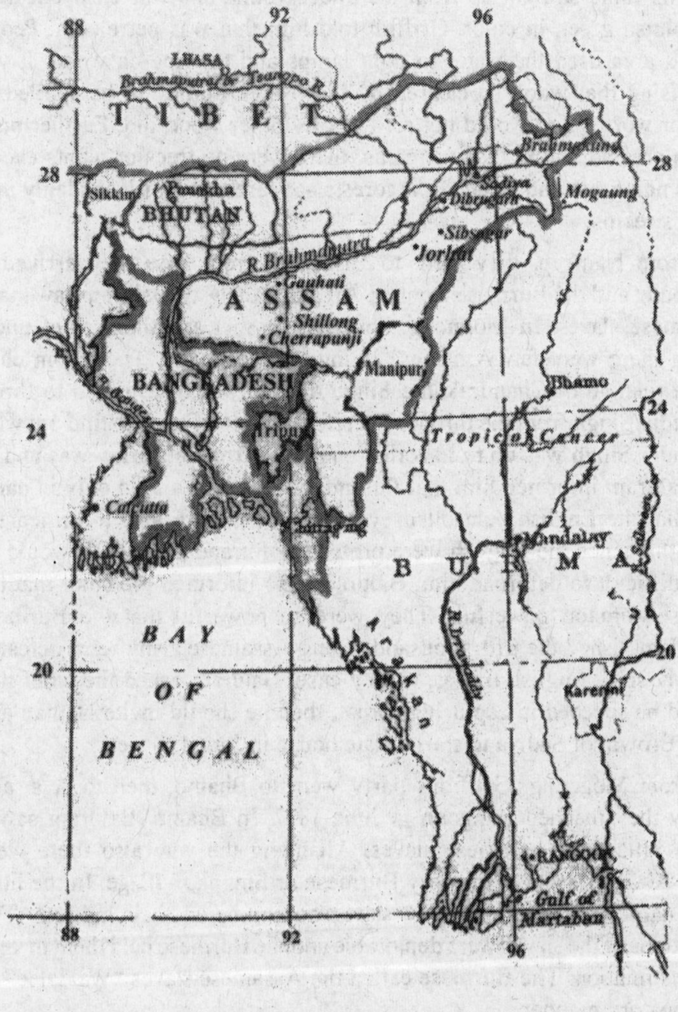

Old map showing the region covered by William Griffith during his tour. [The topography of the region changed considerably after the great earthquakes of 1897 and 1950.]

In Namrup, Baluram saw four strange streams. The water from those streams came straight up from the underground and was clear but thick and bluish green in color. Griffith told him that was petroleum. People in that area used the water to light lamps and to wipe on wood. It was surprising that wood so cleared by that water would not be spoiled by ants or worms and would not rot the way other wood did. Furthermore, in the area adjoining those streams, there were no trees or plants except thin small grass and weeds. The forests appeared to vanish suddenly near those streams.

From Namrup, they went to Bisa, and from Bisa they arrived at Mogoung and the Burmese frontier. All along the way, Baluram saw many Assamese slaves. In Moguong, however, he met an Ahom chief under whom there were few Assamese living independently. The Ahom chief was a relative of Chandrakanta Singh and he was determined to throw Purandar Singh from the throne. Therefore, the chief tried to find out what Purandar Singh was up to in Jorhat and how strong his army was and so on. Baluram informed him that Purandar Singh was a king only in name and that the English controlled everything. Baluram also informed the chief that since the English were protecting Purandar Singh, it would be very difficult to dethrone him. Baluram also informed the chief that the English were too powerful. They were so powerful that the Burmese who demolished the fifty thousand strong Assamese army were defeated by only sixty English troops. In any case, Baluram asked the chief that should he succeed in capturing Jorhat, then he should invite Nathan and Eliza Brown of Sadiya to start a slate house in Jorhat as well.

From Mogoung, Griffith's party went to Bhamo, then to Ava, and finally they reached Rangoon in June 1837. In Bhamo, Baluram saw a whole village of Assamese slaves. All along the way also there were many Assamese slaves in every Burmese or Singpho village. In the little town named Wulla-Khoon, the slaves outnumbered their masters. The conditions of the slaves were deplorable and the Burmese held them in very poor estimation. The Burmese called the Assamese slaves "Waidalee" in a derogatory manner.

From Rangoon, Griffith took Baluram to Calcutta. They left Calcutta on the 31st of August 1837 towards Assam via Dacca and the Khasi Hills, reaching Guwahati in mid-December. In Guwahati, Baluram was allowed to leave the party and return to Jorhat. On December 21, 1837, Griffith left Guwahati for Bhutan and Baluram proceeded towards Jorhat.

Eliza Whitney Brown (1807 – 1871)

Courtesy: The Whole World Kin

2

Eliza Brown: An American Missionary Wife Sows the Seeds of Learning

William Griffith treated Baluram well throughout their travels together. Griffith was so impressed by Baluram's services that he showered lavish gifts on Baluram at the time of their parting. In addition to a good sum of money and clothes, he bought Baluram a pair of new shoes. Even though Griffith gave Baluram the shoes to wear, Baluram always wrapped them well by cloth and carried them either on his head or on his shoulder. He did not wear the shoes on his way to Jorhat.

At Jorhat, he would occasionally put the shoes on and take a short walk on the road but if he wore the shoes for a minute he would clean them for ten minutes. In any case, people in his village did not like the fact that Baluram became a rich man by working for a white man. His good fortune was sore to many eyes and it filled the empty heart of many a jealous soul with envy. As a result, the news even reached the king.

In the Ahom kingdom, none but the highest nobles had the right to wear shoes or to carry an umbrella. So, in the eye of king Purandar, Baluram was breaking the law by wearing shoes. Purandar Singh was having a hard time collecting enough money to pay the British government because of mismanagement and corruption. He and his officers started all kinds of unjust practices to oppress his subjects. Baluram became an obvious target because of his shoes and the highly exaggerated estimates of his fortune. The king sent a Sepoy to arrest him. Getting an inkling of such an event, Baluram fled the night before.

Baluram knew where he should head to—the slate-house in Sadiya. After the travels with Griffith, Baluram had become an expert in traveling. Besides, he knew the road from Jorhat to Sadiya well. Since the major portion of the country beyond Jorhat was under the Matak chief, it was not very difficult for him to travel. As a matter of fact, many of the people there had moved from the Jorhat area to escape the oppressive rule of Purandar Singh since there were no taxes in the Matak country. Many of them offered to keep young Baluram with them, but he denied their help. He told them that he was going to educate himself and do something like Brown and Griffith. He would say, "Just let me rest here for the night, give me whatever little food you can offer. Tomorrow morning, I will proceed on my way to Sadiya. But I will come back to liberate my parents from the clutches of Purandar and to spark everybody with a desire for learning the way Griffith and the Browns have sparked me. Till then, I will not be happy with anything. I do not want land, I do not want money, I do not want a wife, and I do not want any kind of comfort. I want knowledge. That I can get only in Sadiya. To Sadiya, I must go–nothing else matters to me now."

In Sadiya, Baluram went straight to Eliza Brown and begged her to take him as a student in her slate-house. Mrs. Brown was very happy to see her former keen student. She offered to keep Baluram with her, but things had changed quite a bit because she had separated the boys from the girls. Mrs. Brown was taking care of the girls' school while Mr. and Mrs. Cutter were looking after the boys' school, which had more than forty students. There was even an Assamese youth, Nidhi by name, who acted as a teacher's aid in the boys' school. Baluram had met Nidhi earlier and was surprised to see what a scholar Nidhi had become. Baluram also dreamt of becoming like Nidhi and to become a teacher like him.

It so happened that the Brown children were sick and Mr. Brown was very busy visiting nearby villages and writing books. The Browns had also moved to a newer house on the north bank of the Kuril river. They needed a lot of help in keeping things going. So, it was arranged that Baluram would stay near the Browns and help them in his spare time. In return he would get free food and lodging.

Yong and Joni

At the Brown residence, Baluram became friendly with two Khamti youths. One was a young man named Yong who could not only read and write, but also found delight in drawing and engraving. Brown would melt lead and make plain blocks and cut drawings. Yong cut some really beautiful pictures. Yong became so adept at it that one day Brown remarked that Yong was better at it than himself. So, when Mrs. Brown translated Worchester's Primer, Yong did most of the engraving. When a copy of the book reached America, the Baptist Missionary Board went on record to say that the engravings were, "executed with remarkable precision and delicacy." Yong was the artist who later cut most of those beautiful blocks in the magazine *Orunudoi.*

The other person that Baluram met at the Brown residence was a young Khamti girl named Joni, who took care of the Brown children and helped Mrs. Brown with her household chores.

Mrs. Brown one day advised Baluram that he should use the money he got from Griffith to buy a plot of land and settle down in Sadiya, and that if he studied well he could become a teacher like Nidhi in the school. He could get married, raise a family, and bring up children who would be educated. Baluram was pleased to hear all that and to hear more from her he said, "Oh mother, I've run away from home to escape the king's men. I do not know how they might be torturing my parents and other members of the family. I did not want to leave them. But my mother and father begged me in the name of God, 'Go and seek shelter with the Sahibs in Sadiya. We will face whatever befalls us. Don't come back home as long as this king is ruling this land. Come and see us only if the times change.' Here I don't have my father, I don't have my mother, who would find a girl for me and settle me down."

Mrs. Brown assured Baluram, "Don't worry, I'm here. You don't have to worry about finding a girl. We have many good girls here and it will not be difficult to find a suitable match for you."

Baluram replied with delight, "You are my mother, you're my father. Whatever you give me, I will accept as blessings." As Baluram and Mrs. Brown were finishing their conversation, Joni appeared in the yard with a bucket full of clothes that she had washed and started hanging them on the clothesline. Both of them looked at her for a while and then they looked at each other. Mrs. Brown and Baluram could read each other's mind and taking a few steps towards Joni, Mrs. Brown said, "Thank you very much Joni. You're really a nice girl. One day you will really be able to make a man very happy. Whoever has you as his wife will be a lucky man." Hearing that, Baluram was overcome with joy. His blushing face became red and his tongue froze. Unable to express anything, he fast disappeared behind the hut. He, no doubt, had had his eyes on Joni. The thought of future days with Joni brought dreams to his life; and those dreams started making his real life more meaningful. But real life started changing as one unfortunate event swiftly followed another.

Death of a Child

First, misfortune struck the Brown family. Their eldest daughter, six year old Sophia, was taken with jungle fever on September 26, 1938. She could survive the ordeals of the terrible disease hardly for three days and she breathed her last on September 29. The whole Brown household was overcome with grief, for little Sophia was the darling of the household. In addition to her parents and the white people in Sadiya, Yong, Baluram, Nidhi, Joni, and all the students in the schools were very fond of the little angel Sophia.

Sophia's remains were enclosed in a rude coffin, covered with white cloth and was buried in the woods nearby. Mr. Brown built a small brick monument over her grave and set on it a slab of black marble, prepared in Calcutta, with an inscription in English and Assamese.

Baluram was especially fond of Sophia because the little girl would often tell him about her plans of having a school of her own for Assamese children when she grew up. Of course, Sophia could speak Assamese just like the natives. Joni was so struck with grief upon Sophia's death that she would not eat or drink for several days, and Baluram likewise shared Joni's sorrow. Baluram also realized what children meant to their parents because the grief-stricken Browns were never the same again. They would often go and visit her grave and cry holding each other's hand. Baluram also became very sad and he would also often cry in his quarters. His sadness was noticeable to Joni. One day she asked him, "What is the matter with you? The Sahibs have stopped crying, but Yong tells me that you keep crying every night?"

Baluram replied that he was remembering his parents; he just wanted to let them know that he was alive and well. He added, "I know the king's men are harassing them all the time but if they know I am well they would find some solace." Then Joni told him, "Why don't you write a letter, you know how to write. The Sahibs get letters from America. I am sure they would find a way to send a letter to your father. You see how miserable we are. Our people just know how to fight, how to quarrel, how to steal, but they don't know how to make life better. They don't know how to read and write."

Baluram agreed that they would have to teach their people to read and write. As the natives' eyes were being opened to learning, in October, 1838, came the good news that the British finally deposed Purandar Singh and placed his territories under the direct administration of British officers. That brought the reign of the Ahoms to an end. The British divided the area that was under Purandar Singh into two districts, namely, Sibsagar which included the tract south of the old course of the Brahmaputra river, and Lakhimpur, which consisted of the part north of the same river.

At about the same time rumors started spreading that the Khamtis and the Singphos were planning to attack Sadiya. This set panic among the Assamese folks in Sadiya. Yong would tease Baluram saying, "You have nothing to fear because you are becoming a Khamti anyway. But we have to make sure that they don't do any harm to the Sahib, the Mem Sahib and the children." They both resolved to protect them by sacrificing their own lives.

The Khamti Raid

The Khamtis attacked the British stockade on Monday, January 28. It was about three o'clock in the morning that Mr. and Mrs. Brown were suddenly roused out of quiet sleep by the dreadful yell and war-cry of the Khamtis. Mr. Brown sprang to the window and found that the sound came from the direction of the stockade. The noise increased, and soon the sky was red with the light of the burning village. The crack of musketry and the roar of guns filled the silent hours of dawn. In a few minutes the whole of the cantonments and numerous buildings nearby, appeared to be in flames. In haste, the Brown family prepared for flight. They picked up a few warm articles of clothing, a canister of biscuits. Then holding their two infant children, the Browns ran to the bank of the Kuril river.

They reached the waterside just in time to detect a frightened laborer absconding with their boat. They feared that a loud word might betray them to an enemy crouching behind them in the darkness, but the risk had to be taken, and Mr. Brown was obliged to call out with urgency and emphasis before he succeeded in getting his boat brought back. They with their two babies hastily got in the boat and pushed it out into the middle of the stream. In his haste, Nathan Brown forgot the oars. He asked the laborer to go and fetch them—but the frightened laborer refused. Having no other alternative, Mr. Brown jumped into the water and waded back to the shore in the dark. The cowardice of the laborer outraged Joni who was also in the boat. Joni remonstrated the laborer, who sat meantime shivering with fear and cold; "Why do you let the Sahib go back? He will be murdered, but they would not touch you." Unable to start the man, the brave Joni herself jumped into the cold dark water, and followed Mr. Brown to the house, where she gathered a quantity of warm clothing, and hastily tying up the bundle, balanced it on her head and swam out into the stream. The brave girl struggled hard to keep herself afloat under the heavy burden. She disregarded Mr. and Mrs. Brown's repeated peremptory orders to throw the bundle away and save her life. Fortunately, she succeeded in getting it and herself to the boat safely.

The only thing of value that Mrs. Brown could carry was the memoir of Dorothy Sophia which she had finished writing, and which she did not leave in the house, as she expected every moment to see the house in flames. Mr. Brown kept the boat nearly opposite to the house till after the firing was over, and then, rowing softly lest the sound should betray them, proceeded down the river. They approached the stockade; all was now silent there; the sound of the war-whoop as well as the noise of musketry and artillery had ceased. Uncertain whether the British troops or the Khamtis had gained the victory, they decided not to land and, falling in with a group of fishing boats, remained with them till daylight. They were every moment expecting attack from victorious or retreating Khamtis. They feared that a company of Khamtis were lying in wait to rush upon and massacre them, or take them for slaves. Knowing the fate of slaves back home in America, Mrs. Brown dreaded the latter possibility.

An approaching canoe loaded with Khamtis just after the family had taken refuge with the fishing boats made their fear worse. The people in the fishing boats, including Yong and Baluram, did their best to hide the white faces. Luckily, the Khamti boat just rushed by in a hurry. Had the white-faces been caught alone on the river, the family would probably have been massacred. They anticipated the worst—that their English friends were butchered and that they themselves escaped. That was no consolation because then they would have to flee down the mighty Brahmaputra river in that frail canoe without provisions, Completely encircled by danger as they were, and unable to take further steps for their own safety, they could only wait and pray. The trembling mother gathered her sleeping babies to her breast, scarcely daring to breathe a word to her husband, and the time wore on till morning. Mrs. Brown says of her ordeal, "We endeavored by prayer, to commit ourselves into the hands of our covenant-keeping God, and to quietly and resignedly await his dispensations towards us. The night was dark; and the time we spent in this awful state of suspense, was dismal in the extreme."

At last a faint light began to streak the east and to make visible the mountain peaks. A chillier breeze ruffled the water, and the fugitives strained their eyes and ears to catch some sign from the stockade. The dawn grew to daylight, and they heard a sound that was not the scream of natives. A soft, clear, rippling note; it was the English bugle! That must have been the most joyful sound the Brown family ever heard. That was the signal to them that the British troops were in possession of the stockade. They hurriedly made their way to the stockade. There they saw that the British troops paid a high price in defending themselves. The British suffered heavy casualties. Among the dead was Colonel White, the Political Agent, whose body lay with as many as sixty wounds. All around him were the mangled bodies of the slain, the groans of the dying, weltering in pools of blood. The heart-rending cries of the widows and fatherless filled the cold morning with an air of sorrow beyond measure. The surviving sepoys added to the ghastly scene by bringing the heads of the Khamtis by the hair and laying them in a row, to see if any of them could be recognized. To spare Mrs. Brown the agony of the ghastly scene she was carried on the back of one of the boatmen, from a long sand-bank in the middle of the stream, to the opposite shore.

The Khamti attack brought to the region a state of continual commotion. The Khamtis, Singphos, and Mishmis combined, continued to plunder and carry off the peaceable inhabitants. The British troops went scouring the region in search of the enemy, and engaging them in battle wherever possible. The British troops inflicted heavy losses to the Khamtis and Singphos. Finally, the British troops scattered the Khamtis and the Singphos and put them out of harm's way.

Even then, the Assamese population of Sadiya and its vicinity, finding themselves continually subject to the raids of small parties of Khamtis, were daily fleeing in terror from the region. Fields and villages were deserted; and the dispersion went on to such an extent that the missionaries' work was taken out of their hands. With the heat of April and May, the sickness in the crowded cantonments increased. A persistent dreadful odor, and the virulent smallpox, "made the place as deadly as if it had been infested with the plague."

That May, Mr. Brown decided to leave Sadiya and seek another post. Jaipur, few miles away in the southwest direction from Sadiya, was decided upon as the most eligible center of operations, as it was expected that there would be an influx of population through tea-cultivation; and there was also hope of access thence to the Khamtis, Singphos, and Nagas. The decision to remove was not reached without a pang of disappointment, and much unsettling of former plans. Sadiya was depopulated, and afterwards, for a time, overgrown with jungle and effaced from the map. Many years later, it was regarrisoned and became a frontier post.

The Jaipur Tragedy

Baluram followed the Brown's to Jaipur. Meanwhile, they also received the news that the British ended the rule of Purandar Singh and took over the administration of the old kingdom. This was happy news for Baluram. It meant he could go back to Jorhat and look for his parents without facing any harassment. Baluram became eager to go back to Jorhat and expressed his intention to Mrs. Brown. She advised him to go and find his parents. She also advised him to take care of the paddy cultivation on his father's land. She told him that after getting everything organized he should come back for Joni, marry her, and live happily at Jorhat.

Baluram and Joni started making plans for the future. They also promised and swore to wait for each other. Baluram started packing, but before he could start, cholera became epidemic in Jaipur. The natives started falling victim to the dreadful disease and they were dying at the rate of almost one every hour. Some of them were taken apparently in perfect health. It would attack and within six or seven hours, the victim would be dead. One of the earliest victims was Joni.

On August 3 of 1839, the disease suddenly attacked her early in the morning. She moaned and groaned for a little while and then she became speechless and motionless. Terrible pain expressed itself on her face and eyes which she kept closed most of the time. Mr. and Mrs. Brown gave her some medicine. Frightened, Baluram did what his mother used to do when he or his father fell ill—he ran to the tank, took a quick dip into the water, and offered a prayer to the Assamese temple Dhekia-Khowa Namghar near Jorhat. But, nothing worked. Early in the afternoon Joni breathed her last. Suddenly, like a flash of light, the dear friend of the Browns, the future of Baluram, the brave young girl who was with the Brown family on that night of the massacre, who had jumped into the cold January waters of the Kuril river to protect the Browns, was gone—gone as gloriously as she had come. The Brown household was overcast with the same sorrow as when Sophia had died.

For Baluram, Joni's death was as devastating as it was sudden. He, Yong and a few others, cremated Joni. A few days later, broken-hearted Baluram started his lonely march to Jorhat. Yong walked with him for a little distance and then bade goodbye, saying, "Mitir[10], come back again after you find your parents." On his way, his heart would break and tears

[10] Mitir in Assamese means a friend—it usually refers to one who becomes a friend through marriage. Since Joni was a Khamti like Yong and Baluram was planning to marry Joni, Yong and Baluram addressed one another as 'Mitir'.

would come rolling down his cheek when he would look back towards Sadiya and the Khamti land. Sighs and despair were his only companions. But the hope of seeing his dear mother and his kind father gave him the strength to walk on, walk on to Jorhat.

When Baluram was returning to Jorhat, he was still a teenager. Even before he turned twenty, the lad Baluram experienced all the miseries that a man could face—atrocities of an invading army, oppressive rule of a tyrant king, jealousy and envy of his community, and finally a deep personal tragedy. Through all these, Baluram matured into a fine human being mainly because of the thirst for knowledge that the scientist Griffith sparked in his mind, and the milk of human kindness that the noble souls of the Browns filled in his heart. The ray of sunshine that Joni brought to his life brought new meaning of love to him. He felt the strength of love—to do everything for the well being of loved ones and to sacrifice his personal self to make his loved ones happy. He understood why his mother had said, "Go Baluram, go to Sadiya and seek shelter with the Sahib, don't worry about us, just take care of yourself." He now understood why his father risked everything and came with him with a machete to see him reach the bank of Brahmaputra safely and escape into the Matak country, he understood why Joni jumped into the cold Kuril river to bring clothes for the Brown baby, he understood why he could not eat, drink, or sleep for several days after Joni breathed her last, he understood why Yong walked with him for more than a mile to bid him goodbye and parted with tears in his eyes.

Baluram walked to Dibrugarh, where the river port bustled with activity and where there were many boats from Jorhat bringing men and supplies for the British troops. Baluram had deposited his money with Mrs. Brown. Before he parted, she not only returned all of it but also added two extra rupees. In addition, she packed some soft rice and some molasses, telling him, "save this as long as you can. This soft rice is so wonderful, you don't need a fire to cook it and it can give you so much strength. Use it only when you have no other way of getting food." Baluram was able to get into a boat that was coming down to Kokilamukh. The boatmen were very happy to have another hand on deck because they had to unload a few boxes for a Sahib and then take a few boxes from him to another Sahib at Jorhat. The Dibrugarh Sahib arrived, he was none other than Major Bruce, about whom Baluram had heard both from Griffith and Mrs. Brown. Griffith did not like Major Bruce because Bruce was cutting down the tea plants and selling them to make money; Mrs. Brown did not like Major Bruce because he was carrying on liquor and opium trade among the hills people. Mrs. Brown had told Baluram and others that all white men were not good and that there were some bad ones like Bruce, who sold liquor and opium to the natives knowing very well that they were harmful to people.

True, the boxes that were delivered to Bruce were of opium and liquor, and the boxes that he was sending down were of tea. Knowing Baluram could read and write, Major Bruce asked Baluram to work for him. Baluram declined, saying that he had not seen his parents for a long time and that he was going to them first and that later on he would come to Major Bruce if he wanted to work. Baluram added that he was more interested in learning at a slate-house than working. So, Baluram took the oars of the boat and rowed down the big river. This time it was a joyous journey and he greatly enjoyed songs of the singing boatmen as they paddled along. Here are some of the songs and the tunes they sang (courtesy of Major John Butler).[11]

Assamese Boat Songs

I. Keep the boithas cheerily going

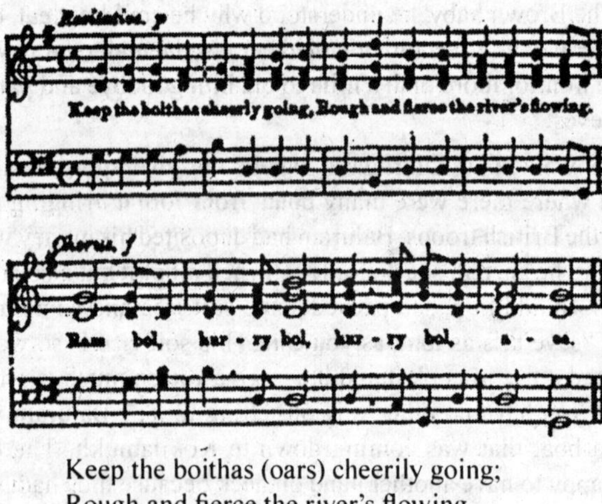

Keep the boithas (oars) cheerily going;
Rough and fierce the river's flowing,
Ram bol, Hawri bol, Hawri bol Aee

[11] Major John Butler was a British officer who had special charge of the hill tribes in the northeast from 1844 to 1865. These songs are reproduced here from Butler's *Travels and Adventures in the Province of Assam* (1855), Reprinted by Vivek Publishing Company, Delhi, 1978.

See! The sun is fast declining,
To the moon his charge resigning,
  Ram bol, Hawri bol, Hawri bol Aee
Pull away, boys, nothing fearing,
Though the rapids we are nearing,
  Ram bol, Hawri bol, Hawri bol Aee

In the well-plied oar confiding,
Safely o'er them we are gliding,
  Ram bol, Hawri bol, Hawri bol Aee
Keep her clear that granite block there,
See, she nears the sunken rock there,
  Ram bol, Hawri bol, Hawri bol Aee

Now the threatened danger's over,
Nothing from her course shall move her,
  Ram bol, Hawri bol, Hawri bol Aee
Soon we'll make the ghat, my heartiest!
Spend the night in jovial parties,
  Ram bol, Hawri bol, Hawri bol Aee.

II. Come and join this merry round

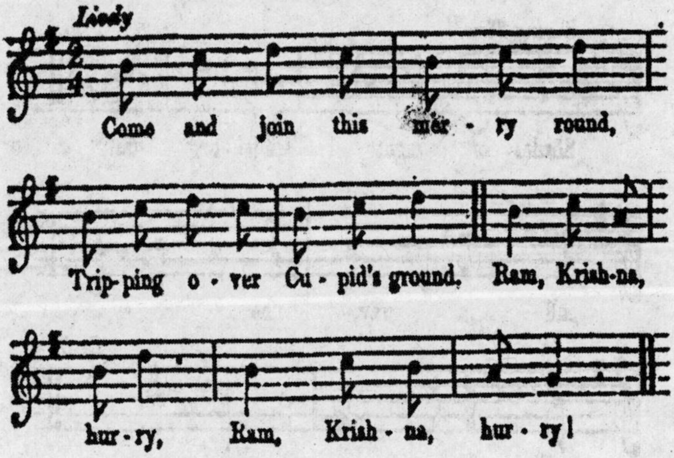

Come and join this merry round,
Tripping over Cupid's ground,
  Ram, Krishna, Hawri.

Dance and sing we all night long'
This shall be the only song,
  Ram, Krishna, Hawri.

Love and music all the theme,
Till the ruddy morning beam,
  Ram, Krishna, Hawri.

Let the ruddy morn arrive,
It shall but our song revive,
  Ram, Krishna, Hawri.

Aided by the solar ray,
Blithe we'll sing throughout the day,
  Ram, Krishna, Hawri.

Let the shadow upwards tend;
Let the weary sun descend;
Still our song shall find no end
  Ram, Krishna, Hawri.

III. An Assamese Air

Shades of night are falling fast-pull away, eh, hey;
All our toil will soon be past - pull away, eh, hey.
Round Thamlya's point we steer - pull away, eh, hey;

See the Puckah Ghat appear - pull away, eh, hey.
Strike together for your lives - pull away, eh, hey,
Towards our sweethearts and our wives - pull away, eh, hey.
First we smoke the fragrant weed - pull away, eh, hey,
Morpheus then will slumber speed – pull away, eh, hey.
We must work if we would live - pull away, eh, hey;
Sahib will our bacshish give - pull away, eh, hey.

Peace at last

Baluram had no trouble finding his parents. They had endured and survived some mean punishments from the king's men. The Burha Gohain prevailed upon the king to set Baluram's parents free because they had not done any harm. The Burha Gohain pointed out that Baluram was spoiled by the British, implying that if Baluram had connections with the British then he might be able to seek help from the British. In any case, Baluram and his parents were grateful to the Burha Gohain for that act of kindness.

Baluram's parents and his parental uncles were very happy that Purandar Singh's rule was over and they were no longer bound to offer services to the king and the nobles. Further, they each got to keep the land where they had their residence and cultivate the land that was assigned to them by the Ahom king. They all became free farmers and they did not have to worry about anything except paying a tax of Rs. 3.00 to the British Government. This arrangement brought joy to one and every paik. However, it created big problems for the nobles. Of course, many of the lucky nobles could get government jobs like tax collector, judicial magistrate, local or district administrator because the British Government made it a point to employ administrative officers from the ranks of the nobles. There was joy all around; soon the granaries were full, people could move about freely, selling their produce and buying simple necessities like salt, oil, etc. But Baluram was not very happy. He wanted to go to school and learn the way the Sahibs had learned. Often he would tell his father that he wanted to know why the white Sahibs knew so much more than the Assamese, why everything they did was better than what the Assamese could do, why they had better clothes, better food, better books, better paper, better ornaments, and above all better guns enabling a handful of them to rule over millions of Assamese.

After years of unrest, turmoil, and immeasurable suffering to the people, peace finally came to Assam. With peace came leisure and idle hours. The idle hours brought emptiness to the youths. Baluram and other youths of his age were happy to work in the fields, help their parents and the village elders—helping them enjoy their opium drinks or the opium smoking. These activities were not enough to fill their idle hours, of which they had plenty. Anything new or different could excite them. Their main interest was the new courthouse in Jorhat and the drama that went on there everyday. They found special pleasure in watching the activities of the Moonsiffs (or native judge), pleaders, clerks, the witnesses and all the rest. The officials arrived at the court punctually every morning at 10 A.M. for fear of losing their salary. Baluram and his friends would also arrive there before that for fear of missing anything. They watched the court-clerk record case by case. They also liked to listen to the lawyers and the witness who could twist truth to a falsehood and a falsehood to a truth. They liked to follow each case to its end. Baluram and his friends were the eyewitnesses of this new drama that became part of life in Assam. They realized that the cruel days of removing knee joints, removing eye balls, chopping ears or hands off that were prevalent during the Ahom reign were gone. Even though the proceedings in the court were often as farcical as the trials during the Ahom rule, they knew well that the days of "killing somebody because you wanted to" or, "hitting somebody because you felt like it" were gone forever. The British administration of justice brought to them a sense of security. They also realized that if they did not get an education, if they did not learn to read and write, they would always remain on the receiving end and would not become part of the administrative process. For Baluram, an education was a reality. He could read and write a little. But there were no books to read nor was there anybody like the Browns to help him learn more. He aspired to find some books to read and learn more. Even when he was plowing the field, even when he was harvesting the rice or even when he was fishing, he dreamt of reading books and yearned to learn more. The spark that Griffith and Brown kindled in his heart kept flickering. He realized that a new era had dawned in the land and that the British Government had brought new promises for the youths of Assam.

Often he would forget everything but the words of Griffith, "These trees, these plants, these fishes, these birds are all our friends and we share this good earth, so we must know them well... Education yes, tea and opium no." Then the assurance of Mrs. Brown, "You can be a teacher in our slate-house, we will teach you everything, Jesus Christ loves you." Baluram realized that the future promise was in education inside slate-houses like the one Eliza Brown established in Sadiya. But there were no slate-houses in Jorhat—nobody knew where the Browns were. Sometimes he thought of going to Jaipur to join the Brown family, but the shelter and security at home after years of helpless wandering made everything far for him. Since he found space to plant his roots, other things distanced themselves from him.

Nathan Brown (1807 – 1886)

Courtesy: The Whole World Kin

3
The American Missionary Nathan Brown Shows the Path for True Refuge

One day when Baluram heard that a white man came to the blacksmith's shop on the outskirts of Jorhat, he ran there. After waiting there for several days, one day the white man did come with two associates and with a bunch of books laden on mules. Baluram recognized him immediately as Nathan Brown. At the blacksmith's place, Brown was having a friendly discussion with a Brahmin pundit.

After some friendly inquiries as to the methods and merits of pujas, the Brahmin discovered that the foreigner was as well versed as himself in his own scriptures, and that he knew that some of them forbade the worship of images. The Hindu and the Christian were perfectly agreed that guilt could not be removed without atonement, and on this common ground the missionary then proceeded to preach Christ, the Holy Incarnation or Avatar. This conversation had taken place in a blacksmith's shop, and the old man at the anvil, who had been listening with the closest attention, now spoke: "Can anything be said against this? Must not this be the true religion?" The Brahmin, to the missionary's surprise, nodded assent. On another occasion Mr. Brown asked a Brahmin,

"Are there three Gods or one?"

"One God," was the reply.

"Were Brahma, Vishnu and Siva all the same?"

"Yes, the same God, in three forms."

"Do not your scriptures speak of a Supreme God, that is above Brahma, Vishnu, and Siva?"

"Yes."

"Is this Supreme God visible or invisible—corporeal or incorporeal?"

"He is invisible and incorporeal—without eyes he sees, without ears he hears, without feet he moves, and whatever is his will, that comes to pass."

"This is the God," Mr. Brown continued, "whose religion I have come to preach—the invisible, incorporeal Being, who is the Maker and Lord of all."

When the Brahmin stopped talking, Baluram renewed his association with Mr. Brown and went with him wherever he went. Often Baluram worked as a guide showing him roads to different destinations.

At another time, the missionary was walking along the road from Jorhat in company with a traveling Brahmin when conversation took the usual turn.

"Oh, I stick to the old scriptures," the Hindu remarked at length good-naturedly. "I shall trust for salvation to Ram and the rest of the Avatars." They had now reached a stopping place and quite a number of listeners gathered around them.

"There are one or two things in your scriptures," resumed the missionary, "that are false."

"Yes there may be one or two," acknowledged the Brahmin.

"I am sure there are; I have read some parts of your scriptures: they say the earth rests on the heads of elephants, do they not?"

"Yes, there are eight elephants that stand on eight heads of a great serpent, and these support the earth."

"Well, people have been all over the earth in the foreign ships, and examined it on every side, and the heads of these great elephants have nowhere been found."

"You do not mean to say that they have gone to the end of the world?"

"Yes, they have been all over it."

"Have they actually crossed the great ocean, and found the other side?"

"Yes, I came from the other side of the earth. My country is directly under our feet."

"What! Do you mean to say that you have come up from the under side? Pray, how did you get here?"

"We sailed directly around on the surface, just as a fly would creep round an orange."

"Is it possible that people live on the underside?"

"Yes, it is night there when it is day here. Perhaps you will wonder why the people don't fall off from the other side?"

"Yes, to be sure!"

"Did you ever see a magnet which draws a needle so that it adheres to it?"

"Yes, I have seen it."

"There is something like this in the earth which draws all bodies towards the center, so that they do not fall off from it, either up or down, on whatsoever side of it they may be."

"This is very extraordinary. Are these things contained in your scriptures?"

"No, our scriptures do not contain geography and other sciences found out by human wisdom; they contain nothing but the words of God, which relate only to religion. This that I have told you of the earth is what men have seen and know, and what you may learn by studying. You will find all the scholars at Gauhati know about these things."

Such discussions were very common, and it is quite probable that many of the Brahmins became secretly convinced that their eight gigantic elephants had a rather small point of support.

"On what does the eight-headed serpent rest?" the padre would sometimes ask.

"He rests on the back of a tortoise."

"And what does the tortoise stand upon?"

"Well you must indeed be unreasonable (with a gesture of annoyance), not to be satisfied yet after all I have told you!"

While at Jorhat, Mr. Brown had an interview with the ex-king, Purandar Singh, and his son Kameswar. The king at first did not like the idea of the foreign padre's coming to change his religion and that of the country. He at length, however, appeared more interested, and made many minute inquiries respecting Christian doctrines and the two disciples who embraced Christianity.

Mr. Brown, however, found the king's son to be a very interesting young man of twenty-five or thirty. He was very inquisitive respecting western theories of geography and astronomy, and earnestly urged Mr.

Brown to come and set up a school at Jorhat. He was anxious to learn English as well as the sciences. Baluram and his friends followed Brown everywhere for a few days, hundreds of people thronged to listen to him. They would say, "The Sahib's words are extremely good and proper; his eloquence surpasses anything we have heard from our priests." Brown, however, was not able to convert anyone. The people knew that he was a great man and that none of the natives could match his intelligence or knowledge. Yet, they were not prepared to give up their religion. For a people so deeply rooted in social customs and everyday life, and for whom religion was a way of life, it was not easy to try the luxury of another faith.

Brown told Baluram that his family had all moved to Sibsagar and that they had set up a school, a press, a church and everything there. Brown invited Baluram to visit them there. Baluram said that things were much better at home and in his village and that he was helping his parents in all possible ways, but that he would like to go to school. He requested Brown to start a slate-house in Jorhat to which everybody agreed saying, "We will all attend your school and we will help you every possible way, we all want to read and write." Brown said he would come back the following winter and see what he could do.

The True Refuge

Brown did come back the following winter (December 1844) but with a different purpose. In December 1844, Mr. Brown set out on a more extended missionary tour through Central and Lower Assam. He made the journey of two hundred miles from Sibsagar to Gauhati, for the most part on foot, in order to visit the remoter villages, making circuits which he could not have done by boat. The little caravan, comprising the missionary, the assistant Nidhi Levi, and eight porters, started down the Dikho road on Saturday the 14th, carrying with them two or three loads of books, and the miscellaneous impediments necessary for a march through the jungles. All were on foot except Nidhi, who, being in feeble health, rode a pony. Two porters carried the sahib's traveling chest between them, suspended from a long bamboo, but after days, re-arranged the load, in more approved Assamese style, by hanging his clothes on one end of the pole, and the empty chest on the other. A single coolie then balanced the pole on his shoulder and trudged along with the greatest ease. Dishes, cooking utensils. and bedding were transported in this manner. If at night the party were fortunate enough to light upon a deserted namghar, which generally consisted of a roof without sides or floor, their hotel accommodations were considered sumptuous. The missionary spread his mat and blanket upon the ground, put up his mosquito netting and carefully fastened it down; fires were built and rice and curry cooked. Sleep came quickly, after a day's march of twenty or thirty miles, or the round of a group of villages distributing, explaining, discussing, and preaching. The winter air was just cool enough to be bracing; the tropic vegetation was tempered by the season to its perfect beauty, and notwithstanding the annoyances and even dangers of wilder portions of the journey—exaggerated reports of which at one point almost raised a mutiny among Mr. Brown's men—still he found it an enjoyable and healthful trip.

The first stop was over Sunday, at the fisher village near the stone bridge at the Namdang. Here, under a tree, the missionary preached to villagers and passers by. The next day, he took the old bund road to Jorhat. Along the way, he saw six or seven hundred laborers repairing the highway, some of whom could read; he gave them Scriptures and tracts. Before reaching Jorhat, his feet were sore from the long march. So, he took his shoes off and walked on the soft grass on the edge of the road. The next morning, he headed to the bazaar, where he expected to see a big crowd. At Jorhat bazaar there were discussions with some Brahmins of Hindu faith; they believed that, "All are but parts of one stupendous whole, Whose body, nature is, and God the soul. The Divine Spirit is inherent in every part of creation; there is an inspiration of deity in every man, beast, bird, and insect; when they live, it is deity that lives; when they move, it is deity that moves; when they die it is the in-dwelling divinity changing its residence."

One day, Mr. Brown exhibited to some Hindu visitors a prism which he had made of pieces of window glass cemented together at the edges and filled with water. The light struck through, and Lo! on the wall a fragment of Indra's bow—Indra, god of thunderstorms, who shoots with that dazzling rainbow the demons that would otherwise shrink up man's needful rain, and whose arrows strike lightening from the eight rocky mountains that sustain the heavens! An explanation of the spectrum followed, which demolished this highly ornamental buttress of the Hindu creed.

Later in the day Mr. Brown sent Nidhi with the prism to explain the rainbow to the young prince who, on his part, sent to the padre a present of a hanging lamp. This was politely declined, however, lest it should be broken in the tramp through the jungles. Just at dark a moonsif, or native judge, called and made many inquiries about these extraordinary foreign stories. He had heard of Captain Cook's going around the world three times, but could not really believe it. Could such a thing be possible? "It is true;" Rev. Brown replied, "and the people of the island where Captain Cook was murdered have since been converted, and have embraced the Christian religion."

The moonsif found it hard to comprehend that vessels might cross the eastern ocean from America to China, coming westward all the time, but was so interested as to repeat his visit the next evening, bringing many new inquirers with him. He and several other Brahmins allowed the Hindu religion to be criticized before all the company without offering to say a word in its defense.

Early the next morning, the foreign preacher was seen to enter the shop of an old goldsmith, an acquaintance of his, and a crowd soon collected. Two Brahmins entered into discussion with him, and finally subsided into silence, but declined to look at his scriptures; and in fact all seemed afraid of the books till after the pundits walked off. Before Mr. Brown left, however, almost every man of the company had a tract snugly tucked into the folds of his suria (native loin cloth). So did Baluram.

The next day, Baluram was looking for an opportunity to tell his parents about the book. The opportunity came while his mother was preparing some parboiled. In the old days before rice mills became popular, villagers usually half-boiled the rice with its husks on in large pots on their courtyard. Then, they dried the rice in the sun. This way, the rice nearly pops out of its husk. The rice is finally separated from the husk on a dheki (a long hammer-like device operated by foot). Rice so prepared preserves more of its nutrition and is very tasty. It used to be a woman's job to clean the courtyard and to prepare the fire and a man's job to do the rest. Of course, during a cold winter morning it used to be a time for everyone in the family to sit around the fire and enjoy a moment of family get together. That day while Baluram's father Jadu was comfortably sitting next to the big fire on the courtyard preparing the parboiled rice, Baluram came and joined his father to start the following conversation.

"Dad, yesterday Brown sahib gave me a book. I can read it quite a bit, would you like to hear?"

"Ok, read, is it written in our alphabet?"

Baluram took the book out from under his shawl and said with a lot of enthusiasm, "Look, this is called the True Refuge, it is printed in Assamese letters. Nidhi taught me all these in Sadiya. Nidhi also came with Brown. He could also read like Brown, knows a lot of interesting things. They have both invited me to Sibsagar. They have started a slate-house there as well."

"What is a slate-house?"

"I told you before—the children go there with their slates and chalk. The Sahibs and their wives teach the children how to read and write. They also sing songs and prayers together."

"Oh! The book is very small," Baluram's father said casting a glance at the book.

"It has a lot of things though—printed letters, they can put ten times more things than our books. Yesterday, the king and the prince begged Brown to start a slate-house in Jorhat."

"Who? Purandar Singh. He is no longer our king. He made us all suffer by leaving us at the mercy of the Burmese. Now, is he trying to destroy our faith and religion by using the white foreigners? God only knows what evil intentions Purandar has in his mind. All these years he had been just tormenting and giving hindrances to king Chandrakanta and now he is trying to interfere with the British government as well. No, I don't trust that scoundrel."

"Even if the king does not, the Company will definitely set up slate-houses everywhere. They put one up in Guwahati, one in Dibrugarh and we have heard that they are putting one up in Sibsagar as well. Now, listen I will read. O Mom! if you wish to hear then come over."

"A conversation about true refuge—one old man told a youth, son, please slow down a little and don't you think it will be better if we walk together by talking to one another? And if you listen, I wish to tell you a couple of things. "

While Baluram was so reading the book to his father, the Medhi, or the representative in the village of Hindu religious leader, stopped by to warm his feet up by the fire and to relax by sharing a few puffs in the hooka. He saw Baluram with the book and immediately started,

"There I caught him red-handed. I heard that last evening some of the youths of our village took some Christian books from the padre. This is a big offense you know. The youths will now destroy our religion. Is that the Christian book in Baluram's hand? O' Lord Vishnu! I think dark days are really upon us. Balu! you better throw that book in the fire right now without further damage to our society."

"No, that's a very small book. What harm can it do? Anyway, I have not allowed him to take it indoors. Are we going to lose our faith and caste if we touch this book?" asked Baluram's father.

"Of course! you will. A book of foreigners all heathens. Then it is about some Sishu or Khisu instead of our very dear Gods."

"No Dad, this book talks only about the Creator and nobody else. Look Mr. Medhi, there is only one Creator—how can you call him Indian or foreign? If He created everybody, who is heathen in his eyes?", asked Baluram.

"Balu, what is all these nonsense you are saying? The Lord who created the four castes, why could not he create heathens? Jadu, if our religious head hears this, God knows what he would do—I think he would put the pots around our necks" Medhi said, referring to the dire consequences that the religious head was capable of putting onto those who had displeased or violated the strict codes of conduct imposed by him.

In a vain effort to win his father to his side, Balu emphasized, "No Dad, the head cannot punish us like that anymore. Only the Moonsif can give punishment after weighing one's guilt. We just have to file a case in the court." Hearing that, the Medhi cautioned Baluram,

"Oh my God! What am I hearing! Even my son says the same thing. File complaint against our religious head in court and find fault with our religion. I tried to make him understand the whole day yesterday. Then only after hours of persuasion, his mother could remove the book from his hand. Look Balu, you don't have to teach me religion—let that book be consumed by our fire God right in front of me while I'm here—if by any power your Jesus can save it let it be so. What do you say Jadu?"

"Yes, that is right, throw it in the fire, there is no need to create more problems." agreed Baluram's father. Baluram's mother also pulled her veil down and stepped into the scene by saying,

"Please Balu, I beg you, throw that book into the fire."

Baluram was startled at the scene they created. He tried to understand what was in their minds. He knew the Medhi was a hypocrite who was trying to maintain his hold on the villagers, which he could do by glorifying the power of the religious head. Ignorant and incapable, the egoistic Medhi could hold the rein of power and control only as the agent of the religious head. For the religious head, it was an age-old strategy to procure economic security for his family and descendants through the business organization created in the name of God. Baluram also knew well that his parents were part of the simple folk who wished to survive peacefully.

Baluram looked around wishing in his heart of hearts that Brown or Nidhi would appear there. He wished to catch a piece of the sun's ray and tell them the truth about the rainbow, he wished to quote from Hindu scriptures and prove that nowhere in it does it say that it would be a sin to touch or read a book by a foreigner. He wanted to prove to them that one would not lose one's faith if one read scriptures of another faith. If the Hindu scriptures contained these kind of statement, then they were wrong, as wrong as their assertion that eight huge elephants are holding the earth up on their heads. But how could he tell them—he had no command over knowledge, no language to communicate what he felt in his heart to be true. Feeling helpless he put the little book in the fire and said,

"OK, I will read our scriptures but who will teach me how to read and understand them?"

"Why! Pundit Hem Sharma is there", said the Medhi.

"But Hem Sharma will teach only the Brahmin children. He would never take a non-Brahmin as a student."

"Then there is our Kakoti, he will take you as a student."

"No, Kakoti charges such a big fee that only the children of the high and mighty can afford to join his school. Don't you understand there is no way for poor and non-Brahmin people like us to get an education and uplift our people?"

"In any case, why do you need to have an education? Our religious leader has arranged for regular readings of the scriptures in the village Namghar (prayer house). If you listen to these you will learn everything you need to know. No, it is not necessary for you to have any other education," said the Medhi.

"But if our people do not learn to read and write then who would take the jobs at the courts—the clerks, the copiers, the lawyers, and the moonsif? They will always be at the hands of non-Assamese. No, we youths are not going to sit with our hands tied. Yesterday, we went and requested Mr. Brown to start a slate-house in Jorhat and he said he would try to do that."

After the Medhi left, Baluram informed his father that hundreds of Muslim and poor Hindu youths would join the school at Jorhat if Mr. Brown started one. Till then, he and some of his friends had decided to go to Sibsagar to learn at Brown's school there. When his father commented that Sibsagar was too far and there was nobody who would look after his work, Baluram quickly answered, "Why! You used to go to Sibsagar to work for the king. We will use the same system. We will form groups of four and take turns—one of us will go to Sibsagar for six months and the other three will look after his work. The only difference is that we will be in Sibsagar not to serve a king or dignitary but to learn reading and writing.

That's what Baluram and three of his cousins decided to do, because Brown could not start a school at Jorhat. Several other youths likewise walked the 36-mile distance to Sibsagar regularly and saw a way to uplift themselves. True the British government freed the slaves and the common folks of compulsory service. But in the beginning, the government could not do anything for the education of the masses or to train them to render services to the government, except as laborers. The American missionaries like Brown and Bronson filled the void. Even though they came to convert people to Christianity, they were not concerned about increasing the number of Christians. They were very genuine souls who believed in having a spiritual goal in life and they found in the gospel the true light for spiritual enlightenment and fulfillment. For them, that was the true knowledge and they wanted to give others that true knowledge. To do that, the first step was to teach the masses to read and write. The second step was to publish books; not only religious books but also scientific books that could broaden the outlook of the masses. Finally, they tried to show through their own acts and deeds how to lead a meaningful spiritual life. They were Christian missionaries serving as messengers of enlightenment. They employed no tricks, no briberies, but true enlightenment as they realized it. That's why youths like Baluram, the children of the freed paiks and slaves, saw the only way to uplift themselves from slavery, to escape from the realms of poverty, and open their eyes to literacy was to join in the slate-houses of Brown and Bronson. For them, Nidhi was the only role model. Soon afterwards Brown started publishing the scientific magazine Orunudoi (which meant the dawn). Baluram and his friends were able to read that magazine and pass on the knowledge they gathered to others.

4

A Good Brahmin Changes Course

The Widow's daughter

One day Baluram witnessed a strange happening at Sibsagar in the Brown residence. An old Brahmin brought a small ten or eleven year old girl to Mrs. Brown and urged her to adopt the girl. He heard their conversation:

Brahmin: Mother! This is my grandchild Parboti—the daughter of my widowed daughter. There is nobody to take care of her. I have come to entrust her future upon you. Please take her and do whatever you think will be good for her.

Mrs. Brown: Why? Don't you have a wife? What is your caste and where is her mother?

Brahmin: I'm a Brahmin by caste. My wife deceased a long time ago. Parboti's mother took another man and left her with me. I have no means to bring her up at this old age. I live essentially by begging. I can't roam around with her. I do not know where her mother is—I do not blame her. After her husband had died, she was encircled by fire all around. She did the best thing for her before the fire completely engulfed her. Now, you alone can save this little girl. Please take her under your wing.

Mrs. Brown: But, don't you know that she would lose her caste if she lives with us? Then she may even accept our religion. We may even get her married to a non-Brahmin. In my household boys and girls of all castes live together without any distinction. Have you thought about all these? Besides, we will need her mother's permission.

Brahmin: Do whatever you think is best for her. I have complete faith in you, and that is why I have come to you. I can recognize good people. You are her only hope. Her mother will give consent. She is staying away from us because she is afraid that people may harm us if they see her with us. In our society, her mother is an outcast.

For a few days after that, there were a lot of discussions between that old Brahmin and the Browns. For example,

Brown: Do you read the scriptures? Do you know Sanskrit?

Brahmin: My knowledge of the divine language is poor. My main guide is the Assamese *Bhagavatam* and I have read few *Puranas*.

Brown: Do you know that there are many false facts in your scriptures?

Brahmin: Vyasa composed the words of Lord Krishna and they have been passed on to us orally. So, surely some wrong things might have crept in. But this ignorant has no abilities to judge them.

Brown: Have you read our scriptures? Have you tried the words of Jesus Christ?

Brahmin: Yes, I have read the books distributed by you. They contain very noble words. But are not there things in your scripture, which are not true? Does your scripture say the Earth is round or flat? What does your scripture say about the Sun and the Earth, I mean whether the Sun moves around the Earth or the Earth moves around the Sun? I did not get any answer to those questions in your scripture.

Brown: Yes, you're right. Some untrue things have crept in our scripture too. But there is no falsehood in the words of Christ. He loves us all, He forgives our sins and He is the true savior.

Brahmin: Sir, I know you are a very learned man. You are more learned than our best scholars. You have read our scriptures as well. Please tell me, have you found anything good in our scripture? Is everything in our scripture wrong?

Brown: No, no. Your scriptures have many good things. They do contain many words of wisdom. They are very heavy and some of them are very difficult to understand. Even the pundits do not understand them. So, many pundits distort them. Many of the pundits are not good people. They do not let the common folks read and write. The pundits and the nobles have been trying to secure a good life for themselves by keeping the common people ignorant. Our scripture is easy to understand. We are writing them in Assamese so your people will understand them easily. We will teach every Assamese to read and write. It will be good for the Assamese.

Brahmin: I have found comfort in my religion. I am happy to think of myself as a servant of Lord Krishna and I have taken refuge at his feet. But in my society and in my religion, there is no hope for this little girl. So, please take her and shelter her under your religion.

Brown: If your granddaughter wants to be a Christian, will you object?

Brahmin: No, never. I have seen with my own eyes how you people have been educating the helpless girls. You have done benevolent work. God alone has brought your people to our midst. May God bless you. Let this girl take refuge in Christ. That's all I wish. She is doomed as a Hindu. I have only one request—if possible, please do not make her eat beef.

Brown: No, don't worry. Even though our people eat beef, we have told our people not to eat or kill cow. We know that you Hindus do not like cows to be slaughtered. That's why we have asked our people also to desist from doing that. We wish to live in peace and harmony. Christians will not lose anything if they do not eat beef. But Hindus, Christians, and Muslims must learn to respect each other—that is more important than what we eat.

Mrs. Brown agreed to keep and to educate Parboti, the grandchild of that Brahmin. Parboti's mother also came and gave her consent. Mrs. Brown made it clear to Parboti's mother and Parboti's grandfather that they would baptize Parboti as Christian only if Parboti showed her willingness and abilities to live as a Christian. The Brahmin promised to keep visiting Parboti every month or so. However, after parting with his granddaughter, he continued to stay in Sibsagar sleeping under a tree on the riverbank.

Baluram was thrilled to see a devout Brahmin trust his granddaughter to the cares of the missionary with so much confidence and faith. He found it hard to believe. So, Baluram followed the Brahmin around in Sibsagar helping him by doing little errands for the old man. Baluram also felt admiration for the Brahmin because the Brahmin's questions led Mr. Brown to admit that even the Christian scriptures contain wrong things. Therefore, he tried to acquire some knowledge by nagging the Brahmin with questions.

Salvation through Education

Baluram: Sir! How could you leave that little girl with those people from an unknown land? Aren't you afraid that they may cause harm to her?

Brahmin: Why should I fear anything? Don't you see how kind and generous they are? Mr. Brown is like Lord Ram not only in looks but also in benevolence. The love and piety they are demonstrating

I have never seen in India before. They are very religious people. I have no worries about that. My only regret is that I could not do anything for the little girl.

Baluram: You're right. They are truly kind and generous. The way they are embracing the orphans, the poor and the little children despised by our society is really admirable. Their love and affection will win trust and goodwill from anybody. Sir! for quite some time I have also been seriously thinking about becoming a Christian with them but I am very afraid that by so doing I may be forced to eat some food that my ancestors had forbidden us to eat. Please, will you give me some advice as to what I should do?

Brahmin: You see, I have traveled all over India. Nowhere would a Brahmin sit and eat with me. They say the Brahmins of Assam eat meat and fish, so, they are untouchables. In a way, that is true. If one reads our scriptures then one can easily conclude that since the soul dwells in every living being, it is wrong to kill an animal. Since we cannot give life, we should not take life away. One should not eat any kind of fish or meat. But in this land of ours, in this country we call Assam, almost every Brahmin bites meat or fish. Assamese Brahmins have adopted many rules like eating meat for their own convenience and to satisfy their own greed and self-interest. How shall we know about these foreigners? What do we know of the land beyond the seas that they have come from? How can we know about their Gods and religion? For some reason or other they allow people to eat beef, who are we to judge? But, I have a hunch that some day our people will do likewise. We, the Assamese, are really without backbones, we always take up anything that is easy or that serves our sense-gratification. Our religious leaders do not care for true knowledge—who can deliver us from this darkness I don't know.

Baluram: Do you think I will be delivered if I become a Christian?

Brahmin: If you trust in the Supreme Being, and do your duties sincerely and in a steadfast manner, then you will find salvation through any path.

Baluram: What is the way up for people like us? People who have been ignorant for ages. Our rulers and religious leaders have always oppressed us and always did everything to keep our children and us ignorant. They don't even teach us the alphabet. It is by the grace of Griffith and Brown that I have seen some light and

I've come to realize that education is our only recourse—we will never be able to get out of our bondage without education. It is good that the government has set us free but the government has not shown us the way for our salvation. In old days we used to sit down or stand up as the King's men told us—otherwise, we would end up losing our eyes, knees, or even our lives. Nowadays, we don't have to do that. Now, we need education. We need education to read books and gather knowledge, and we need education to be eligible for government jobs—jobs in the courts, the police, the postal and other departments. But how can we get education? The padres have come forward to give us education. I often think of joining the padres and becoming a Christian. But something holds me back—I don't know what. Sir, please tell me would you consider becoming a Christian?

Brahmin: By the grace of Krishna, I have come to understand him a little and I have put myself under his lotus feet. I have found peace and harmony with my life by becoming a servant of the Lord Krishna's servants. So, I do not have to become a Christian. But, if you or anybody else wishes to become a Christian, then I would not stop him.

Baluram: Sir, will you please teach me how you found Krishna, how one can know and find Him? Will you teach the scriptures to a non-Brahmin like me?

Brahmin: Surely, come and I would be glad to tell you the knowledge I have gotten from the *Gita* and the *Bhagavat*. I'm not afraid of the Brahmin scoundrels of our society. They are despising a young widow because she has remarried and they want me to sever all relations with her. Not only that, they want me to throw out this eight year old baby girl from my house. What would happen to her? Where would she go? They do not care. How can you tolerate such neglect of children in the name of religion? The Lord Almighty is all merciful—if we have faith in Him we also must be merciful and show our love not only to follow beings but to all beings—men or animal. Yes, Mr. Brown is right. Many of our pundits have really distorted the true knowledge of our scriptures. I wish I had the strength and the resources to change all the distortions. In any case, the few years that I have left on this Earth, I wish to spread the words of Krishna and His glories. I am not afraid of anybody now. I will teach those who are willing—be he a Brahmin or a non-Brahmin.

Knowledge has no caste

Baluram: Sir, please tell me one thing. Is it really true that our scriptures are forbidden for the sudras like us and do the scriptures really forbid remarriage of widows? Which scripture contains these rules?

Brahmin: They are stated in Manu's book. That is not a scripture but garbage. Who knows who wrote it in the name of Manu. Whoever wrote that cannot be an accomplished soul—he must be a depraved person. Those words cannot be the words of the Lord or of a noble person.

Baluram: Then sir! How did you feel when your widowed daughter took a second husband? Was it a shock to you?

Brahmin: No, not the least. In my heart of hearts, I feel that whatever she did was for the good of everybody. I would have been very happy if she and her second husband took the responsibility of bringing up Parboti. They should not have deserted this poor little girl in my custody. No mother or father should give up the responsibility of raising his or her children.

Baluram: I am really afraid to get màrried after seeing all of this. If I die young my wife may take a different man and desert our children. What kind of life that would be for my children?

Brahmin: No, no, this is not something to be afraid of. Birth and death are in the hands of Lord Almighty. Who knows what fate has in store for him or her? But one should not be afraid of the shadow of death in every turn. No person should use death as a factor of one's duties. If you really take refuge in the lotus feet of Krishna, all your fears will disappear. Marriage is a very sacred institution, it is an act of divine character. Every male should find a female life partner and every female should find a male partner for life—it is a wise thing to do and it is wiser to serve the Lord as husband and wife. Of course, the ideal should be to marry once and once only. A man should not take a second wife if his wife dies, just as a woman should not seek a second husband if her husband dies. This ideal is clear from the teachings of our scriptures. A person should decide his or her course of action based on this ideal. If for some reason a man or a woman gets married a second time, then who are we to blame him or her? We cannot denounce a person simply because he fails to live up to the ideal. A man's ideal is to become a noble person—does that mean that we should denounce or kill everybody who fails to achieve that ideal? The ideal of love and kindness is to touch with love those who have never known love.

Sibsagar Temple: on the spot drawing by Nathan Brown. Re drawn by Sukanya Basu

Baluram: These are very heavy things and they are beyond my understanding. Will you please explain it one more time? I understand that a man should have a wife and bring up children with love. I understand that a man should be devoted to Lord Krishna, the Almighty God. But what I cannot fathom is what he should do if the wife dies, or what the wife should do if the husband dies young?

Brahmin: Everybody has to go in his or her own time. How often have you seen a husband and wife dying together?

Baluram: I understand that—there is the question of age as well. What I mean to ask is if one of a married couple dies young what should the surviving partner do? One girl with whom I was engaged to be married died of Cholera before we could tie the knot. Now I have no desire to find another because her memory always comes to me. Often I think that I should not remain a bachelor like this. Everybody at home and in the village always keeps telling me, "Get married, get married." I am afraid; afraid that my wife may die very young. It is a great affliction—I suffered a lot last time. Even now I remember her. She even appears in my dreams and tells me, "Don't sit idle, Balu, do your duty." But what is my duty? She never tells me, nor can I figure out. Please tell me if you know what I should do.

Brahmin: You are a good man. God will bless you. What happened to you does not happen very often. People do not usually die young. These are called the exceptions. Our rules and ideals were not made keeping the exceptions in mind but they were made keeping in view what normally happens. The ideal is to be married once, to bring up children keeping Krishna as the role model. If one of them passes away, then the other partner must continue the responsibility that he and she promised to uphold. But in something like your case, there is no doubt that you should get married. Only thing is that you should keep the ideals of married life in tact. In any case, these are up to the individual—the ideal provides the guidelines.

Baluram: So, you are advising me to get married and settle down.

Brahmin: That's really up to you. In your case, it is kind of easy. Since you were never married and you do not have any children, just think whether you wish to settle down with a woman and bring up children. You need a woman to take care of the household affairs.

Similarly, every woman needs a man who can provide. Men and women need one another. But one should enter into married life with the spiritual goal in mind. You should never forget Lord Almighty, the supreme personality of Krishna. That's the most important thing.

Baluram: In a way, I do wish to start a household. The British Government has set us free. In the future, we won't have to be anybody's slave. Despite this, I have not been able to do anything in this life. It is my hope that I shall have children whom I can educate with the padre so that they may be learned and spread true knowledge among our people. Just look at the white man's yearning for knowledge. They cast their searching eyes on everything - trees, plants, fruits, river, fish, rainbow, women, children, stars, planets. Then they gather knowledge from all things big or small. Then again, see how they desire to distribute knowledge. Within a few days they learn the language of the natives and then they try to educate everyone—the poor, the downtrodden, and people from the lower castes. They say everybody can learn—knowledge has no caste. Sir, please do not blame me. I trust every word they say. Our pundits have been really misleading us—the pundits say to us, "You miserable paiks, you plowmen, you sudras you will never learn anything," but that is false. There is no truth in it. Look at Nidhiram. He is of lower caste. Now he is translating books from English, Bengali and writing so many wonderful things in Assamese. Don't you think it will be great if more pundits emerge from among us? That is why I think of getting married. But every time I get ready to take the plunge, the fear of death stops me from doing so. I fear that after we have children, either she or I may die young, making the children completely helpless.

Brahmin: No, you should not think like that. I have told you that birth and death are in the hands of the Lord. You should not make death a factor of your decisions. You should decide your course of action based on what normally happens. If I did not get my daughter married fearing that she might be widowed, what good might have happened? Fate made her a widow, so different responsibilities became her lot. I told them that as long as I could, I would take care of them. She lived with me several years in complete despair. She cried every day holding Parboti in her arms. Her late husband's relatives completely turned their backs on her. When this fellow came forward to marry her, I told her "Be like Tara, try to find a course of action with faith in God and ultimate goodness. I told her, no matter what, I would be with her.

Baluram: Sir! Who is Tara? Why you asked Parboti's mother to be like Tara?

Brahmin: Why, the Tara of Ramayana, the wife of the great warrior Bali. Lord Ram himself conspired to kill Bali. The fault was Bali's—his own power and strength made him too proud and vain. Bali tried to give his brother Sugrib a lesson for a betrayal that Sugrib did not commit. But Bali was completely blind to reason and truth. Bali would believe no one but his own pride and vainglory. He became mad to take revenge on his brother Sugrib. His wife, the wise and devoted Tara, tried to stop Bali by all possible means—but to no avail. The much-vaunted Bali succumbed to a single arrow of Lord Ram. Hearing of her husband Bali's death, Tara became completely desolate. Her grief and heart-rending cry saddened the whole Earth and the heaven. She prepared to die with her husband by throwing herself in the funeral pyre of her husband. Then somebody brought Tara's baby Angad, and he ran to Tara's arms. Tara's grief was displaced by a realization of her responsibility towards Angad. She realized that the resolve she and her husband Bali had made to bring up Angad, to make him a hero and to set him on the throne, needed to be fulfilled. With Bali dead, the whole responsibility was on her. She decided to shoulder that responsibility. Later she married Sugrib—not so much to secure her well being but to ensure that Angad would become the crown prince. That was the condition on which she took Sugrib as her husband. Of course, in those days it was customary in that society to marry a late husband's brother. I also thought that my daughter remarried to secure her daughter Parboti's future. Now, I am sad that my daughter completely gave up her responsibility towards her daughter Parboti, and I am beginning to doubt her.

Baluram: How can we know all that? We don't even know all the episodes described in Ramayana or the Mahabharata. I just heard a few stories from my father, that's all. My father tells me that before the Burmese plundered our country, people were very cultured. People regularly staged dramas and musical evenings. The singers and players from the monasteries used to visit every village regularly. They told, staged or displayed the stories of Rama and Krishna. With their help even the villagers used to stage dramas. In my village, even now there are few old persons who can still recite the dialogues of those dramas. The discourses with that

Brahmin gave immense pleasure to both. The Brahmin was an outcast of the Brahmins in Jorhat because his widowed daughter remarried and because he did not throw out his granddaughter the eight year old Parboti. After he put Parboti in the care of the Christian missionaries, the wrath of the whole Hindu society fell upon him. Nobody would take or share food with him, nobody would visit him except his poor students like Baluram and others who were sons of poor farmers or former paiks. The Brahmin felt an inner urge to spread his knowledge to whoever was willing to receive that knowledge. So, he welcomed Baluram with open arms, because Baluram had a spark for learning and because he brought others to listen and learn from the Brahmin. The youths provided him constant companionship and gave him a sense of security.

Baluram became well versed in the scriptures, the spark that Griffith had produced in his heart found immense satisfaction through the door that was opened by the Browns. The spark started burning like a regulated fire under the tender care of the Brahmin pundit. However, the liquor-consuming, fish-meat-eating, devoid-of-learning Hindu society had literally thrown the Brahmin pundit out of their fold. The upper caste Hindu society resented the fact that the Brahmin was opening up the Hindu scriptures to the people from the lower castes. However, the saner Brahmins realized that what the Brahmin pundit was doing was right. They also realized that whether they liked it or not, the door to literacy was being opened to the people of the lower caste as well. The tide had come. So, some of them followed the example of the Brahmin pundit and started setting up their own private schools. One such school known as "Kon Bamun's School" on the western part of Jorhat town, became an inspiring place for the residents of Baluram's village.

A few years later, the religious leader who had established his authority over Baluram's village, instructed the villagers to stage a play glorifying the activities of Lord Krishna. The responsibility of staging that play fell upon Baluram. For the first time since the Burmese had plundered the state, Baluram's life became alive and vibrant with cultural activities. Once more the gentle tide of Sankardev's cultural renaissance began to flow through Jorhat. Again the villagers started participating in cultural activities such as singing, dancing, organizing religious festivals, staging plays, etc. This became part of the village life. Through all those activities, Baluram found new meaning in life. In the mean time, since his father was getting old, Baluram had to take full responsibility of the fields and of seeing that rice, vegetables, and other necessities were produced on time. That, too, brought new meaning to Baluram's life. He felt that it was best to lead the simple life of a farmer because it made him self-sufficient and provided complete leisure time to pursue knowledge and creative activities. He also realized that the goal in life had to be spiritual, and found immense pleasure in seeking true knowledge from his religious leaders and the Christian missionaries. From his Hindu priest, he learned service to the Supreme Lord, and from the Christian missionaries, especially the Browns, he learned service to humanity. Even though many of his friends did not like to praise the Christian missionaries, they could not openly argue with him, for they knew that Baluram was better than them in many respects. Unlike them, Baluram could read and write, he had a lot of self-respect, he was always very enthusiastic in whatever he was doing and above all, he did everything with confidence.

Baluram finally was able to overcome his anxiety about getting married, and got married later in his life. One of the first things he did in his married life was to take his wife to Sibsagar and introduce her to the missionaries. He showed her the press, the Assamese books, and the little boys and girls that the missionaries had taken under their care. He also went to the Brahmin Pundit, and the newly married couple sought his blessings by kneeling down and touching his feet. Later Baluram accompanied the Brahmin to witness the Baptism of Parboti. Baluram did not become a Christian, but he truly believed, like that Brahmin Pundit, that Christ was an incarnation of the Supreme Lord like Krishna was. He thought that Christ also demonstrated the supreme strength of the Lord during his appearance, and enlightened people with supreme knowledge about love, service, and subordination the way Krishna did as the Chariot driver of Arjuna. In addition, he realized that the missionaries truly understood the messages of Christ. Finding them meaningful, they had braved the hills and the seas to go to the corners of the world and spread His messages. Baluram could appreciate very well how they could cheerfully bear all their troubles and hardships in Assam.

Later on, Baluram saw many other foreign Christians in Jorhat. Many of them came to start or manage tea plantations around Jorhat, and some of them vere military or police officers of the British Government. He saw that those white Christians were not like the Browns—many of them were simply mean, ruthless, uneducated drunkards. Seeing their distasteful nature and uncivilized behaviors, Baluram realized that all Christians or all whites were not necessarily good people, and that there were dark sheep among the Christians as there were bad people among the Hindus or the Muslims. Baluram realized that religion was not what was in the scriptures, but how you could put it into practice. Therefore, it was not necessary for him to become a Christian. The white tea planters and the police officers completely destroyed any desire that Baluram had to become a Christian. But Griffith and Brown remained for him the true gurus from whom he always tried to draw inspiration. The desire to acquire knowledge that they sparked in his heart remained with him forever.

From Griffith he learned to develop an inner urge to seek knowledge. From the Browns he learned the truth about love and human kindness with God in his mind. From his contact with Brown and Griffith, Baluram realized that it was a curse to remain illiterate. Baluram became determined to teach his and other children in the village how to read, write and to seek knowledge.

Nanda Datta, the eldest son of Dandiram Datta who, they say, looked just like Dandiram Datta and who also worked in the same tea garden as his father. We do not have any picture of Dandiram Datta so this may give some idea of what Dandiram Datta looked like.

5
Dandiram Datta: An Indian Father Makes a True Sacrifice

In 1866, soon after President Lincoln waged war in America to free the slaves, Baluram's only child, Dandiram, was born. By then, the slaves and paiks in Assam were completely free. Due to the fact that the former king had allotted each of them a plot of land for residence and a plot of land to cultivate, they were able to live by producing their own food and other necessities. This was a luxury the freed slaves in America did not have. In addition, the women in Assam were traditionally very adept in spinning cotton and silk threads, and in weaving them into beautiful clothes for themselves. As a matter of fact, many women in Baluram's village could produce extra cloth that earned some income. In particular, many of them were able to produce the rich and durable silk shawl known as *Eri Kapur*[12] that always fetched a very good price.

The village prayer house used to be alive with regular cultural activities like congregational chanting, one-act plays, religious festivals, and so on. Baluram took an active role in these activities and all the villagers participated wholeheartedly. These factors brought a climate of socio-cultural security that was also assured by a stable government.

Dandiram was born into this secure world. By the time Dandiram was able to speak, the British Government had established many elementary schools and a high school in Jorhat. As a result, it was ensured that Dandiram would be able to get an education. Baluram dreamt that his son Dandiram would become learned like Brown and spread knowledge all over Assam. The peace and discipline that the British Government established in Assam brought new promises for the likes of Baluram and Dandiram.

---

[12] Assamese or other Indian words, used in this book, are explained in the Glossary

Baluram felt secure that his son Dandiram would be able to live on the land owned by him. In addition, there was plenty of bamboo, timber, and canes in the forest, which they could always use to maintain their small huts, or build new ones if necessary. Baluram was determined to give his son the necessary education to allow Dandiram to read and acquire knowledge from the bottomless store of Orunodoi. The world of art, music, and drama were also open to Dandiram so that he would be able to cultivate a creative and meaningful life.

As Dandiram grew up, the world around Baluram started changing rapidly. Baluram's dream started crumbling due to the onslaught of the realities of the changing time. The upper class that the British government created to run the affairs of the state slowly nibbled away at the hopes and aspirations of Baluram. Under foreign rule, a slave mentality had crept into the thinking of the people, and, this gradually destroyed Dandiram's personal spirit and freewill.

After finishing his elementary education, Dandiram entered the government high school that was started in Jorhat and was built on the land that once housed the royal family. This alone brought about new problems. In those days, the facilities that the British government provided for the people were through the native officials, lawyers, and others with connections to the British rulers. Most of these privileged natives were former high-ranking officials of the Ahom king and their descendents. Many of them were from the privileged castes that had opportunities or access to get some traditional education. The British government usually appointed them to such positions as police sub-inspectors or inspectors, collectors, district administrators, teachers, and so on. In the beginning, even school-children were from those families. Therefore, many of the teachers and officials did not like the idea of former laborers' children entering into their schools for education. These children were not welcome in the government high school. Many teachers thought the children were merely attempting to break the barriers of the caste system. However, neither the teachers nor the Head of the school could refuse to admit those children because, in the eye of the British ruler, education was for one and all who were able and willing to learn. Thus, the teachers resorted to other methods to drive those children out of school.

The children of the poor or the farmers were made to sit on the floor while the children of the upper class sat on benches. Of course, they all had to sit together whenever a British official or the inspector came to visit the school. Discipline of the poor was enforced with a merciless cane. These children were never to treat the children of the rich on equal terms. If they ever picked a quarrel or teased rich children, then it was their fault and they received physical punishment for that. Of course, rich children could tease or abuse poor children in any manner or form they liked without fear of punishment.

The teachers hired upper class and bigger boys to keep the other students in check. Those bigger boys formed a sort of gang, which terrorized poor students. In addition, poor children were mentally tortured as well. Verbal abuse was the rule of all dealings with them. All the efforts of poor children to do well were always met with derision, discouragement, and punishment. They were always given lower marks than those given to rich children.

In class, most teachers paid attention only to the rich children, perhaps to gain favors from their influential parents, or, perhaps to keep their old traditions of class privileges alive. Many teachers also shared with bureaucrats the uneasy feeling that the children of former paiks or laborers would soon have the same opportunity to become government officers, teachers, and landlords. This kind of thinking produced immense panic in the hearts of the teachers and the people of the privileged class, and this apprehension left its mark on the backs, faces, and heads of the students from poor families in the form of the beatings they received from their teachers.

Ever since Dandiram started going to the high school, it became routine for him to come home with a bleeding nose or ears and other marks of beating he received from teachers. If his father asked Dandiram why his teacher beat him, he always gave the same answer, "For nothing." If he was asked, "Does the teacher do the same to every student?" Dandiram would reply, "No, in my class the teacher roughs up only us." "Us," of course, included the son of an Ahom soldier, one Mising, one Nagamese, a couple of other farmer boys, and himself. In addition to beating them up for any or no reason, the teachers used degrading terms to call them. For example, they were called "the dumbheads," "the tom cat," "the fox," "the donkey," "the thickheaded," and so on. The other students, namely the children of the rich and the dignitaries, picked the same epithets from the teachers and referred to their classmates in the same way. In addition, they took every opportunity to mock and make fun of the degraded classmate, which often resulted in physical abuse.

Baluram was very much grieved to hear about the abuses that his son was being exposed to in the high school. He had wished that the government high school would be a center of learning, a place of love, comfort, and of true knowledge. Baluram felt that something was not right. He went and met with the fathers of the other abused kids, but they saw no way to put an end to the abuse. There was no king and they had no way of approaching the British administrators. The Daroga, or the police chief, was a terror—it was difficult to even look at his eyes. Having no way out, they went to the Burha Gohain (the son of the former Prime Minister of the Ahom King). After narrating the plight of their children, they asked the Burha Gohain if he could do anything. The Burha Gohain told them, "We no longer have any say in any matter. Did not you see what happened to King Kandarpa? You never know who is trying to trap whom. You may go and talk to the teachers and tell them not to beat your children black and blue."

So, Baluram and the parents went to the teachers. One of them said, "You think you have become babus (gentlemen) simply because your kids are in high school?" Another teacher commented, "It is no use trying to be equal with gentlemen's children. Tell them to learn some good behavior as well." One of them proudly declared, "You see, real learning is on the tips of canes. If you want your kids to learn anything they must be prepared to receive some good beating." The other comments made by the teachers were,

> "Why are you sending these dumbheads to high school? Simply because they have somehow managed to pass the elementary school, it does not mean that they will be able to pass high school. High school education is very difficult."
>
> "Your kids' heads are full of garbage. It is difficult to hammer any knowledge in there."
>
> "Take my advice. Take them out of high school and teach them to farm the land well. Then you will at least be able to have two good meals everyday."
>
> "What will they do by coming to high school? They will never be able to pass the entrance examination. Even if they pass the entrance examination, how will you send them to Calcutta for college education? Where will you get the money?"
>
> "It is better that a plowman's son become a plowman and a soldier's son become a soldier. Then, everybody becomes educated."

In short, after meeting with the teachers, Baluram and the other parents came to realize that the high schools had been established for the rich only, and the children of the former paiks of the Ahom Kings were not welcome there. As a result, some of the kids from the poor families did drop out and others, such as the tribal children, started attending missionary schools, where they said that, "The Assamese teachers in high school treat us very bad."

Baluram thought that since his son was able to read scriptures, the newsmagazine *Orunudoi*, and was able to measure the area of a plot of land, there would be no harm if Dandiram dropped out of school. He thought that Dandiram and the other youths of the village would be able to take an active part in the cultural life of the village. But the youths thought otherwise.

The Eyes of the British and the Minds of the Natives

Dandiram and his friends asserted that the British regarded every human being as equal, and that the British government set all the Paiks (the drafted soldiers) and the slaves free. They even knew that the white government in America fought with the white supremacists of the country to free the black slaves held in captivity by the slave owners. To them it was obvious that the privileged people during the Ahom rule found it a hard pill to swallow that those whom they had been treating as lower class should so suddenly try to be their equals. Unfortunately, the native officials of the British government were also picked from the dignitaries of the Ahom rule. These people continued to enjoy power and privileges. Even low ranking petty officers, teachers and clerks looked upon themselves as enjoying privileges that they owed to the former dignitaries and British officials. It was in their interest to keep the underprivileged in status quo.

Dandiram and his friends resolved that the high school was for everybody and they would continue their studies in spite of the cruel teachers. However, Dandiram and the other poor kids had to contend with other kinds of abuse as well. Some of the kids from the privileged families always teased them and tortured them with mental and physical abuse. Dandiram and his friends decided to take care of that as well. One day when some of the kids of the privileged class were teasing a poor Mising boy, Dandiram and his friends came to rescue the boy. They returned the favors of the privileged kids in kind. A fight ensued and even though Dandiram and his friends received a few minor blows, they were able to beat the kids of the privileged class black and blue. The clean clothes of the rich kids were smeared with dirt and dust. As a result, the rich kids tasted the fragrance of mud and the poor kids tasted life in prison because the local police officer rounded up Dandiram and his friends and took them to the prison. The parents of the rich kids including the magistrate, the tax collector, a lawyer and others, advised the Police Chief to teach the 'bad boys' a good lesson so that they would never dare to raise a finger against the privileged kids again. When the Chief was just about ready to do that the British officer in charge of the district came to know about it and went to the police station. Baluram and the other parents of the poor kids were frightened beyond wits.

The British officer, however, scolded the Police Chief saying, "Why did you have to wag your tail when some school children were having a skirmish? Then why did you round up just about everybody from one group and you didn't pick a single fellow from the other—have not they done anything wrong? Don't do anything like this again. Don't enter the high school again without my permission. The Headmaster will take care of everything within the walls of the high school."

The officer released all the students and let them go home with some kind words. Dandiram and his friends were overjoyed. They realized that in the eyes of the law they were equal with others. The incident opened the eyes of everyone in the former capital of the Ahom Kingdom. They realized that a more humane and just system of law was taking root in the country. The high dignitaries and the people in power could no longer have their way just by force. Dandiram's father, however, was apprehensive. He was afraid that even though Dandiram and his friends escaped unscathed that time, there could be trouble later on. He told them, "We are equal only in the eyes of the British but not in the minds of the native officers. The British live like kings and we have a hard time catching their eyes. Native officers and dignitaries run the government. Most of them come from Brahmin, Kalita or Kayastha castes. They regard these castes as the upper castes. Most people coming from the so called upper castes think that they are the only civilized people on this Earth, they are the only Hindus and they are the only ones who deserve all the good things in life. They regard us—the paiks, the Miris, the Nagas, the Kochs, the Abors, the Ahoms, the Kacharis, the Mataks, and the like, as the downtrodden undeserving uncivilized brutes whose destiny it is to suffer and to serve the Brahmin-Kayastha-Kalitas. They despise us and hate us with a passion. They cannot tolerate the idea that our kids will become educated and be equal with them. So, they will always resist your education and will always try to harm you with all the resources they have and they can muster. It is better that you take care of yourself and maintain your distance."

"Our fore-fathers were newly converted Hindus. Even though the present day people of the upper castes do not follow the Hindu religion, they are full of prejudices and hatred against the new Hindus. Because of their spiteful attitude, many of the new Hindus have embraced Christianity or Islam. So the number of Hindus is slowly decreasing in India. If things continue like this, it is certain that one day this pious land will go to hell. Thank heavens the Guru Sankardev gave us the wisdom of dharma and taught us to understand Krishna and his teachings. The Guru has given us music, drama, and congregational chanting. We would never give those up. In the future, we would have to save this religion of wisdom. The upper castes would bring their own ruin by going after wealth, power and good living. They would self-destruct by abusing, torturing, and exploiting us, the so-called people of the lower class. God will pass the final judgment on these abusive teachers and rulers. Now the British government is giving us education. We must use this education to uplift ourselves and uphold the best of the religion of wisdom."

Dandiram did not drop out of school. He continued to attend the high school. Somehow or other destiny kept urging him to continue his education. However, after three years, the learning environment became so intolerable that even the urges of destiny could not keep Dandiram in school. Because of the inhumane treatment they received from their Assamese language teacher, Dandiram and his friend Puwali Saikia of Chowdung village quit school for good.

It happened like this: The Assamese language teacher was actually a Sanskrit scholar. He was steadfast in his beliefs such as:

"Sanskrit is the best language in the world",

"Assamese is derived from Sanskrit,"

"Sanskrit grammar dictates the rules of the Assamese grammar, "

"the more Sanskrit you use in Assamese compositions the better it sounds,"

On the other hand, Dandiram, Puwali, their parents and many others received their early training from the missionaries and the missionary newspaper *Orunudoi*. The Assamese books published by the missionaries constantly inspired them. At that time the only books that were accessible to the vast majority of the Assamese people were the ones published by the American missionaries. The American missionaries, under the leadership of Brown and Bronson, had established that even though the Assamese language owed the greater portion of its vocabulary to the ancient Sanskrit, the original native stock formed the language itself. Therefore, the Assamese had a very distinct pronunciation and grammar. Nathan Brown had also observed, "The native pundits, in fact, make no scruple to introduce, whenever necessity or convenience requires, any word, however unusual that may be found in their sacred writings. This is a license which is often abused; native writers being apt to adorn their compositions with a profusion of Sanskrit that is quite unnecessary, and renders their productions wholly unintelligible to the common people" [13](*GNA* vi). This was true of the Assamese language teacher of Dandiram's high school.

Dandiram, Puwali, and others could easily read and understand the books and magazines published by the American missionaries because they were very similar to the language they spoke. The language that their Assamese language teacher taught or they were forced to learn was hard for them. The rules of grammar, mostly from Sanskrit grammar, were beyond their comprehension. Those rules simply did not make any sense to them. So, they always made mistakes in saying, reciting, or writing—and each mistake brought harsh punishments that included twisting ears, caning, kneeling or standing in awkward positions for a long time. So Dandiram and his classmates belonging to Naga-Mising-Ahom-Koch-Kachari and other native tribes came to the conclusion that the Assamese language teacher was making the Assamese language very difficult for them because he (the teacher) did not want to see the likes of them become educated. They felt that the Assamese language teacher was almost trying to destroy their native tongue. So, they decided to write a letter of complaint to the British officer. Unfortunately, the teacher got an inkling of it and appeared while they were drafting the letter and started beating them right and left with the passion of a raging bull. Everybody except Dandiram and Puwali fled the scene, but those two held their ground and boldly told the teacher that he had no right to treat them like that. Hearing that, the teacher got more enraged and gave them a few more blows on their faces. With swollen and bleeding faces they ran out of school. Puwali was determined to take revenge and waited outside the school gate with a machete in hand. Dandiram threw his Assamese text at the teacher saying "Keep your knowledge to yourself", and ran home to his parents.

That day many of the students left the public school. Two students of the Naga tribe left saying, "The Assamese teacher does not wish that we learn the Assamese language." A Miri student left saying, "The Assamese always try to belittle and find fault with us and that's why they are even making the language difficult for us." Some others left saying things like, "Our teachers and these pundits are going to kill our language," "In the future, if the Assamese find it hard to read and write their own language

---

[13] Nathan Brown, *Grammatical Notices of the Assamese Language*, 1848, hereafter referred to as *GNA vi.*

and become disrespectful of their language, then these teachers are responsible for it." Puwali's parents came and persuaded him to leave the teacher alone and instead they gave the teacher a piece of their mind.

For Dandiram that day proved to be his last one in school. His cuts and bruises were painful, but the mental trauma of the incident was more painful—the pain, the agony, and his suffering made him so unwell that he ran a high fever. His mother washed his feet with warm water, massaged his whole body with mustard oil, and gave him some herbal medicine to bring the fever down. While his mother was so tending him with all her affection, Dandiram kept pouring his grief out in mournful numbers.

"What kind of teacher is he? He does not know any kindness. We don't even beat a bull or cow like that."

"In front of the dignitaries, he wags his tail like a dog and in front of us he becomes a tiger. It would have been good if Puwali had cut him into pieces."

"He is trying to teach Assamese. But he does not even know the language well."

"He says everything is wrong in the Orunudoi; only what he writes is correct. We understand everything in Orunudoi but we don't understand anything he writes."

Money does not grow on trees

After dropping out of high school, Dandiram devoted his energies to farming. He thought of increasing their food production so as to earn some money by selling the surplus. It was not easy, however, to acquire more land for cultivation because most of the farmland in and around Gayangaon were deeded on copper plates to the Brahmins of various religious institutions. So, the best they could do was to farm extra areas on a 50-50 basis. That is, the farmer had to give half of the produce to the owner of the land. Therefore, it was not possible for one to earn enough befitting one's labor. However, everyday the need of money increased for the likes of Dandiram.

The British government had freed the paiks and allowed them to make a living without being anybody's slave—but, that liberty was their only wealth; prosperity remained an impossibility and upliftment was nothing but a dream. Since they led a simple life, their material needs were negligible. They themselves produced most of their basic needs like mustard oil, molasses, clothing and building materials in the village. The village was economically independent. However, as life began to flourish in that independent environment, their dependence on other needs began to increase. Knowingly or unconsciously, they started giving up producing their needs one by one and allowed their need for money to increase by one or two rupees each day. Finally, money became the most important thing and the ultimate necessity in their lives.

Following the advice of scientist Griffith, Baluram .never took a sip of tea, but for Dandiram, drinking tea had became such a habit that he could not start the day or start any work without first drinking a cup of tea. The shopkeepers and owners of tea stalls tried to push the sale of tea by telling people that tea was a stimulating and invigorating drink. The rich Assamese imitated the tea serving, tea drinking culture of the Englishmen as a status symbol, and the poor Assamese tried to imitate the rich as a show of vain prosperity. As a result, the young boys and girls of Assam acquired the tea drinking habit one by one. But tea was not something that you could grow at home; one needed to buy it from the store. Then for a good cup of tea you needed sugar, cups, teapots, tea strainers, etc., none of which were produced in the village.

With tea came snacks like *luci* and *bhaji* for which one needed flour and all kinds of spices. For Dandiram's father, the usual snacks were soft rice, ground rice (Sandah), rice crispy (Muri), rice flakes (Chira), all of which were produced at home. His son Dandiram, however, began to like loaves, biscuits, cakes, which had to be purchased. In Baluram's youth, salt was almost a rarity in Assam, and the people of that time did not develop any taste for salt except for what was extracted from banana peels and other vegetable products. But Dandiram developed a taste for salt, which, however cheap, had to be purchased. The clothes Baluram and his son Dandiram used, such as the dhoti, shawl and towel (Gamucha) were all woven and tailored by his wife. But for high school-educated Dandiram, those kinds of clothes were of no use—he wanted to wear shirts, shorts, and coats professionally tailored from mill clothes. Thus, as tea, sugar, salt, bread, flour, and mill clothes became necessities of life, so every household became more dependent on money. Whenever Dandiram had a chance he would tell his father: "You know dad, nowadays you really cannot survive without money. I think it will be better if I give up toiling on the soil and instead take a good job."

But his father would discourage him by saying, "Office work is not a good way of life. The whole day you are confined to your table in a room. In addition, a job may be there today but may disappear tomorrow. But if you have your grip on your plow, you never have to worry about your daily essentials. Your land will always be there. Thank God that we have a plot of land to live by. Money is a curse. To live a simple, happy and peaceful life you do not need money. You young folks are looking for money because you have picked up the habits of purchasing tea, sugar, salt, refined flour, shoes and mill clothes. If you give up these bad habits then you will not need any money. I believe Griffith when he said that tea is harmful to health, consumption of sugar may result in Diabetes, and if you start using salt daily you are bound to have high blood pressure."

Dandiram would interrupt saying, "But Dad, we need money to buy books, slates and chalk."

Dandiram's father would assure, "You don't have to worry about those. Your mother has always been making enough money by selling Eri clothes to pay for your educational needs, and if we expand our cultivation a little more, we can make some money by selling the surplus food. If you need to go and study at the mission school in Sibsagar, Guwahati or Nowgong we can pay for that as well."

Dandiram would say, "How long can mom and you continue to work so hard?" So, Dandiram would always look for jobs. He would vigorously look for jobs towards the end of summer after the rice was planted, until it was harvest time. He did manage to get some odd part-time jobs, including delivery work for the post office at Kakilamukh.

In spite of his father's words of caution, Dandiram continued to look for jobs. His mind was set on securing a job at one of the tea plantations. He knew that that was where well-paid jobs were. Once in a while he used to go to the river port near Jorhat and watch the big steamer boat load and unload passengers and cargo.

The Plight of Tea-garden Laborers

Often, the river port was not a pleasant sight because that was where laborers for the tea plantations were brought in. The misery of the laborers was heartbreaking. They were packed in the bottom part of the boat like cattle, and the men, women, and children had hardly any clothes on. During their transportation, and off the boat, they were thrown old and rotten food to eat. Everyone suffered from diseases and malnutrition. Many of them died on the journey and their bodies were thrown into the river. Those who survived the perilous trip would be in miserable shape and health when they arrived. Dandiram used to be curious about what kind of jobs those laborers did and how the plantations managed to earn all the money that everyone talked about. He did not have to wait long to find out.

One day at high noon, a tea garden laborer with a couple of little kids came and fell prostrate on Baluram's feet seeking shelter. The laborer asked, "Babu, please save us, please give the kids something to eat. I will serve you like a slave, help you in the field. But, please give us shelter." The man's name was Sivarao. Seeing their distress and believing that guests at high noon are like Narayana (the Hindu God), Baluram's family treated them well and let them stay in the house till everything was sorted out.

Sivarao and many others were brought to the plantation with a contract for twenty years. They were promised free transport to the place of work, regular supplies of food and other essentials for daily life and a fair salary. Since the laborers were not literate, the tea plantation owners exploited them in every possible way. They had to work from dawn to dusk every day, come rain or shine, be it unbearably hot or unbearably cold. While at work, they could never take a break because the supervisor, or Sardar in the native language, was always standing over them with a ruthless whip. For food, all they received was rice, lentils, salt, and a little oil. Sometimes, the British planter would kill a crocodile or an elephant and would give them the meat. The cottages where they had to reside were worse than cowbarns. There were no medical services of any kind to treat the laborers. If they became disabled because of poor health, or because of injuries, no attempt was made to help them. Those who could not work were thrown out of the plantation and put at the mercy of tigers, wolves, and other wild elements. The tea planters were interested only in getting the services of the laborers by squeezing the last drop of blood from them. Once in a while, a kind manager would try to do something to help them. But this was rare. The only taste of kindness they received was from the missionaries. The missionaries always took up the cause of the tea garden laborers and would advise them not to enter into anymore contracts once the initial contract was over. The missionaries would take care of those who embraced Christianity. The Hindu laborers did not own any land that they could make a living from outside of the tea plantations. As a matter of fact, the clever owners of tea gardens and tea companies did everything in their power to ensure that the laborers and their children would have no choice but to work in the plantations. In 1900, Sir Henry Cotton, the then Chief Commissioner of Assam, gives a vivid picture of the plight of laborers in his labour Report. He dutifully recorded tales of grievous misery and wrong-doing. Sir Cotton wrote :

> It is needless to say that it was only a small percentage of abuses which could come to my knowledge. But I had cases brought to my

notice where contracts of sickly and unfit labourers were cancelled for the purpose of keeping down the rate of mortality among contract labourers, and of others where deaths had been treated as desertions for the same reason. I knew of cases where it was the practice to expel sickly coolies who had become unfit for labour. I have seen with my own eyes a Government hospital full of sickly and dying coolies whose contracts had been cancelled and who had just been expelled from his garden by one of the oldest and most respected tea planters in the province. I have seen dead and dying coolies lying in the ditch by the roadside and in the bazar. I knew of cases in which coolies in the fourth year of their agreement were not paid higher rate of salary to which they were entitled. In other cases, rice was not provided at the statutory price and the subsistence allowance prescribed by law was not paid to sick coolies or pregnant women. Advances were often illegally debited against coolies on account of subsistence allowance or sick diet, as well as on account of rewards paid for the deserters, and labourers were thus bound hand and foot to the garden service. In some instances only a few annas (or pence) found their way into the hands of a coolie as wages in the course of the whole year, the managers having deemed that they were justified in making deductions right and left so long as they kept their labourers in good condition like their horses and their cattle.[14]

The laborers were not given any incentive to save. There was no banking arrangement of any kind. Instead, the management established or encouraged the establishment of liquor stores where cheap country liquor was sold. So, by and large, the majority of the laborers, both men and women, spent their money on alcoholic drinks. Thereby, they made themselves weak both physically and mentally.

Few, like Sivarao, managed to stay away from alcohol and were able to save some money that they could spend on buying a few things for the comfort of their children. Sivarao was a positive-thinking man and he always thought of uplifting the laborers. He pinned his hopes on the Assamese people. He was attracted by the Vaishnab culture that grew out of devotion to Krishna and centered on the village congregational center (the *Namghar*, or temple, of an Assamese village). Sivarao's forefathers had similarly embraced Vaishnavism under the influence of Guru Purandar Das. Like the majority of the Assamese, the ancestors of Sivarao were also

---

[14] Cotton, Sir Henry. *Indian and Home Memories*, hereafter referred to as *IHM* (265-266).

newly converted Hindus. They were also despised by the so-called upper caste Hindus.

One of the Assamese clerks in the tea-plantation was very kind to Sivarao. From this clerk, Sivarao came to know that many Assamese farmers were not able to cultivate all of their land because of the lack of laborers. So, Sivarao had decided that when the term of his initial contract was over, he would move out of the plantation and go to an Assamese village where he would try to make a living by helping a needy family in farming. He would also put his children under the care of the Assamese families as servants. He had already put his elder daughter with the kind Assamese clerk, and she was having a much better life there than she would have had in the tea-plantation. That Assamese clerk was willing to help Sivarao, but could not do so, because of the fear that the British manager of the tea-plantation might be offended. The manager was quite mad because quite a few laborers joined Sivarao and did not want to renew their contract.

Dandiram's family was happy to help Sivarao. Another villager agreed to keep Sivarao's son and Baluram's brother also took the daughter. Baluram put up a little shed to serve as Sivarao's living quarters. Sivarao helped Dandiram in the cultivation of rice and vegetables. Sivarao also cleaned the yard. In this way, Baluram was able to produce more, much more than what Sivarao himself consumed. The other tea garden laborers who had left the plantation with Sivarao were also similarly established in that and other neighboring villages.

In any case, all those laborers were completely desolate and poor. They owned nothing and were without any roots after being uprooted from their native homes. Even in the Assamese villages, the laborers were completely under the mercy of the Assamese head of the household. Many Assamese, instead of treating them with kindness, took advantage of their helplessness. For those Assamese, tea garden laborers provided cheap labor and, soon, there were plenty of such cheap laborers. Gradually, the Assamese came to look down upon those laborers as a class of lower beings and referred to them as "Coolie" in a derogatory manner. Ordinary Assamese people gave those "Coolies" the same prejudicial treatment as they themselves were receiving from the wealthy upper class. The class of people that the ordinary Assamese despised, the upper class, had become the role models for the Assamese.

Sivarao was of course fortunate. He received good treatment from Dandiram's family. Dandiram gathered all the information about tea plantations from Sivarao as he could get. He came to know from Sivarao that since he could read and write, he could become a Babu (a clerk), and the life of a Babu was very good. Since Sivarao was there to help his father, Dandiram expressed a desire to become a Babu in a tea plantation. This time, his father Baluram consented.

Dandiram Babu

Dandiram was able to become a clerk in the Saru Saikota garden near Jorhat. As a clerk, his job was not only in record-keeping, but also in supervising the work assignment and development of projects of the industry. Due to his dexterity and because of his desire to learn the running of the industry, he soon got promoted to head clerk. As the head clerk, he was given a comfortable house, household laborers and he received a handsome salary. Since he also received food, clothes, etc., all on subsidized rate, he could save a good percentage of his salary. So, when he was 23 years old, he married Damayanti, whose family he had known while working at the Kakilamukh post office. He soon became the proud father of a boy and a girl whom he could raise comfortably on the tea plantation. His only worry was his old father Baluram.

Baluram was managing everything well on his farm with the help of Sivarao. Since Dandiram was also helping him financially, everything was fine. As age crept in, Baluram was not able to work as hard as before but he did not need to. As a matter of fact, he had enough money to buy all his needs. But he kept himself busy at home and in the village Namghar. Things changed when Sivarao passed away. Since his wife had died earlier, Baluram was left alone in the village. So, Dandiram asked his father to come and live with them in the tea garden, but Baluram would not leave his village and give up his activities in the Namghar. Instead, he would implore his son to come back and start living in the village. Baluram would emphatically declare:

"Jobs in the garden are there today but may disappear tomorrow."

"True, you are living in comfort but you are living without the taste of good social life or cultural activities. You don't even get a chance to do some congregational chanting with your village folk."

"You spend half the time saluting the sahib."

"What will the children do? There are no schools for their education, no society, no relatives in the garden. How will they learn social obligations and good behavior?"

"If everybody works in offices, who will do the cultivation? Who will supply food and produce? You are not doing a good thing by giving up your hold on the plow."

Because of opinions like the above, Baluram went to the tea garden only once in a while. He could never stay there for a long time. After spending a few days in the garden he would become restless and impatient to come back to the village. While he was at the garden he would always advise his son to come back to the village, send the children to school, and take an active role in the cultural life of the village.

Dandiram was mindful of his father's advice and saw the truth in them. But, it was not easy for him to give up the sense of security and the comfortable life he was providing for his family. He used to assure his father that he would not stay in the garden forever but would return to the village after saving some money. Because of that assurance and because of his advancing age, Baluram finally agreed to move to the gardens for a few years. At that time, Dandiram was in charge of the two elephants that belonged to the tea garden. He got permission to use an elephant to fetch his father, but his father insisted on walking. That was a mistake.

Meanwhile, some Assamese rich men had also become tea planters and were becoming phenomenally rich. So, they imposed rules on the common folks as if they were the dignitaries of the Kings. As Baluram was walking past one of the tea planters house with his umbrella opened, the servants of the planter came and harassed Baluram saying no one was allowed to walk by the big man's house with an umbrella opened. At another place, he saw some high school students drinking tea in a tea stall. Remembering what Griffith had told him, Baluram thought that perhaps those students were becoming sick at the high school. As he walked past a Namghar of a village, he saw some older persons drinking opium water. One or two of them even offered a cup to Baluram, saying "Have a sip, you would feel so good as if divine nectar is flowing through your veins."

Along the way he also met many tea garden laborers heading towards Jorhat. Most of them were old or maimed, and one or two of them were suffering from incurable diseases. They were all being thrown out of tea plantations because they became useless for the tea industry. So, they were hoping to survive, if possible, by begging in Jorhat town.

A lady who was crying hysterically caught Baluram's attention. The night before while they were sleeping by the roadside, a tiger had taken her husband away. She and her companions had all worked in the garden for forty years. Since they could no longer work as profitably as before, the owner would not enter into anymore contracts with them and sent them out giving each a ration of food for three days. Food for three days was all they got after forty years of service. They had no choice but to go begging and expose themselves to the elements. Some of them did fall prey to the tigers, crocodiles, and snakes that roamed freely in the Jorhat area in those days.

The owners of the tea industry did not feel any obligation to take care even of the old and sick laborers. The owners would say, "If they had saved their salaries instead of wasting it on liquor, then they would not have to become beggars. It's their own fault." The truth was, the owners themselves made liquor available to the laborers. The owners made sure that liquor was available in plenty but they did not make any provision or give any incentive to the laborers to save money or to plan for retirement. Baluram felt that the tea industry was doing immense harm to the Assamese. Already valuable forestland had been cleared for the plantation of tea, creating havoc for the wild animals that once lived in those forests. The wild animals started roaming around the neighboring villages in search of food.

Laborers for the tea plantations were brought from all parts of India to the tea gardens and then let loose in their old age, making beggars and sick people a large part of Assam's life. So, Baluram and Dandiram discussed the issue:

"When you grow old, will they throw you out of the plantation like they throw out these old laborers?"

"Yes, when we are unable to perform to satisfactory standards, we will also have to leave the garden."

"What will you do then? Where will you go?"

"Oh, we will get some money from the company. I will go back to the village and till the land."

"How will you work in the farm? If your children always live in the garden, how would they learn to work in the field? There are no schools there. Where will they learn to read and write?"

"Don't worry, as soon as they become a little bit older, we will send them to Jorhat and they will be able to go to school there."

"You mean your family will be in Jorhat and you will live here alone? What kind of a life is that?"

"No, no, I would go and visit them frequently."

"You know, the best thing a man can have is a family. If you always have to live away from your family, there is no point in being alive. Children growing up without their father, a father living away from his wife and children; I hope these things will not happen to you and your family."

"Well, well, I will also move back to Jorhat soon. Actually, I also have been thinking about it for some time. Just let me work for a few more years and save some money. We will all be out of here."

Dandiram had to make the move from the tea garden back to his village sooner than he had thought.

Birth, Destiny, and Karma

On Thursday, December 12, 1901 (26 Aghun), Dandiram's fourth child Phanidhar was born in the tea garden. The pundit, who made the horoscope of the newborn, emphasized again and again that the boy's signs were exceptional and that he should be a very bright learned man from whom the society could benefit a lot. The pundit said, "Don't neglect to educate him. The signs that I see in him for education are exceptional. If God permits, he will be able to light up this land with his education." One reason why Baluram decided to come to the gardens was to be near his grandson who charmed him. Baluram saw many good indications in the baby. However, Baluram did not live long enough to see the child grow up. He passed away when Phanidhar was only about three years old. But before he breathed his last, he told Dandiram, "Look after this child well. He has the potential to climb very high. You are getting a son like him after the good work through many births. Don't shut him up in the garden—send him to school, educate him at all costs. Remember that it's my last wish that you do whatever possible to educate this boy. He will accomplish whatever I was hoping you might accomplish in your lifetime."

By the time Phanidhar was four years old, his father was determined to give up his job in the tea garden and move back to his village in Jorhat. The manager Mr. Silmon and his wife both took a liking for Phanidhar and would always say, "What a smart kid, he is going to be very bright." More than that, Mr. Silmon did not want to lose the services of Dandiram who was like his right hand. So, he tried to stop Dandiram from leaving the garden and said to him, "Listen Dandiram, we will pay all expenses to keep him and educate him at the mission school in Jorhat."

But Dandiram relented saying, "We Assamese do not like to part with children at such an early age, Plus, we feel that we would deprive him of our affection and the interaction with his brother, sisters, and other relatives. What fun is it to give birth to children and be unable to bring them up? No, we cannot let our children get out of sight. I would rather starve than part with my children."

So after twenty years of service, and after living in luxury for twenty years in the garden, he decided to give up that life and embrace the rugged life of a farmer. Mr. Silmon and all other officers of the company tried to persuade him to change his mind. But, for the education of his child and to fulfill the last wishes of his father, Dandiram was steadfast in his decision and plodded homewards with his wife and four children. This was a momentous journey, one that would prove to be of immense benefit to the cause of education in Assam and for Dandiram's descendants.

6
Acts of Kindness: British Tea-Planters Silmon and Ward

There comes a time in the career of the Anglo-Indian when he must face the alternative of separation from both wife and children or from children alone. His children cannot be reared in India , and it may be that all the duty of their management and education is thrown off by parents. Or it may be that the mother in a conflict of duties is torn from her husband and devotes herself to the children. In either case there must be a laceration of domestic ties and the family bond is broken. It is this family dissolution and the domestic anxiety following from it that are the most painful accompaniments of an Indian life. The crisis had now arrived in our case. My wife's health was delicate, and she was now entering on her seventh consecutive hot weather in the Bengal plains. The boys had grown too old to remain any longer in India with safety. And so it was decided that they should go home together. A third and last son was born to us in the September of this year in England. To the care and education of these three boys my wife bestowed for many years the most exemplary devotion, and to her is due the whole of the credit of any successful career to which in after life they may justly lay claim. (Sir Henry Cotton, *Indian and Home Memories,* T. Fisher Unwin, London, 1911, hereafter referred to as *IHM* 125).

In the previous chapter, we saw that Indians, and, indeed, parents of all ages and from all walks of life, face the same predicament Sir Cotton has described above. Of course, in the case of the Anglo-Indians, the problem is more pronounced because of their approach to solve it. Here is another view that issued from Dandiram's decision to give up his life of luxury in the tea garden so that he could educate his son (Phanidhar) and also fulfil his father's last wishes.

Sir Henry Cotton (1845 – 1915)

From a painting by Hugh G. Riviere, presented by the people of Bengal, 1903. Courtesy: Indian and Home Memories

The Bet

The weekend after Dandiram left the tea plantation, Mr. Silmon, the senior manager of the company, visited the Wards at Saru Saikota garden. As the two families sat and drank, they had the following conversation:

Silmon: So, you could not persuade Dandi Babu to stay. Now we will have a hard time finding a man who can take over the job.

Ward: I did everything I could. But nothing would change his mind.

Silmon: Stubborn old man I guess. Did you offer him more money?

Ward: Yes, I did. I could not buy him. It is funny you think he is stubborn. Dandi Babu is the last man I would call stubborn. He is very amiable, very accommodating. No, he is not stubborn.

Silmon: Then, why wouldn't he change his mind?

Ward: I think he values two things more than anything else. First, respect for his father. Second, deep faith in education.

Silmon: What do you mean?

Ward: The poor fellow has a lot of respect for his father. Apparently, the old man's last wish was that Dandi would go back to his village immediately and educate his children. The problem is with the youngest son, Phanidhar. The astrologer making his horoscope predicts that Phanidhar has great potential to be highly educated and spread learning among his people.

Silmon: Dandi believes all that, and is prepared to give up everything to send his son to school? He is a stupid fellow.

Ward: There you have it all. I admire those natives who are so respectful of their elders and so willing to be guided by astrologers.

Silmon: Even if he wants to educate his children, he can send them to the school at Jorhat. Did you tell him that we could arrange that?

Ward: I offered that we would send his wife and the kids to Jorhat. We could give them a nanny and a laborer, and he could take the company elephant to visit them every weekend.

Silmon: Stupid! Isn't he?

Ward: Don't say that loud. My wife thinks otherwise. She says Dandi is a very wise man and he did the right thing.

Silmon: Why does she think so?

Ward: She says, "A man or a woman's greatest pleasure is to give birth to children and raise them with love and affection." This she got from Dandi Babu.

The two wives joined in the conversation.

Pat Silmon: That is wonderful! Those are exactly the words in my heart. Ever since we sent little John to the boarding school in Calcutta, my life has been a long yearning to be near him. I see now why the Hindus have a child God.

Betty: I think so. Isn't it wonderful? Don't put the natives down. They may not be clever but they are wise. I will never send my children to boarding school and expose them to child molesters, homosexuals, and abusive matrons.

Silmon: No, they are not that bad. Anyway, it is better than living a poor and destitute life in a cold frigid country.

Ward: No, I am not going back to England to live from hand to mouth.

Betty: You know, I have been thinking a lot about it. I have found a solution. I am going to teach my children at home. Since I am certified to teach up to the junior level, I will teach them at home. I will bring all the textbooks, some sample exams and teach them at home. When they grow up they can go and take the junior Cambridge exam and then they may continue higher studies in England. How does that sound?

Pat: That is wonderful. If you mean it, I would bring John home and let you teach him as well. I can help you as much as I can. But, tell me one thing, will the education authority back home recognize this kind of at home schooling?

Betty: Sure they will, if the kid can pass the exams. As a matter of fact, if the kid can pass and prove his worth, everybody will recognize him, but if he fails and has nothing much to show, then nobody will recognize him.

Ward: I support that wholeheartedly. But, please tell me one thing. Do you folks believe in astrology the way the natives believe? Look at Dandi Babu. The astrologer who predicted that the little fellow had great potential for learning started the whole thing.

Silmon: I think astrology is just a humbug. Dandi Babu will soon realize that he made a big mistake. Wait two or three years. He will come back begging as soon as the little fellow fails an annual examination.

Ward: No, I don't think so. I can bet he will never fail. I can already see signs that what the astrologer says about Dandi Babu's son is true.

Silmon: I can bet that it is not going to be true.

Ward: How much money do you want to put on that bet? How about 100 rupees?

Silmon: Sure, let us do it. I bet 100 rupees that Dandi Babu's son will fail sooner or later in school.

Ward: Okay, I bet 100 rupees that he will not. That is a deal. You better start saving, man; the little fellow is quite a kid. He is not even four and he already knows his alphabet. He can already count, add, and multiply.

Silmon: Okay, that's a deal. I wish him luck and wish you luck too. I know the natives, their thinking, and their jealousies. They will create an environment that will not let him go beyond elementary school.

Man proposes, God disposes

Upon returning to his village, Dandiram formally started Phanidhar's education by arranging a congregational chanting at home and taking the blessings of society. At such a ceremony, the child kneels down before the congregation and is blessed by the village elders. The child then starts writing a few letters and words on a slate or on a piece of paper using chalk or fountain pen made of birds' feather. The next day the child goes to school. Phanidhar first went to a private school run by a benevolent Brahmin known popularly as Kon Bamun, whose school was near Phanidhar's village. After spending a few months there he went to Union School in the heart of Jorhat town. At that school, Phanidhar proved to be a very sharp student with special dexterity in arithmetic. Such was his skill that once, when school inspector G.A. Small visited the school, he was so impressed by Phanidhar that he gave Phanidhar a reward of one rupee (a big sum of money in those days).

Phanidhar's success in school made Dandiram feel that he made the right decision by leaving his job at the tea garden. With the money he had saved, he was able to buy several plots of land to which he added several acres of farmland. He was able to cultivate the land for rice and vegetables. In addition, he had enough money to buy other necessities. There was no hardship in the family and they lived comfortably. Meanwhile, he had one more daughter and a son. After everything was settled, he decided to build a bigger house with a permanent structure and bought an acre in a residential area. So, he procured some big timber for posts, and other building materials. Unfortunately, Dandiram could not begin the construction on his new house. When Phanidhar was not even eleven years old, Dandiram caught pneumonia and died suddenly at the young age of forty-seven. At the time of Dandiram's death, his wife was carrying his seventh child.

All of a sudden, the world collapsed around Phanidhar. On his deathbed, Dandiram told his wife's brother, "If I die, please educate this unfortunate child of mine by whatever means you can. That was the main purpose of my return to this village." Two days after his father's death, Phanidhar had to sit for the primary examination that determined who would get a scholarship to go to high school. He did take the exam. Although the results came with the news that Phanidhar topped the list of successful students, there was no happiness in the Datta household. Phanidhar wrote about that day:

> Results of the scholarships were announced. Jumping with joy I went and told my mother, told everyone in the village. My mother and everybody at home started crying the same way as they did when Dad had died. My mother cried saying, 'If your father was here he would have done this or that—how unfortunate you are, who will educate you?

Sadness and poverty encircled the once prosperous household of Dandi Babu. The big wooden posts and other building materials started rotting—the house could not be built. Though inexperienced, Phanidhar and his elder brother Nanda took to the fields to feed the family. Their father had lent some money to some relatives, but instead of being grateful and returning the money, the borrowers completely denied the loan and paid them only unkind words.

Nanda thought of dropping out of high school because there was no money to pay his school fees and buy books. However, when the news of Phanidhar's scholarship came, it was agreed that Nanda's fees would be paid from the scholarship money. The two brothers took all the responsibilities of the family on their shoulder and did everything together with understanding, trust, and a kind of affection that would last all their lives.

As a child, Phanidhar used to resent the authority of his father for yelling at him if he did not get up early to study, or if he played with his friends till late. He was especially mad for the beating he got from his father one morning for sneaking out of the house to play soccer with his friends. It was more upsetting to him because he had spent hours making a soccer ball out of old clothes. Phanidhar used to be upset because his father would insist he study regularly for an hour or so every morning and every evening. After his father's death, all the rules that his father used to discipline him became very meaningful to him. Phanidhar felt the immense pressure his brother Nanda was under and admired the attitude with which Nanda undertook the family's responsibilities. Nanda told Phanidhar, "Now we will have to do everything for our mother and our sisters. But, don't you worry; I will manage the work in the field. I am not doing very well in my studies, whereas you are doing excellent in your schoolwork. So, you study with devotion and then you will be able to get a good job."

Phanidhar's desolate mother would sometimes say in despair, "Forget your education, first we have to find ways to survive." Nanda would then interrupt and say, "No, no, he must continue his studies. Even his horoscope says that he will be learned and do a lot for the upliftment of his people." Phanidhar's uncle was of the same mind and said, "Yes, Phani must continue his studies, don't you remember what his father said on his deathbed? 'Educate him at all cost.' I am with you Phani; I will help you every possible way. Try to fulfill your father's hope, for which he gave up the best things in life. Act according to his last wishes."

"Education at all costs," "Education for the upliftment of the people." Those words of his father and the knowledge that his horoscope predicted great potential for learning were encouraging to Phanidhar. In addition, his elder brother's love, affection, and assurances remained a true inspiration throughout his life. He took to his studies diligently and took the strong resolve that he would leave no stone unturned to acquire higher learning. He was confident that he would not allow anything to prevent him from reaching his goals.

He faced many obstacles both in acquiring education and in uplifting his people through education. In his efforts, he received help and encouragement from many quarters both western and Indian. But behind his success was the inspiration of a benevolent British administrator and a British educator. Mr. Ward came to know about the death of Dandi Babu. He immediately sent a messenger to fetch Dandi Babu's eldest son, Nanda. Mr. Ward not only offered the family some sympathy both in cash and kindness, but also offered Nanda a job at the tea garden any time he wanted it. Nanda told Mr. Ward that as soon as his younger brother was big enough to work at the field, he would take a job in the tea garden. When Phanidhar was a little bit older and stronger, he was able to take care of all the work in the field by himself. As promised, Nanda went to

Mr. Ward looking for a job. He decided to earn some money to support the family, especially since he had to arrange the weddings of his two elder sisters. Mr. Ward gave him a job in a tea garden near Mariani about twelve miles away from home. He would come home Saturday afternoon and take a train from Jorhat to Mariani very early in the morning on Monday.

To catch the train, he had to walk a distance of about two miles before daybreak. Since it was very dark when he left home for the station, Phanidhar would walk with him and, along the way, they would talk and discuss their future and that of their sisters. According to Phanidhar, those were some of the happiest moments in his life. It brought to both of them a sense of security, a sense of responsibility, and a deep feeling of attachment to one another.

Prejudices of Teachers

On one of those days, Phanidhar confessed to his brother that he had had enough of school life, and that he was just about ready to quit. Phanidhar was facing a fate similar to his father's. In those days, there were many teachers who abused their power and status to rough-up students. More often than not, children of the poorer section or lower stratum of society were the victims of their abuse. These teachers often derived sadistic pleasure from beating up school children, and even extended their authority beyond school. Those teachers were completely unaware of the harm their rude behavior caused the tender children, some of whom had not even reached their teens. The effects on older students were worse. Their rebellious minds sought revenge on their teachers. Since they were powerless against the teachers, they turned their anger against society. Subsequently, if they could not do anything against the teachers or the society, they would lose interest in learning, and became negative in their attitude. What was worse were the prejudices of the teachers against children coming from what society regarded as the lower castes or from poor families. Most of the teachers in those days were from the upper castes and most of the people of the ruling or the upper class were from the upper castes. Many teachers thought that the English education was only for the children of the upper class or the upper castes. They regarded attempts by a lad coming from poor background as an encroachment of forbidden land. Of course, their prejudices were expressed in somewhat violent ways.

In the words of Phanidhar, "In high school, I never got any beating for my misdeed or fault but I received many beatings for no fault of mine."

Such beatings from his Sanskrit teacher became routine, and that routine led to deep despair. Phanidhar left a description of his despair in his biographical note:

> Every day he not only beat me up on any pretext, but also called me by such derogatory names as bamboo stump or tree stump. Almost every day Madhab, Suren, Indra Sandikoi and I wrote the same thing. In translation work, we all wrote exactly the same thing. My handwriting used to be better than anybody else's and I did most of the translations; others providing only nominal help. When he graded them, Madhab (brother-in-law of the Deputy Inspector of Schools) would get 8 out of 10 and some advice with kind words like, 'You can use such and such a word,' etc. Suren (grandson of the former Prime Minister of the Ahom King) would also get 7 or 8. Indra Sandikoi (son of the tea planter Radha Sandikoi) would get 7 or 8 but would be told, 'Improve your handwriting. If the examiner sees this kind of handwriting he would not give you a good score', etc., and when he would look at my paper, he would always begin like this, 'You! Where did you learn to put the short vowel sign u like this? Where did you learn to put the comma like this?' Creating such faults, he would either slap me a few times or twist my ears several times.

In the beginning, Phanidhar took this treatment as an amusing act of the teacher. When it became a routine, however, he started feeling sad. He could not express his sadness to others, especially to Suren, Madhab and Indra because they were his very close and dear friends. Even those friends could not help noticing the way the teacher was roughing up the brightest among them. They discussed the matter together, but could not come up with any motive because, as teenagers growing up together, they were not aware of some of the prejudices of caste, religion or class, that their elders harbored in their minds. They, the teenagers, also did not understand why a teacher would treat a poor student differently than a rich man's son. They, the teenaged friends of Phanidhar, saw themselves as very much alike. In fact, they did everything together: they sat together, they played together, and they even ate from the same plate. The net result was that they all hated the Sanskrit teacher and hated the subject he taught. They came up with such reasons as:

"Because Phani is smart,"

"Because Phani knows more than him,"

"Because Phani is skinny,"

"For nothing,"

"Because Phani does not have a father," etc.

In addition, Madhab, who himself was an orphan and who was being brought up by his elder sister, was very sensitive to such unkind treatment. He was frightened that maybe the teacher was beating Phani because the teacher knew that Phani's father was dead. Madhab thought that perhaps the teacher did not know that his father was dead and that once the teacher found out that he also did not have a father to protect him, the teacher would start roughing him up as well. But Phani would assure him that was not the case; it was that the teacher hated him. So Madhab and Phani planned a ploy to find out. One day, Madhab took Phani's answer book to the teacher, and as before, the teacher gave it a score of eight. Then Phani took Madhab's answer book, and as before the teacher found fault with his vowel signs, etc., and started to hit him. Phani explained the answers were not in his handwriting but rather in Madhab's. That made the teacher very angry and gave Phani a double dose of a beating. That day Phani felt very despondent. It left no doubt in his mind that the teacher hated him with a passion. He knew that it was not his handwriting nor his ability to learn Sanskrit that caused his teacher to hate him. It was simply Phani as a person whom the teacher hated, perhaps due to the fact that he was poor. He expressed his realization to his friend, Madhab, who also realized the sad truth. He told Madhab that he would not come back to school.

Madhab was deeply disturbed by the whole thing because he realized he was fatherless like Phani, and because he, too, would have been poor and helpless like Phani if he did not have his elder sister and her husband. His sadness so permeated his person that his sister sensed something was wrong. When pressed, Madhab told the whole episode to his sister and her husband, Sarat Goswami, who was then the Superintendent of the Normal School, and previously the Deputy Inspector of Schools. Mr. Goswami was a very learned man and especially trained in education. In addition, he was a very progressive person who gave leadership to the educated Assamese in many directions. He founded the Assamese Literary Society, Teacher's forum at Jorhat, and provided guidance in primary education in the neighboring hill areas. Mr. Goswami immediately made a trip to the teacher's house and told him to change his age-old thinking. Mr. Goswami told the teacher why it was so important for a teacher to be kind to all his students, and why a teacher should not have prejudices of any kind—religion, caste, or class.

Then Mr. and Mrs. Goswami and Madhab went to Phanidhar's house where Mr. Goswami assured Phanidhar that he would always keep an eye out for him, and that the teacher would not wrong him. Phani was most moved by Mr. Goswami's revelation that he was also very poor and that he had also lost his father a year after he had entered Collegiate High School at Gauhati. Mr. Goswami told Phanidhar that both he and his brother had to go begging in order to be able to stay in school and make ends meet. Mr. Goswami told Phani that many people helped him to get his education and he was determined to help Phani get the education he deserved. That was the start of a long and lasting relationship between the Goswami family and the Datta family. After that, the Goswamis became regular visitors to the Datta house. Phanidhar found in Goswami a real role model and one which he tried always to emulate.

English System of Education produces a rigid class system

When English education was introduced in India, the British Government must have had the self-interest to produce a class of educated people who would help the Government rule India by producing literate soldiers, clerks, teachers, administrators, and so on. That is why they kept the education system limited in scope so that only a privileged few could get its benefits. As a result the poor always had to struggle to get an education. Even in England, until recently the English education system has consistently reinforced a pretty rigid class system. In India also it has done the same ever since the day it was introduced. This can also be inferred from the difficulties that Phanidhar Datta faced to get an education. Education in India has always been very difficult, if not impossible, for the poor.

The British Government had established high schools at several towns in upper Assam. In addition, Govind Bezbarua, a bold educator, had established private high schools at Golaghat (1886), Sibsagar (1888), and at Jorhat (1893). Those high schools enabled youths from those areas to receive an education that could qualify them to go for a college education. For a college education they could go to Cotton College at Gauhati, which was established in 1901. In those days it was not easy for the poorer section of the people to send their children to Gauhati for a college education. They could afford to pay for high schools selling their produce, but their produce could not earn enough to pay for post-matriculation studies. The experiences of Phanidhar described below will provide a better understanding of this.

> I had not collected enough money to pay the examination fees—mother sold two eri pieces (native homemade shawls) she had produced for 16 rupees to a Bengali merchant who had come to sell cows. Taking

those sixteen rupees I went to school. There I came to know that my friend Madhab Chandra Bhattacharya had already paid my fees. He had collected that money from his sister, the wife of Inspector Srijut Sarat Chandra Goswami. I had no idea that noble Mrs. Goswami would pay my fees. The noble Mr. & Mrs. Goswami treated me with a lot of kindness like they treated Madhab. I will always remain very grateful and indebted to them.

After taking the exam on time, I passed it in 1921 in first division. Srijut Sarat Goswami brought the exam result a few days before others could get it, by writing to somebody in Calcutta. Our telegram contained the results of Madhab, Surendranath Burha Gohain, Sailendranath Nath and mine. All three came to my house with the telegram—their joys knew no bounds—they were talking about who would take what courses in college, when they would go, where they would stay, etc.—the very things that were in my heart, but how could I think of going to college?

Let me mention here that after our father died, our enemies and some people in the village made our lives miserable. My elder brother started his job training in our birthplace, which was the Saru Saikota garden. Our old acquaintance, the English manager, called him in, paying only six rupees a month. I went to the town with my friends. Most afternoons, we used to go and sit on the beach in the northern side of the Rajmao tank—the school boarding house was not there then. On that side there were two bungalows for the Sahibs—the Sahibs were not there. There I joined my friends with the joys of successfully passing the examination and started planning for the future till 8:30 p.m. Then we got up to go home. Sailendra Nath used to live in the residence of Nabin Phukan across from the present girls' high school. I went there chatting with him and when he entered his house I went back to Rajmao tank and worried about higher education, my financial situation, and how I could go to college. I spent the whole night on the pool bench crying in despair.

That sleepless night, Phanidhar Datta took the strong resolve that if he could ever acquire higher education he would definitely do something to make education more accessible to poor students. Before that, however, it was necessary for him to arrange money for his own education.

He decided to approach some of the rich men of Jorhat. Many of them were encouraging, but, even after a lot of hustle, nobody offered him more than a few rupees. He walked from one tea-planter to another and met the same fate. One of them even gave him a huge lecture, gave him five rupees and said he could not help anymore. After trying like that for some time and being unable to collect enough money, he gave up all hopes of ever going to college and took to the plough.

However, after finishing all the planting, the desire to get a college education started gnawing at him again. He decided that he must find a job and earn money to pay his own way in college.

> First I went to the office of Jorhat Railroad Company—because I heard that they were going to hire a clerk paying forty rupees a month, and that the selection would be on the basis of a written test. The headclerk Babu Surendranath Ghosh knew me because I played cricket with him. He said he would try whatever he could to help me get the job. The test was held—consisting of a piece of dictation and a few math problems—I did all the math problems correctly and made no mistake in the dictation. Suren Babu told me that I would get the job. However, after a few days, I came to know that Sri Lalit Mahanta, B.Sc. was hired because he was a B.Sc. All those who took the test were ignored. After that I joined Jorhat Mission school as a teacher with a salary of 25 rupees a month—I had to give up that because of involvement with the Non-cooperation movement[15]. Then I made acquaintance with DSP Babu Monmathnath Ghosh. I used to carry his gun during his hunting trips to Malow field hoping that by making him feel good I would be able to get the job of a police sub-inspector. Even there after some exams, they informed me that they could not offer me a sub-inspectors spot but could employ me as an assistant sub-inspector. They had simply replaced the name Havildar by assistant sub-inspector. Then I decided not to take the police job.

Arranged marriage

Since help from the rich was not forthcoming, and since there was no prospect of getting a decent job, Phanidhar thought of another plan.

He thought that if he agreed to marry the daughter of a rich man, then his rich father-in-law might agree to pay for his education. When he suggested the idea to his mother, his mother laughed and said, "You have got two unmarried elder sisters and an unmarried elder brother. How can you think of your marriage?"

> "No, I am not thinking about my marriage, but about my education. Even the noble Sarat Goswami married soon after going to college

[15] See Appendix for an account of the Non-cooperation movement

and that was a big help."

"But he did not have any unmarried elder sisters. Don't even think of such a thing. People will think you are becoming crazy."

"OK then don't wait, try to arrange the marriages of my elder sisters"

"Well, how can I think of marriage when there is not a penny in the house? Who can go and look for grooms I don't know what God has in store for us and what God will bring for the girls."

In those days, arranged marriages were the rule. A marriage was usually looked upon as a social obligation. So, interests of the family, the village and perhaps the caste were very important factors. Parents would teach their daughters to work in the field, to cook, to take care of the whole household , to weave and to sew. The parents tried to find a suitable match for daughter in a family and village that would assure their daughter a happy life. In the same way, a young man's parents tried to find a suitable match who would help him and the family every possible way. It usually worked well because the parents always tried to do the best for their daughter or son. However, if one is orphaned by one's mother or father or both, then things may prove bad because the self-interest of the guardian often dominates other considerations. There are abundant stories in Assamese society of abuse of authority by people who force unpleasant partners on wards under their care.

For once God was kind to Phani's mother. Her brother in Charigaon met a young man who was looking for a bride. The young man wanted somebody who would be adept in running a household. He had lost his mother a year earlier and there was no woman in the house who could hold the household together. Phanidhar's uncle talked the young man into starting a dialogue with Phanidhar's family. It clicked, and the wedding was settled. What's more, the young man wanted a simple marriage and asked Phanidhar's mother not to waste money on ornaments and clothes. In those days, all the villagers helped when a wedding took place in a household. Each family had a set quota of rice to give to the family of the one that was getting married. In addition, they would supply banana trees to make disposable bowls, bamboo to set up a gazebo, and above all everybody (both old and young) would come and work to prepare food. The parents simply had to give some ornaments and clothes according to their abilities. There was no tradition of supplying furniture, beds, etc., as happens nowadays. Marriage, by all accounts, was a social event in which everyone participated and everyone cooperated wholeheartedly.

Since the groom's family did not want to make any demands, marriage was no problem.

The only problem was that there were two persons willing to marry the same girl. The same week that things were settled in Gayangnon for the eldest daughter's wedding, Nanda unaware of the developments at home, started a dialogue with a young man's family near the garden as a match for his sister. That weekend, when Nanda came home and told his mother that he had invited the boy's parents to come and visit the girl's family, the Datta's faced a dilemma:

"It's good that Aimon's wedding is all settled, but what do I tell the folks from Parbatiya when they come tomorrow?"

"Oh! Don't worry, I will do all the talking. I will go and meet them half way and bring them here."

"No, you should not bring them here. We should let them know that Aimon's wedding is already settled and they should look elsewhere."

"No, no! You can't do that. God is finally smiling at us and we should help God to help us."

"What do you mean?"

"It's simple: we start a dialogue with them to marry Bhani the younger one."

"No, no, she is not yet ready."

"Why not? She is only two years younger than my eldest sister."

"Maybe, but she is not prepared mentally. How can she think of marriage when her older sister is not married?"

"I'll prepare her mentally."

So he did. The mother and his elder brother were apprehensive of arranging two marriages at about the same time, but, Phanidhar prevailed saying it would make things easier and cut down expenses. The younger of his elder sisters also agreed to tie the knot because she was convinced that her marriage was going to help Phanidhar's education. The two sisters were soon married.

A Groom for Sale

After that, Phanidhar decided to set out in search of a bride whose parents would agree to finance his college education. The first person he thought of was a rich lawyer, Bhabanath Hazarika of Sibsagar. Mr. Hazarika had once met Phanidhar when Phanidhar was in class VIII. At that time, Mr. Hazarika had encouraged him to study well and had promised that if he did well in exams, Mr. Hazarika would help him later. Phanidhar thought that encouragement was a hint that Mr. Hazarika would like to have him as a son-in-law if he was academically successful. Phanidhar also knew that Mr. Hazarika had seven daughters, five of whom were unmarried.

So, one day, Phanidhar made the trip to Sibsagar, a distance of 36 miles, on foot. He went straight to Hazarika's house and told Mr. Hazarika very frankly and with a lot of self-confidence that if Mr. Hazarika would pay for his college education then he would marry one of his daughters. Mr. Hazarika was quite receptive to the idea, but Mrs. Hazarika was of a different opinion. For her daughters she wanted rich and handsome young men and for her sons she wanted fair complexioned beautiful girls whether they were literate or not.

At that time Phanidhar was skinny and sunburned from all the work in the field. Malnutrition and hard labor had robbed him of his youthful appearance. At the very sight, Mrs. Hazarika was repelled by the idea of having him as a son-in-law. Mr. Hazarika could not make her change her mind. So that Phanidhar would never think of her daughters, she treated him very rudely. That was a big shock to Phanidhar. He was completely devastated. His consolation was that one of the daughters treated him with a lot of kindness and even had the courage to tell him, "Please don't take offense at my mom's words." The rich and prosperous Mr. Hazarika was not really keen on helping the poor, but simply wanted to help a prospective son-in-law if he was poor.

The shock of that episode told hard upon Phanidhar, and he did nothing for some time. When finally he recovered, he decided to write to some other rich people about whom he had known. He decided to write to them instead of visiting them in person. He wrote boldly that he was looking for someone who would pay for his college education—in return he was prepared to do anything possible including marrying their daughter.

The replies came. One of them wrote,

> "No, we do not want to buy a son-in-law. Our son-in-law will be someone who can stand on his own legs."

Another wrote,

> "No, we do not want to give our daughter in marriage to a village farmer boy."

The one that shocked him the most wrote,

"No, we will never give our girl to a beggar."

Being so insulted again and again, Phanidhar's resolve to go to college became stronger and stronger. After failing with the native resources, he decided to approach the British tea-planters.

The English Act of Kindness

This time, he met with success. We quote his own words to describe how he experienced kind and encouraging help from the English officials of the tea plantation where his father had worked and where his elder brother was working.

> First, I went to the Manager of Saikota garden. He was happy to receive my application and he called my brother and said, "I want to help your brother—but I have no money. I am giving you leave for two days and I will give you a letter. Both of you go to the Superintendent in Chinamara, for he may be able to help you.' So saying he gave us a letter—I did not know what he wrote in the letter. Since we did not have money to go by train, I walked with my brother to the Chinamara garden, met Silmon Sahib and gave him the letter. He read the letter with keen interest and smiled. Mr. Silmon seemed very happy to know of my success and told us how he and Mr. Ward had bet on me. Apparently, Mr. Ward reminded him about that bet in the letter and asked Mr. Silmon to give me the money that Mr. Ward had won. Mr. Silmon was exceedingly happy and said that he would give me much more than that. He agreed to pay me six rupees a month. Our joys knew no bounds.[16]

The question may be asked why it was so important for Phanidhar to go to Cotton College. The simple answer is that in those days the dreams of Assamese youths for a fruitful life centered around an education in Cotton College. To understand why, we have to look at how the college was born under the leadership of a noble Englishman named Sir Henry Cotton and how the College was shaped brick by brick by the vision and diligence of a great Educator named Frederick William Sudmersen.

---

[16] The Jorhat Tea Company for which Mr. Silmon worked sent that amount regularly every month for six years.

7
The liberal British Administrator Sir Henry Cotton Inspires A Spirit of Devotion

The White Baboo

During the British rule, many Englishmen held coveted posts in India, especially in the Indian Civil Service (now known as the Indian Administrative Service, or, IAS). For many educated Englishmen it was a life full of pomp and power. They would come over from England and lead a luxurious life in India. They sent their children to England for their education, and would themselves return to England after retirement, by which time they would have collected enough wealth and treasures to spend their old age in style and comfort. Such was the case with Sir Henry Cotton (1845–1915). Henry Cotton's father, Joseph John Cotton, was a British Civilian in the Madras Presidency from 1831 to 1863. Henry was born at Combaconum Tanjore district of Madras (now known as Chennai in the state of Tamil Nadu). He was educated in England and, after graduating from King's College, London, he followed his father's footsteps and took the Indian Civil Service Examination. He was successful. He then very sincerely tried to prepare himself for his task by meeting and learning from some leading personalities of his time. For example, he read John Malcolm Ludlow's *British India: Its Races and its History* and *Thoughts on the Policy of the Crown towards India*. According to Henry Cotton, "These books, written at the end of the fifties, were far in advance of any contemporary writings on the subject, and it is a pleasant duty to acknowledge my indebtedness to their author, whose ninety years have not obliterated his sympathetic and liberal instincts" (*IHM* 51).

Henry Cotton
From a photographic study by Julia Margaret Cameron, 1867

Courtesy: Indian and Home Memories

He also attended lectures on Positivism which were conducted by Dr. Richard Congreve. In those lectures, he was among such noteworthy companions as George Eliot. The net result was that by the time he arrived in India with his bride, he was deeply in love with India and its people and felt a deep commitment to serve India.

Henry Cotton joined the Bengal Civil Service in 1867. He rose rapidly as a diligent and efficient administrator. He also demonstrated a deep devotion to the people of India and took up the cause of uplifting India's masses. In 1885, he set forth a bold vision for India in his book *New India or India in Transition.* This book contained daring statements such as: "The waves of the ocean of Indian progress are dashing against the breakwater of English prejudice", "A spirit of devotion to the people of the country is not inconsistent with, and has never obliterated, my sense of official duties." After his retirement he published *Indian and Home Memories* which was reprinted eight times before his death in 1915. About India, Cotton wrote: "To India the whole of my mature life has been devoted, and when I retired, after thirty-five years of official service, I did so with the profoundest regret, for I owe a debt to India I can never repay " (*IHM* 56). It is quite clear that a British administrator who felt so indebted to India must have had both a lot of inspiration from India and much to offer it during his entire life spent there. To illustrate this, I quote a few incidents from his own writings:

> I am bound to say that this pernicious practice of striking natives, and especially domestic servants, prevailed as a common and general habit during the whole of my residence in India. I believe and trust that it is far less common now. It was much less common at the close of my service than it was in the early days. But it was always a gross and flagrant evil. I remember once when I was walking through the streets of an up-country city with a high official, and a few miserable petitioners blocked the way by throwing themselves prostrate before him and endeavouring to clasp his feet, he struck them right and left with his stick, and thought nothing of it. On another occasion when I had ventured to remonstrate with a distinguished officer for striking a lazy or careless gardener, I was met with the reply that there was no harm in it, and that everybody did it. When I retorted that I did not, I was told that I was the only man he had ever met who could say that. These are not reminiscences on which I love to dwell, but they serve to illustrate how subtle and unconscious is the poison of demoralisation in Anglo-Indian life. (*IHM* 65)

> I wrote an article entitled "Has India Food for Its People?" which to my delight was at once accepted by Mr. John Morley, and appeared in the *Fortnightly* for December, 1877. I followed this up with another paper which was published in September, 1878, entitled "The Prospects of Moral Progress in India." (*IHM* 147)

Sir Henry Cotton, by his own account, was a disciple of Dr. Richard Congreve, the Director of Positivism, "who, endowed with learning, abilities, and character of the highest order, abandoned all worldly prospects and ambition and devoted a long life of self-sacrifice to the service of his fellow men"(*IHM* 149). Dr. Congreve's teachings had a lasting influence on Henry Cotton and he sought to emulate many traits of Dr. Congreve's characteristics.

Sir Henry Cotton's book *Indian and Home Memories* was dedicated, by permission, to Lord Ripon, the popular viceroy of India (1880 - 1884), who made valiant attempts for the emancipation of the Indian people in right earnest. According to Henry Cotton, Lord Ripon was instrumental in infusing a spark in the then nascent Indian nationalist movements. Like Ripon, Henry Cotton did his part to see the development of Indian nationalism. Here is how Henry Cotton saw it, "The Marquess of Ripon left India in December, 1884, and the first Indian National Congress met in 1885. The date of his departure is the natal day of a New India. 'His journey from Simla to Bombay,' writes Meredith Townsend, 'was a triumphal march, such as India has never witnessed—a long procession in which seventy millions of people sang hosannas to their friend.' This homage that was never before tendered to any foreign ruler. The spectacle of a whole nation stirred by one common impulse of gratitude was never before beheld in Indian history. I took my share in the great demonstration in Calcutta. No public movement could have been more characterised by unanimity and spontaneity. No sign could have shown more clearly that the germ of a nationality had already sprung into life" (*IHM*185). Most British administrators and businessmen in India did not like Lord Ripon's pro-India policies and many of them bitterly opposed them. Sir Henry, however, did not conceal the fact that he identified himself with Lord Ripon's policies and, for this, he was widely ridiculed by Englishmen as 'a white Baboo'.

The Protector of "Dumb Coolies"

The true test of Henry Cotton's mettle came after 1896, when he was appointed the Chief Commissioner of Assam. First came a blow from nature as Assam experienced its worst earthquakes in history on June 12, 1897. Thousands of people lost their homes and all belongings, hundreds lost their lives, and hundreds of villages were obliterated. Henry Cotton emptied the royal exchequer to help the disaster-stricken people.

Sir Henry Cotton met his doom for taking up the cause of the tea garden laborers. Some time in 1900 the Government of Bengal decided to consider the proposal to raise the coolies' statutory wage and Henry Cotton was asked to inquire into it from all points of view, and to probe the issues to the quick. Cotton wrote of his findings that:

> In undertaking this investigation I learned many things of which a Chief Commissioner may remain, and often has remained, in ignorance. I was distressed beyond measure at the tale of suffering which came to my notice, and I felt it my duty not to conceal the truth. I reported on the facts. Although, when indignation is aroused against injustice and wrong, it is difficult to refrain from strong language, I wrote and spoke with moderation (*IHM* 262).

Starting with that kind of humble beginning he boldly wrote exposing the terrible conditions of the tea-garden laborers (or coolies as they were referred to by the British):

> Coolies of good physique and constitution, willing to emigrate to Assam under a penal contract, had never been obtainable at the statutory rates, and, to meet the demand, contractors were compelled to search far and wide for people who were in such a state of destitution that they were prepared to emigrate on any terms as a last resource. The recruiter was accustomed to lie in wait for wives who had quarreled with their husbands, young people who had left their homes in search of adventure, insolvent peasants escaping from their creditors. In carrying on his business he had to display considerable activity and resource. He had to incur unpopularity and even physical danger, to bribe police underlings, and to run the risk of Government prosecution and punishment. . . . In too many instances the recruiters resorted to criminal means, inducing their victims by misrepresentation or by threats to accompany them to a contractor's depot or railway-station, where they were spirited away before their absence was noticed by their friends or relatives. The records of the criminal courts teemed with instances of fraud, wrongful confinement, intimidation, and actual violence—in fact, a tale of crime and outrage which would arouse a storm of public indignation in any civilised country. In India the facts were left to be recorded without notice by a few officials and missionaries.(*IHM* 262–63)

As the Chief Commissioner of Assam, Henry Cotton was appointed to the Viceroy's Legislative Council which had three Indian and fifteen European members. Cotton's appointment to that Council was good for the tea-garden laborers. He, however, faced a tough battle when, in 1900-01, the Council took up the new Assam Labour and Emigration Bill. Cotton writes that:

> My position was a difficult one. An acute issue had been drawn up

> between the interests of Capital and Labour. The labourers in Assam are an ignorant and voiceless community, and they had no organ to press their demands. On the other hand, the whole of society and all the newspapers of the British Press were united in their support of the tea industry. The term is used to denote the interests of the proprietors of the tea gardens, of the shareholders of companies, of the agents in Calcutta and London, and of the employers of labour; and this customary use of the expression is a true indication of the fact that we are too apt, not only in language but in thought and action, to contemplate the interests of the industry exclusively from the capitalists' point of view. The capitalists were represented on the Council by many members of energy and ability; but there was no labour member to argue the coolies' cause, and I therefore felt it peculiarly incumbent on me, as representative and head of the province concerned, to state the case on their behalf as completely as possible and without reserve. (*IHM* 259–60)

Other liberal members of the Council did not want to incur personal unpopularity with the British Press or with the tea planters in Assam. So, Henry Cotton had to fight the cause of labour single-handedly, but fight he did. He was bitterly disgusted at the passive attitude of the Viceroy Lord Curzon and challenged him across the Council Board with the charge that he was stultifying his own policy. On his part, Lord Curzon timidly cautioned him that he was exceeding the limits of decorous debate. Of course, the result was obvious—Cotton received the support of only the Indian members of the Council. Later, Lord Curzon went so far as to say on record that, "The Government of India is reluctant to believe that the Hon. Mr. Cotton can be correct in his rejection of the views expressed by an unbroken series of his predecessors and endorsed by himself."(*IHM 276*) Henry Cotton also received an intimation that the sooner he vacated his appointment, the more convenient it would be for the Government of India. Because of his broken health, he did not wish to protest. Thus, he obtained leave from April, 1902 to the end of October of the same year, when his thirty-five years of service would have expired. The Government of India could either promote him to a higher office or allow his Indian career to terminate automatically. The Government chose the latter and Cotton returned to England.

This part of the battle had been lost, but Henry Cotton's fight remained an inspiring deed for all days to come. He earned the love of the tea workers and was called "the protector of the dumb coolie." His departure from India was regretted by all Indians and was accompanied by demonstrations of popular sympathy. In the annual report on the Indian National Congress at the Calcutta session in 1901, mention was made of the services rendered by this British civilian for the betterment of the down-trodden laborers of the tea gardens. India did not forget him. In recognition of his liberalism and love for India,. Sir Henry Cotton was elected President for the Bombay session of the Indian National Congress held in 1904. He was the fourth Englishman to preside over the Indian National Congress. The three predecessors in this office were George Yule (1888), Sir William Wedderburn (1889), and Alfred Webb (1894). Dr. Annie Besant, the venerable English lady who settled in India, later became the President of the Indian Congress in 1917.

The following extract from the Presidential address of Sir Henry Cotton demonstrates his love for India and the Indian people:

> The Indian National Congress has its own functions, which, I take it upon myself to say, as a watchful eye-witness from its birth, it has discharged with exemplary fidelity, judgement and moderation. Yours is a distinguished past. If you have not in any considerable measure succeeded in molding the policy of Government, you have exercised an immense influence in developing the history of your country and characters of your countrymen. You have become a power in the land, and your voice peals like a trumpet-note from one end of India to the other. Your illustrious leaders have earned a niche in the Temple of Fame, and their memory will be cherished by a grateful posterity. (S.C. Kakaoti in the Cotton College Centenary Volume, 2001, hereafter referred to as *CCC*)

After returning to England, Sir Henry Cotton entered political life in England as early as 1903 and was elected to the British Parliament in 1906 from East Nottingham as its Liberal candidate. Even today, Sir Henry Cotton is cherished and revered as a pro-India administrator. He died in 1915.

The Birth of a College in Assam

In Assam, Sir Henry Cotton is remembered for the College he established in Assam, which also bears his name. Initially, the rich folks in Assam rose up in arms against his decision to establish a college in Assam, but Henry Cotton wanted to give the people of Assam the opportunity for higher education by establishing its first college. Till then, a college education was just about impossible for the common folk of Assam, as it meant going to a college in Calcutta, whichmost people could not afford.

The few rich and influential individuals, who could send their children to Calcutta, thought that a hostel in Calcutta served their interests better. Naturally, they demanded a hostel in Calcutta rather than a college in Assam. Having no other recourse, Henry Cotton took an opinion poll of the people of Assam, and, the people favored his proposal. Thus, in 1901, he established the first-ever college in Assam, which has proved to be a milestone in the history of education in Assam. About his Assam days, Henry Cotton later said, "To the encouragement of education I devoted the best of my energies. I regard it as a great honour that my name should be associated with a first-class college which I inaugurated at Gowahatty. It made a good start, even in my time; it has thriven since, long may it flourish!" (*IHM* 245). Cotton College today stands as a fitting memorial to this friend of India.

The college was declared open by Sir Henry Cotton on Monday, May 27, 1901. To lay the foundation of the college, Henry Cotton invited a tested educator named Frederick William Sudmersen. Sudmersen started his career at Bareilly College in the heat-belt of North India. He served there for four years and in early May of 1901, he moved to Mussourie, a nearby hill station, to escape the heat of Bareilly and to ponder his future. So, when the invitation came to take the responsibility of starting the newly established college in Assam, an area kept cool by monsoon rain and the monsoon clouds, he gladly accepted. However, he had second thoughts after arriving in Assam. He soon found out that Assam was much farther away from home than he thought and that the monsoon cloud also sheltered such dangerous elements as mosquitoes, snakes, malaria, cholera and the like.

After travelling several days and night by train or boat he reached Gauhati on 28 May, 1901, the day the town was celebrating the establishment of the first college in Assam. The proposed college building was decorated with colorful crepe papers. The natives had planted banana trees and hung mango leaves as signs of good omen. Colorfully dressed native men and women were running around in joy. Formally dressed Englishmen of all sorts were roaming around with majestic tread. Pompously dressed native dignitaries and Maharajas were vying to see who could hold his turban higher than the rest. The whole town had a festive look. Sudmersen was not moved. As Sudmersen walked to his temporary residence, the government band played such English tunes as "He is a jolly good fellow", "Mary had a little lamb". He walked by a thatched cottage that was designated as the college hostel. At the Dak Bunglow (official transit House), where he was to stay, Sudmersen was met by English tea-planters and tea-garden employees, who had come to join in the festivities and who were by and large uneducated Englishmen unwanted at home. Sudmersen found the whole scenario very repulsive and decided not to unpack. Instead, he resolved to head back home to England.

In the evening, there was a cultural function. Again native singers and musicians vied to show who was a more versatile maestro than the others. The English-speaking audience tried to hide their discomfiture by pretending how much they liked classical Indian music. All this was too much for Sudmersen and he did not see any prospect of creating an environment for learning in Gauhati. Luckily, Sudmersen was accompanied by a Gurkha peon, who was a very good flute player. At the urging of Sudmersen, the organizers allowed the Gurkha peon to play his flute towards the end of the cultural function. The peon mustered all his courage and talent, and played a vibrant tune that signaled the dawning of a new era amid the chaos and disorder of the present. The tune captivated the audience and held them spellbound. After it was all over, the talk of the town was how enjoyable the flute player's music was, and how it had filled their hearts with new hope and a feeling of great joy. Almost everyone declared that the Gurkha peon's performance was the best and that it truly signaled the dawning of a new era in Assam. With that dawning came Sudmersen's change of heart.

The Gurkha's tune completely overwhelmed Sudmersen with a new determination. He decided to give a try to start the college. In November of 1902, he went to England to recuperate his health. He came back with a new vision and worked with a passion to make that vision a reality. Except for that year's sojourn, Sudmersen stayed as the Principal of Cotton College for nearly twenty-five years, from 1901 to 1926. What he did as the Principal is now a legend. Sudmersen showed the way a college should be established and run.

Principal Sudmersen showed the same spirit of devotion to the people of India as shown by Henry Cotton. He set for himself the goal of producing educated men of character who would be able to uplift the common masses through education. Therefore, it was very important for him to build an exemplary college. He built the college brick by brick and put it on a solid foundation of academic excellence and integrity. He set high standards not only for the students but also for the teachers. He could infuse a zeal for learning both among the students as well as the teachers. Soon, Cotton College came to be regarded as one of the best colleges, if not the best, in Eastern India. Within a few years it became the dream of every Assamese high school graduate to go to Cotton College. Otherwise, there was no future no hope of ever achieving anything meaningful in life.

So, to realize his dream and to fulfil his father's last wishes, it was imperative that Phanidhar get an opportunity to study in Cotton College under the golden wings of Principal Sudmersen.

Frederick William Sudmersen (1870 – 1953)

Courtesy: Cotton College

8
British Educator Principal Sudmersen Demonstrates Leadership

Sudmersen envisioned a residential college where students and teachers would live like one family and engage in the pursuit of knowledge. He built spacious dormitories, each under the care of a Superintendent, who would be selected from among the teachers. He himself demonstrated the duties of a Superintendent. He visited the hostel twice a day, once in the morning and once in the evening. He looked after the well-being of students just as a father would do to his children. The Superintendent would be like a father for each student under his charge.

Principal Sudmersen emphasized that there was no short cut to learning one's lessons, only hard work. He set high standards for the students and wanted them to work very hard. He made no compromise on academic standards. In addition, he firmly believed that college education could not be meaningful if it did not build the character of the student—truthfulness, discipline and sportsmanship were all part of college education. A college student must try to acquire them.

Principal Sudmersen emphasized the value of sports in developing an all-round personality. He made sure that the Cotton College hostels provided good facilities for the popular games of the time, like soccer, cricket, volleyball, etc. He himself took an active role in encouraging students to participate in sports. He expected the Superintendents to do likewise.

Principal Sudmersen wanted to create good athletes out of good students and good students out of good athletes. He strongly demonstrated that games and sports were not only great entertainment for the athletes, as well as the spectators, but also effective tools to build the character of youths.

By 1922, Sudmersen's Cotton College had already produced many educated young men who were already rendering invaluable services to the cause of education in Assam. Wherever they went the Cottonians carried with them a spirit of devotion to the people, exemplary integrity, and admirable capacity for hard work. We need to look at one such product who left his mark on the academic and literary life of modern Assam and who was briefly mentioned earlier.

Sarat Goswami

Sarat Goswami was born in 1887 in Nalbari. His father and his ancestors were well known educators who were committed to knowledge and the disbursement of knowledge in true Brahmin tradition. His father was both the head of a religious monastery and a teacher of a Sanskrit school. The family was not rich but very highly respected. Like Phanidhar, Sarat Goswami was the fourth child and lost his father when he was a little boy. Sarat's father lived by the truest of Hindu traditions, and believed that English education was essential to expand and enrich the people of Assam. So, in spite of opposition by the conservative elements of society, he sent his son to have an English education at Collegiate High School in Gauhati. However, he did not live long enough to see his son fulfill his dream.

Sarat Goswami was a brilliant student. He passed the Collegiate Entrance Examination in 1904 with flying colors, earning a competitive scholarship and three gold medals, and continued his education at Cotton College, Gauhati. In 1906, he passed the first part of the college exam (called FA in those days), again securing gold medals and topping the list of candidates from Assam. Before that, he had married a daughter of Naryan Chandra Bhattacharya, the chief priest of the Hoigrib Madhab temple at Hajo. In 1908, he passed the BA examination from Metropolitan College (now Bidyasagar College) of Calcutta with honors in Philosophy. Then, to finance his MA education, he had to go and seek help from others. To go and beg money from others, whether to borrow or as a gift, was not an honorable thing to do. However, for the sake of education, Sarat Goswami was prepared to do that. He went to Calcutta with borrowed money and even took a job. However, he did not finish his MA because the Assam Government offered him a job as a Deputy Inspector of schools. It was in that capacity that he first came to Jorhat. Later on, he was deputed by the Assam Government to study BT (Bachelor of Teaching) at Dacca College. In 1911, Sarat Goswami passed the BT examination, receiving the top position in Calcutta University. In 1915, he was appointed as the

Superintendent of Jorhat Normal School, where he served for twelve years. Sarat Goswami brought with him the younger brother of his wife. This was perhaps one of the luckiest things that happened to Phanidhar in his otherwise unfortunate life. Madhab became his dearest friend—through him the Goswamis developed a special affection for Phanidhar. For Phanidhar, Sarat Goswami was both an inspiration and a constant source of support.

In the mean time, things were rapidly changing in Jorhat. The old folks tried to keep up social divisions by caste. The old dignitaries and new dignitaries alike were trying to start a division by power (lost power) or wealth. But, a younger generation was growing up with English education that enabled them to acquire some western values. The younger generation was becoming more aware of scientific knowledge, creativity through art and literature, and above all, a sense of brotherhood. The conflict that Dandiram faced in high school was unthinkable by the time Phanidhar was in high school. Teachers or students who would display prejudices of the old time usually became the laughing stock.

On the contrary, during the third decade of the last century, a group of youngsters hailing from different backgrounds were vigorously active in uplifting the society through education. The person who gave the leadership to make the youths socially aware was Sarat Goswami, the new Deputy Inspector of schools. Goswami had the foresight to see that the future of Assam depended on the spread of modern education and he urged the youths of Assam to acquire as much education as possible and to dedicate their lives to uplifting the masses through education. What Mr. Goswami and a few friends did to help Phanidhar get a higher education is an inspiring story.

As days rolled by and all his efforts to collect money to go to college were spent in vain, Phanidhar's urge for higher education became slimmer with each passing day. Then his friends came home after completing a year in college and brought new hopes. These friends had promised him before leaving for college that they would definitely do something for Phanidhar's education. True to their words, those friends did not forget their brilliant but poor friend.

During the first year of their stay at Cotton College, Madhab and his friends told Principal Sudmersen about Phanidhar and requested him to grant Phanidhar a tuition waiver of some kind. Of course, their strategy was to impress upon Sudmersen the fact that Phanidhar was not only a brilliant student but also a very good soccer player. Principal Sudmersen assured them that if Phanidhar was good enough to be included in the college soccer team, he would offer him some waiver. Luckily, most of Phanidhar's friends from Jorhat were staying at the second mess of Cotton College. "They arranged with the monitor of that mess if Phanidhar came, they would keep him in second mess and charge him only half of the monthly meal charge. The encouragement and the enthusiasm of his friends once more added fuel to Phanidhar's then dimly flickering urge for higher education. He sold a piece of land for 119 rupees. (His father had bought this piece of land near his wife's birthplace). Since this was quite far from Gayangaon and it was lying unused, he sold it to his uncle. His friends also promised to help him raise some money.

Binanda Barua (later, an Assamese poet of reputation) took Phanidhar to his uncle Kamal Chandra Barua (then a head clerk at Mariani and a litterateur of reputation). Mr. Kamal Barua was very kind to Phanidhar and promised to send 2 or 3 rupees every month for him along with what he would send for Binode. Madhab Bhattacharya took him to Golokchandra Bezbarua, the owner of Bor Saikota tea garden. He was a friend of Madhab. On Madhab's request, Mr. Bezbarua also agreed to help him by sending him four rupees per month, and paid him 16 rupees then and there. Mr. Bezbarua said that he might not remember to send him money every month, so he would send him the amount for 4 or 5 months together. After that Phanidhar had no obstacle except his mother, who implored him not to go to Gauhati—she was really afraid that he would die of starvation somewhere. His uncles in the village also tried to stop him by saying that education was not in his fate.

But Phanidhar was determined to pursue higher education at all costs. The assurance of six rupees per month from Chinamora tea garden and the four rupees per month by Golok Chandra Bezbarua were enough to give him the courage to face the uncertain life of college education. Phanidhar noted in his memoir, "In addition to the help from these two places, the promise by Sri Sarat Chandra Goswami that he would help by whatever way he could, the assurance of help by Kamal Chandra Barua of Mariani, and above all the assurances of my four friends, Madhab-Suren-Binanda and Sashi, were my resources and inspiration for my college education."

Encounters with Principal Sudmersen

Phanidhar joined Cotton College in 1922 and came face to face with the mighty educator Principal Sudmersen. The two developed a relationship from that first meeting which had a lasting influence on him.

Phanidhar's friend Binanda Barua documented many incidences

involving the two. Binanda Barua told these to the present author in a taped interview and later published them in the Assamese monthly Prakash, (1987 – 1989) issues, published by The Publication Board of Assam. According to Binanda Barua, "Phani was not afraid of the Principal, but loved him and respected him a lot. The Principal also came to know Phanidhar well. Whenever the two met, it appeared that Principal Sudmersen liked Phani. The students liked many things that they saw in him or heard from him. He (the Principal) gave the appearance of a hard hearted person but he was not actually so. His heart was not hard, but very soft."

There are many legends and interesting anecdotes about Principal Sudmersen that are still current in Assam. Many of them are scattered in the biographies or reminiscences of former students. Here are a few narrated by Binanda Barua that involve Phanidhar.

The Toothbrush Tree.

In one story told by Binanda Barua: "There was a mature tree near our hostel. We used to brush our teeth with little twigs from that tree—Phani and I. One day, Mr. Sudmersen brought a laborer with an axe in hand. He started axing that tree. Phani saw it, he only had a small cotton towel wrapped around his loin. He ran towards Mr. Sudmersen like that and begged, 'Sir, Sir, please spare that toothbrush tree – poor student, Sir, please remember.' Mr. Sudmersen decided not to cut that tree and went away."

The Slip of Bijoybabu

Binanda Barua narrated another funny story: "Our Superintendent was Bijoybabu. He was really afraid of the college Principal Mr. Sudmersen. He used to forget everything at the very mention of Sudmersen's name. One day Mr. Sudmersen sent for Bijoybabu. In his hurry and fear Bijoy Babu put on his wife's slip as a scarf around his neck and ran to meet Mr. Sudmersen. On the way, somebody pointed to his mistake, so, he dropped that slip right there. Phani picked up the slip, put it on and had the whole hostel rolling in laughter by acting as Bijoy babu's wife."

Fancy-dress Football

In the following story told by Binanda Barua, we get a glimpse of how Principal Sudmersen tried to create an environment of interaction between students and teachers. "Phanidhar always used to look for opportunities to catch the eye of Principal Sudmersen. Once the Principal organized a

Phanidhar Datta in Cotton College (1926)

fancy dress football match on the open space between the hostel and the college. Principal Sudmersen and some other professors also took part in it. Phanidhar dressed as a farmer working in the field, he carried a spade on his shoulder. As soon as the game started, Phani started digging the field, the Principal jumped on him right way and asked him not to spoil the field. Phani stopped but only after digging a little with his spade."

A match

We can see how Principal Sudmersen tried to maintain a strong hold on students' behavior from the following incident described by Binanda Barua "One day, there was a big soccer match on the judge's field near the college. Principal Sudmersen was among the spectators. Phani took his position near the Principal to watch the game. We were also nearby. A shabby student named Sarukon was also watching the game with special keenness. If some player kicked the ball, Sarukon would also raise his leg, if somebody headed the ball, he would also raise his head and pretend to head the ball; in that manner he was playing the game by himself outside the playing field. Then the inevitable happened. Once, when the ball was near, Sarukon could not resist. He ran into the field and started playing for real. The embarrassed Principal, finding Phani nearby, asked him to drag Sarukon away from the field. Phani wasted no time. He jumped in and dragged Saukon away. The spectators found the ensuing tussle between Sarukon and Phanidhar more fun to watch than the soccer match."

Because of his friends' help, Phanidhar did not have to starve in Cotton College, and was able to study with a lot of intensity. But to ensure that others in his family did not starve to death, he went home every summer to plough the fields and cultivate rice. Everything was fine until it was time for the intermediate examination. Again, he could not afford the high fees. Then his roommate, Binanda Barua borrowed some money by offering his family ring as collateral. But, just before the final examination, Phanidhar fell ill. In those days, if you failed to appear in the scheduled final examination, you had to wait a whole year before you could take it again. This would have been impossible for Phanidhar—so, he took the exam with a very high fever. Again, his friends literally carried him on their shoulders to the exam room. Overcoming all these obstacles, he passed the examination in the first division. Then destiny took a strange turn.

9

A Poor Indian's Efforts To Receive Education At All Costs

Even though Bhabanath Hazarika's wife had insulted Phanidhar by saying that she would never have a skinny, sunburned poor guy like Phanidhar as a son-in-law, destiny had a different plan.

Bhabanath Hazarika had seven daughters. The two eldest ones were already married. Of the remaining five, three were already of marriageable age and it was imperative that Mr. Hazarika start looking for suitable matches for the daughters. To make matters worse, people in Sibsagar used to say things like, "Where will lawyer Bhabanath find good matches for his dark-skinned daughters?" Even though those words were said behind his back, it did not take long for them to reach his sharp ears. Mr. Bhaba Hazarika resolved to find promising young men for his daughters. He was clever enough to catch them young. Mr. Hazarika would have nothing to do with smart kids who perhaps had eyes on his wealth. He knew how to find young men of character and with a good future.

While Phanidhar was preparing for his intermediate final examination, Bhaba Hazarika once went to his hostel to check on some prospective grooms. When the students heard about his presence, many of them came forward to meet and talk with him. Some came because they felt a sense of awe towards a very rich man. Others came because they liked to revere a successful elder person. Still others came because they liked to boast, "Lawyer Bhaba Hazarika wants to offer his daughter to me." In any case, most of them were glad to talk to him and show him around. Only Phanidhar did not move from his study table. As a matter of fact, he was studying with so much concentration that he did not even know Mr. Hazarika was standing and peering over his shoulder. Mr. Hazarika admired Phanidhar's concentration and his neat, clean, beautiful handwriting. Bhabanath Hazarika had the ability to judge a young man. So, when he returned to Sibsagar, the first thing he told his wife was, "The fellow Phanidhar whom you said you would never have as son-in-law is the best of them all. He would be the best match for Aidhan. He would be able to appreciate Aidhan's qualities."

Aidhan was Hazarika's very dear and most trusted daughter. He even trusted the keys to his iron safe to Aidhan. Even though Aidhan was a good student, he did not send her to high school after she completed her primary education. In those days, parents had to choose between a traditional education and a high school education for girls. The traditional education consisted of teaching the girl weaving, knitting, cooking, the basics of good house keeping, good behavior towards people of all ages and all classes, and above all, spiritual values through regular study of Vaishnab scriptures. At school, on the other hand, they learned how to read and write English and Assamese, some geography, history and math, and a little bit of English literature. Even though these were essential for a college education, they were not regarded as being of any use to a girl who would not be looking for a professional job as a doctor, lawyer, or engineer. Only parents who desired to make their daughter a professional sent their daughters to school. Even this was very difficult because, for college education, the daughter would have to go to Gauhati or to Calcutta. Having a daughter go to a college away from home was an impossible thought for Assamese parents. So, for Aidhan, Mr. Hazarika decided to give her traditional education at home. However, after Aidhan, Mr. Hazarika changed his mind. He sent his other daughters to high school with a half-hearted effort to make them culturally enriched. Culturally enriched in those days meant the ability to play the harmonium and sing (this was a pure imitation of the Bengalis) and be able to set up the house like that of an aristocrat (imitating the Bengali or the rich Assamese who imitated the uneducated Englishmen of the tea-gardens). Perhaps he also thought the girls might grow up to be schoolteachers.

Actually, in those days people like Bhaba Hazarika were on the threshold of change. They were brought up with Hindu traditions, but Hindu thinking and Hindu philosophy never took root in their lives, which is why a sense of insecurity was reflected in the lifestyle they chose for themselves. The money, power, and material success that the British rule brought for them was pulling them towards a different way of life. They were not able to design a way for themselves that synthesized Hindu ideas and Western culture. Though they did not quite despise their spiritual upbringing, they were unwillingly entering a materialistic world. Even when they were most immersed in the materiality, in their heart of hearts they revered the spiritual world of their elders.

For Bhaba Hazarika, Aidhan was at the borderline of the spiritual world that he was leaving behind. He sent all his daughters younger than Aidhan to high school, emphasized their English education and sought for them husbands who were likely to be rich, namely doctors and engineers. He wanted those daughters to live comfortably. However, he respected and trusted Aidhan who was brought up through traditional education. For her, he wanted someone who was down to earth and who could respect the sincere devotion that Aidhan had for spiritual values. In the case of Aidhan, he was not disturbed by the poverty of the prospective groom. When Phanidhar's mother expressed her apprehension about bringing a girl from a rich family as her daughter-in-law, Bhaba Hazarika sincerely declared, "I am telling you very truthfully that for your son, I am not offering a girl, but a real diamond—she is my diamond. If your son has to live in a shed made of leaves, she will create a heaven there." Mr. Hazarika expressed this kind of respect for his daughter to many others.

The question is, if Mr. Hazarika had so much respect for the traditional upbringing of his daughter, Aidhan, then why did he not try to bring up his younger daughters in the same way? Even though in his heart of hearts he saw the merits of an education guided by spiritual values, he could not help but push the younger children towards a materialistic world. Even though it is hard to answer why he and many others elected to act that way, it was quite clear that the Assamese society of the time was slowly moving away from the strong Vaishnab culture that Sankardev and others had firmly established in Assam. In Bhaba Hazarika's family, Aidhan was literally the last link with Vaishnab culture.

An Artist's view of Phanidhar Datta's resolve to get an education at all costs.

Courtesy: Dr. Satyendra N. Das

When she was asked which of the suitors she would like to marry, Aidhan replied, "The one that came from Jorhat, the one mother had laughed at as being skinny, poor, and half-starved. We should not be so rude to one who is so sincere. Whatever is in my destiny, I will face. Even if I have to live by begging, that will be okay. Arrange the doctor and the engineer for my younger sisters. Let them live in comfort. We will be able to manage somehow."

Aidhan expressed her desire to marry Phanidhar. Her father Bhabanath also thought Phanidhar would be the best match for her. Bhabanath was afraid that Phanidhar might refuse since he was rejected once. In any case, he was determined to go and talk to him personally. Bhabanath had several obstacles. First, his wife wanted a good-looking and well-to-do young man as her son-in-law. On the other hand, Bhabanath wanted a man of character who had a spark for knowledge and education. He told his wife, "I actually think he is good looking, tall and slim. He looks a little skinny and sunburnt because he always works in the fields under the bright sun, and perhaps he is a little under nourished. If you feed him luci (rolled and fried Indian bread) and bhaji (vegetable medley cooked Indian style) and keep him away from the sun and rain for a few days, his looks will be more than satisfactory to you." His wife did not buy that argument, but agreed to see Phanidhar one more time and to find out a few more things about him.

The chance came when her second son, Indra, had to go to Jorhat to play soccer for his school. One of Mrs. Hazarika's sisters lived in the same village as Phanidhar. She was married to the Head Clerk of a tea garden. She had an affluent life and never visited Phanidhar's folks after they had sunk to the level of poverty. Indra came to her and asked if she knew Phanidhar and could show him Phanidhar's house. She replied, "I know him but they don't have a house. That shed made of palm leaves is where they live. You should not go there. If you wish to meet him, we will send for him."

Indra Hazarika dropped the matter there and did not go to meet Phanidhar. However, the next day there was a problem about the referee for their soccer match. The assigned referee was very partial to the Jorhat team in an earlier match. So, the Sibsagar boys refused to play. The Sibsagar team, of which Indra was a member, had high hopes because they were coached by Bhuban Gogoi who had a big reputation as the first Assamese to play for a reputed Calcutta team Mohan Bagan. They did not want to lose a game because of a bad referee. Somebody suggested, "You know Phanidhar who plays for the first team of Cotton College is at home for vacation. He is a good referee. Maybe we can ask him to be the referee today."

In those days, people looked up to the players of the Cotton College team as exemplary. They were good students who played the game with true sportsmanship. Principal Sudmersen took pride in his students and always endeavored to instill in them a spirit of learning, whether in the classroom, on the soccer field, or in the outside world. It was suggested that if Phanidhar became the referee he would be fair. So, two of them hopped on their bicycles to bring Phanidhar. Indra Hazarika also accompanied them.

Along the way, Indra Hazarika came to know a lot of things about Phanidhar:

"He is a very poor farmer boy. In spite of his hardships he is showing brilliant results."

"In math, he is even better than his teachers.'

'He is a very cheerful chap, full of humor."

"He is a very good actor."

"He is not ashamed of his poverty or of the fact that he has to work in the fields like a laborer."

Indra Hazarika and the others went and found him in the field plowing with a big watch on his wrist (he had won the wristwatch in a college lottery). Indra Hazarika and Phanidhar were attracted to each other from the moment they met. The two had very similar personalities. They were both kind, honest, hard working, and believed in higher education. In addition, both of them were true sportsmen. From that moment, a true friendship developed between the two and they remained good friends all their lives.

After returning to Sibsagar, Indra Hazarika told his mother that of all the people he had met, he liked Phanidhar the best. Hearing praises from his favorite son, his mother agreed to take another look at Phanidhar. Meanwhile, Bhaba Hazarika had decided to tell Phanidhar to marry Aidhan and that he would pay for Phanidhar's education.

In Assamese society, third parties usually play an important role in marriages. A marriage is normally arranged through a third party that is normally a well-wisher of both families. Then there is the other kind of third party, which becomes very active and tries to break the marriage. These third parties usually do it out of their own unhappiness or out of a strange sense of jealousy which does not allow anything good happen to others.

In the case of Phanidhar and Aidhan, the active third party was the sister-in-law of Bhabanath, who lived a few houses away from Phanidhar's. She was the one who had stopped Indra Hazarika from meeting Phanidhar during the soccer incident in Jorhat. With his intention to offer Aidhan in marriage to Phanidhar, Bhaba Hazarika first stopped at his sister-in-law's house and told her the purpose of his visit. She discouraged him by saying,

"What! you are going to offer your daughter to that dark-skinned guy with big eyes? If you seal a bond with that half-starving family, then it would so disgrace us that we may have to move from this village to some other place."

Bhaba Hazarika was unmoved. He said, "Since I have come so far, I will pay them a visit just to say hello." Phanidhar was not home at that time. Bhaba Hazarika met his mother and gave the marriage proposal. He also invited Phanidhar and his mother to come and see the girl in Sibsagar. On the way back, he did not even stop at his sister-in-law's. His sister-in-law got the message, and her jealous self rose up in arms. She immediately got dressed and went to meet Phanidhar's mother, a family from whom she always used to distance herself.

"I guess Bhaba Hazarika must have come with a marriage proposal."

"Yes, that is what he said. But I asked him, how can I think of bringing a girl from such a well-to-do family to this house."

"What did he say to that?"

"He said that his girl was a real diamond, if my boy has to live under a palm leaf shed, she will keep him happy there as well."

"I guess he must have meant the eldest one at home."

"I don't know how many daughters he has or which one is his real diamond. I didn't even ask."

"Don't be fooled by that lawyer's words. The eldest one is too old—the next one, you can't even touch. She plays the harmonium with her fingers as well as with her toes. The one younger than those two is better looking and good-natured. If he offers that one then you may consider. Your son is the real diamond, don't settle on an old maid for him."

Hearing those conniving words from her neighbor, Phanidhar's mother simply said, "Lord only knows. It is all up to Phani. His eyes are not set on girls but on his education. Whoever is prepared to pay for his education, he is willing to marry the daughter no matter what she is. I am sure one of these days he is going to bring a strange girl home." Before leaving the third party cautioned Phanidhar's mother "A good young man has emerged in the village. We will not let him bring a strange girl or an old maid. That's why I thought I should let you know."

Phanidhar's mother was easily influenced by the third party and told Phanidhar to seek the hand of the younger daughter of Bhaba Hazarika. Realizing that, Phanidhar decided not to take his mother along on the

Sibsagar trip saying, "Mom, I am the one who will marry, I am the one whom he is going to educate, so, why should you worry and take this long trip? Let me go alone. Just give me the gold ring that you have been saving and please clean up the house a little. If possible, I will bring the girl along."

"What a scoundrel I have given birth to." So saying, the mother decided not to accompany Phanidhar. Only she told him again and again, "Mrs. Bora has told me that the one younger than the elder two is the right one for you. Fix up with that one only."

During the Ahom rule, the ordinary citizens were not allowed to wear any shoes. After the British came, everybody was free to wear any shoes or any clothes. However, the villagers, or the ordinary citizens could not afford to buy shoes. Those who could afford to buy shoes were rather shy to wear them. It was not easy to throw away a centuries old practice. The lawyers, the judges, and the other dignitaries did wear shoes. Of course, every Englishman always wore shoes. For a long time, shoes remained an elitist symbol. Those who studied in college started wearing shoes half as a necessity, and half in vanity to distinguish themselves from the rest. Many students, especially those in their senior year of high school, would start the practice of wearing shoes early—almost to signal that they were ready to go to college. When all of Phanidhar's friends started wearing shoes, he also had the desire of trying a pair of shoes on.

Phanidhar found a good opportunity to buy a pair of shoes with the money that his mother had given him to pay his fees for the Entrance Examination. So, he used part of that money to buy a pair of shoes. The pair of shoes, however, was not much fun because his feet were not used to the luxury of such a tight cover, and his toes and muscles were not used to gripping with shoes on. So, he had a mighty fall after taking a few steps. The blisters on his feet and the impact of the fall hurt him badly. But the scolding he got from his mother hurt him more. She was furious that he had wasted the money meant for a different purpose. Above all, she said there was already a pair of shoes in the house that he inherited from his grandfather. She said those shoes were like new since his grandfather hardly ever used them.

Phanidhar took that pair of new shoes to college but he could hardly ever wear them. In those days, except the few students from the rich families, most of the college students went either barefoot or used wooden slippers. So, like his grandfather's pair, Phanidhar's first pair of shoes lay unused like a valued treasure. When he got invited to meet his likely bride, he saw a good opportunity to wear his shoes. He trotted barefoot to the nearest railroad station (about seven miles away) carrying the pair of shoes on his shoulder and then took a train to Sibsagar.

Sibsagar was quite a few miles from the nearest railroad station of Simaluguri. Bhaba Hazarika sent a bullock-cart to Simaluguri to meet Phanidhar. Before he left Sibsagar, Aidhan called the cart driver aside and asked him, "How will you recognize the person?" Since the driver had no clue, Aidhan wrote his name on a slate and told the driver to hold it high up near the entrance to the station. Phanidhar was quite moved to find somebody waiting to receive him at the station. After getting into the cart, he put on his shoes and felt a pleasant feeling that all the obstacles for his education were over. He felt a genuine sense of love and gratitude for the girl who had brought that promise to his life. He also realized that his labor and his education enabled him to so cross the age-old barrier that the poor faced. He thanked his stars and his friends. He resolved that he would do everything to bring education to the poor. He would teach the poor to work hard for a better education.

Phanidhar also wondered if he was making a mistake by choosing his wife on the basis of the single fact that the girl's parents would pay for his education. He convinced himself that it was not a mistake. Sooner or later he would have to find a 'life-partner.' He would have to choose a girl for one reason or another. So, why can't that reason be higher education? After all he was very frank and honest about his intentions and was merely accepting the proposal that the girl's father brought to him. His only worry was whether the girl had accepted him wholeheartedly or not. The thought that she might have been forced to accept him saddened him. So he started a conversation with the cart driver:

Phanidhar: Do you know the eldest girl in the Hazarika household?

Driver: Of course I do. She is the Lakshmi (the goddess of good fortune) of the household.

Phanidhar: Does she know whom you are coming to pick up today?

Driver: Of course she does. She herself wrote your name on the slate. That is her handwriting.

Phanidhar: She knows me then.

Driver: Of course she does. The Hazarika house is very famous. You see there are many suitors—one doctor, one engineer, and one handsome son of a priest. From all of these Aidhan chose you. She started liking you the first time she saw you. She says her mother did not treat you nice. Her mother is very different.

Phanidhar: Forget her mother. Did Aidhan say anything about me?

Driver: She gave me a whole description of you. I could have picked you up from among a thousand men.

Phanidhar: How did she describe me?

Driver: She said you were tall and very pleasant looking, that you were slim and that kindness was written all over your face.

Overjoyed, Phanidhar started to sing the famous Assamese song praising the Lord. The cart-driver also joined in the doleful tune.

Foremost I prayto thou the Lord of the Universe!
Thou art Narayan the cause of all incarnations,
From thy lotus-navel Brahma took birth,
Thou incarnate in many forms through the ages.
First you incarnated as a fish and
saved the Vedas from the Great Flood,
Thou showed thy power to King Satyabrata,
The Ocean was not big enough to hold thy body.
As the Tortoise incarnation on the bank of Khirododhi,
Thou stretched over million miles of path,
Thou held the Meru Mountain on thy back,
Awestruck men, devils, angels, snakes and
All creatures prayed for thy mercy.
In the bright shining Boar incarnation
Thou rescued the Earth on your teeth.
Thou killed the mighty devil Hironyakshya
tearing him apart with thy teeth.
As the Lion-man thou tore apart
the heart of the mighty devil Hironykashipu.

Then the two continued their conversation:

Driver: I hear you are a poor farmer boy like us but you are very good in your studies. That's why you caught the attention of our master, the lawyer. It is great to see someone like us become so diligent in school and college. My son is also studying in elementary school. Do you think he will also be able to get a college education?

Phanidhar: Why not? Everybody has the potential to be educated. The only thing one needs is complete dedication to learning. But college education is very expensive. You should start saving right now. Save every penny you can by selling vegetables, rice and whatever you can. Education is everything. It is the duty of every parent to see that his or her children are educated.

Soon afterwards they crossed some covered bullock carts that led to the following conversation:

Phanidhar: Who is coming in these carts?

Driver: It must be a marriage party. Are you planning to take the girl away on this trip only?

Phanidhar: What do you think? I am just going back after looking at her face.

Driver: O my God! If you are in such a hurry then you will have to run away with the girl. If you would like to do that let me know. I have a boat as well. For a rupee or two I will be able to put both of you across the river Dikhow. No problem. I got my woman like that only because I was in a hurry and the parents of my wife did not consent.

Phanidhar: Don't talk like that. The father of the girl himself had proposed to me and has brought me here by paying all expenses and has made all these arrangements. So, why should I run away with his daughter?

Driver: No, no, please don't blame me. I am just offering my help thinking that you are in a hurry. In any case our Aidhan sister is not the kind of girl who would run away with a guy without getting married. You see, she is the most trusted lady in the household. The lawyer trusts all the keys to her. What's more, all the servants and household helpers like me are attached to the household mainly because of her. She treats us very kindly. Would you believe that she taught us all to read and write? She says every Assamese must be able to read the 'Kirtana.'

As soon as they reached the Hazarika house, the cart-driver went and informed Aidhan, "He is really the right match for you. He is very jovial and, like you, very religious. We two chanted spiritual hymns all along the way."

So, everything was all set. Phanidhar finalized everything with a ring and completed his studies with financial help from his father-in-law. He passed his BA with mathematics honors and secured a gold medal (Rajani Kanta Barat medal).

Then on April 23 of 1926, (the ninth day of Baisakh), he married Aidhan. So securing gold and "diamond," he went to Calcutta where he earned the MA degree in Mixed Mathematics.

While studying for his MA, he also prepared for the law examinations. So, while working as a temporary lecturer in Cotton College, he passed the first two law examinations in 1929. He passed the final law examination in 1930 and earned the qualification to practice law. After he became an MA,BL, the government offered him the job of a Sub Deputy Collector. Many of his friends like M. Sultan, Madhab Bhattacharya accepted government jobs but Phanidhar returned to Jorhat to do something there.

10

Some Native Graduates Start a College of Their Own: JB College

Principal Sudmersen left Cotton College the year Phanidhar graduated. In his farewell message, he took pride in the fact that he was leaving behind a good band of educated young men in Assam who would be able to guide the destiny of Cotton College and also do a lot for the cause of education in Assam. Principal Sudmersen's message was clear, "Education is only of value if it leads to greater service to mankind." That message kindled a little spark in Phanidhar's heart which remained a constant source of inspiration in his later life.

It is noteworthy that through his hardships in obtaining a college education, Phanidhar realized the obstacles that poor students from upper Assam faced in obtaining a college education. In a way, Phanidhar was lucky that he had some very good friends who were prepared to do everything for him, but there were many unfortunate ones who could not afford to go to the college about 200 miles down the road. So, many of the students from Upper Assam and studying in Cotton College often discussed how it would be possible to start a college in Upper Assam. They not only had discussions but also organized formal meetings to discuss the issue.

The educated youths of Jorhat were for a long time discussing the possibility of establishing a college at Jorhat. However, nobody could take any initiative mainly because of the difficulties of raising substantial funds. In addition, there was a lack of qualified teachers. An opportunity came when Murulidhar Barua, who inherited the large and rich estate of tea-planter Jagannath Baruah, indicated that he would donate the Borpatra Cottage in the center of the town to the college. He mentioned his intention to Tulashi Narayan Sharma. Mr. Sharma, in his turn immediately informed Phanidhar Datta. The two discussed all the possible avenues. They first wrote to their friends Mr. Gunagovinda Datta, MA, BL. who was practicing at Gauhati and to Jogneswar Sharma, MA, who was then studying law at Gauhati. They were all students together first at Cotton College and then in Calcutta, and knew of each other's commitments for higher education in Assam. The two promptly replied in the affirmative.

Phanidhar Datta and Tulashi Naryan Sharma then went to Krishna Kanta Handique who was managing his family's tea-garden and who had, by then, established his reputation as a Sanskrit scholar. Mr. Handique at first had doubts about starting a college at Jorhat. He finally consented to teach in the college if the founding teachers would form a registered body as, "Jorhat Council of College Education" and would legally bind themselves to the responsibilities of running the college. After that, things started moving fast. A meeting was held on August 19, 1930 in Chandra Kanta Hall with Keramat Ali as President and Tulashi Narayan Sharma as convenor. Two important announcements were formally made in that meeting. First, Datta, Handique, and the two Sharmas (Tualshi Narayan and Jogneswar) declared that they would teach in the college for a few years without any remuneration.

Second, Murulidhar Barua announced that he would donate the Barpatra Cottage with its estate to start the college. Since the question of a building and teachers were so settled, a decision was taken at that meeting to start a college at Jorhat. They decided to name it the "Upper Assam College."

The founders were concerned about the students from Upper Assam and their dream was to start a college in that area. Nevertheless, when that dream became a reality and at a later public meeting held on September 4, 1930, the majority of those present voted to name the college as Jorhat College.

The college came into being soon afterwards on October 10. The teachers—the two Dattas and the two Sharmas, requested K. K. Handique who was senior to them in age to act as the Principal. In the beginning, there were 14 students, most of whom were sons of poor farmers who had passed the college entrance examination but could not afford to go to Gauhati. Jagannath Barua (or JB as he was popularly known), the first BA from Upper Assam, built the Barpatra Cottage during the years 1884-1893. Mr. Barua had brought the steel posts for the building from England and had the doors and windows built in Calcutta. The plot of land measuring nearly 5 acres was purchased in 1880 from the family of Barpatra Gohain, one of the three ministers of the last Ahom King. Mr. Barua had a good sense of history and promptly named it, "Barpatra Cottage"—it was only after JB's death that people changed the name to its Assamese version, "Barpatra Kutir" wiping out a page of history.

Till the time the college was started, Barpatra Cottage was used by the Agriculture department to sell and distribute seeds. The Agriculture department maintained a skeleton service in the cottage for a long time even after the college was started. Therefore, for a long time, farmers would often come in and interrupt a class in progress asking, "Where can I find vegetable seeds?" Once in a while, Professor Datta would have the class rolling in laughter by replying "Brother, we don't have vegetable seeds here, but, we have a few Kachu[17] seeds that we need for ourselves."

It is hard to describe the obstacles that the founding teachers faced after starting Jorhat College. First and foremost they needed to get the support of the people both in cash and in kind. In the words of Jogneswar Sharma, "Some of us went into the interior areas and tea-gardens not for collecting money, but for spreading the news and also to open future avenues for donations. . . . They mocked and fingered at us as 'college-makers' and gave us names." (Jagannath Barua College Golden Jubilee Commemorative volume, 1982, hereafter referred to as *JBG* 41-42). Often they had to endure humiliation and discouraging comments like:

> "There was no need for a college,"
>
> "A college in a Mofassil town was most likely to limit the outlook of pupils who would be in the dark about the outside world. It would encourage a parochial outlook."
>
> "These college-makers will soon be looking for places to hide the money they have collected."

The professors in their spare time started a collection drive. They started to visit every house and every town within their reach. Other young men like Suren Buragohain also came forward to help, but Tulashi Narayan Sharma and Phanidhar Datta shouldered the brunt of the trouble.

---

17 Kachu is a leafy plant. The Assamese eat both its leaves and its roots and refer to naughty kids as Kachu seeds – perhaps because if a Kachu-root is not properly cooked it can cause a lot of trouble.

They bicycled as far as Sibsagar (a distance of 36 miles) seeking donations. Jogneswar Sharma and Prafullapran Changkakati collected money in the Dibrugarh area as well.

The teachers were very much encouraged by the attitudes of the poor village folk. They offered whatever they saved by selling vegetables, bananas, and whatever they could produce. They offered their savings with great reverence with all the native rituals of putting their donations on a Sarai and falling prostrate on the ground. Even then what they could collect was very nominal. So, they had to teach without any remuneration for several years. They had to find other means to make both ends meet. Tulashi Narayan was a mauzadar, but that was more of a responsibility than earning. Gunagovinda was practicing law, but in those peaceful days amidst law abiding gentlefolk, his earnings were nominal. Jogneswar Sharma was not a native of Jorhat, so, he suffered greatly even in procuring his daily bowl of rice.

Phanidhar Datta's legal practice was no better than that of Gunagovinda. So, he had to work in the fields to feed his family. He would work in the field from dawn and then go and teach after taking a hurried bath in the water tank. Often his body would carry traces of dirt or mud from the field. On occasion some students, especially those from the town, would tease him for that. On one instance, a student jokingly said, "There is a big speck of mud on your ear lobe." Professor Datta unhesitatingly replied, "You see, we have started this college so that you people can get a good education and become an accomplished person. For your sake, we did not accept government jobs. We are not taking any salary, so we have to work in the field. This is just a reluctant evidence of turning soil up and down."

An artist's view of a founding professor of JB College

Courtesy: Dr. Satyendra N. Das

Hearing that, the village boys clapped and put the teasing student in his right place. Being moved by the dedication of the founding professors, Prafullapran Changkakati of Sibsagar joined the college in 1931, and Padmeswar Gogoi of Lakhimpur joined two years later in 1933. They were promised some salary but they accepted much less than what was promised. Jogneswar Sharma, Changkakati and Gogoi were not from

Jorhat. They lived in an empty house belonging to Durgeswar Sharma and ate with the students in their hotel. Once in a while they would go home and bring rice, rice crispy, rice flour, etc. and give them to the boys. In short, apart from mauzadar Tulashi Narayan Sharma and tea-planter K. K. Handique, the early teachers of the college took a lot of hardships on themselves to put Jorhat College on a firm footing.

Then came the question of affiliation. It was not likely that Calcutta University would grant affiliation without sufficient fund. So, the teachers thought of a novel way to create a fund – they signed a registered deed to work without remuneration for four years. Quinquennial Review, 1931-32, pp. 210-211 contains a comment about this fund:

> The new institutions are not beginning their career with even approximately adequate resources. One of the conditions of affiliation actually laid down by the university in the case of Jorhat College which seems to be financially far better off than Habiganj College, is that the authorities should obtain an undertaking from the staff that they will serve the College without remuneration for the next four years commencing from the session 1931-32.
>
> To expect educationally well-qualified but poor men to teach conscientiously for years for nothing at all seems to me very extraordinary.

Calcutta University deputed Dr. H. C. Mukherjee (later Vice Chancellor and then Governor of West Bengal) and Deva Prasad Sarbadhikari to inspect the college. Since there was no library, a rubber stamp bearing the name JORHAT COLLEGE was immediately made and the teachers brought all the books in their possession, stamped them, and put them in one of the rooms of Borpatra Cottage. They showed it as a library to the Inspectors.

K. K. Handique best described this by saying, "The most urgent problem confronting the organizers at the outset was that of affiliation of the institution to the University of Calcutta, an uncertain factor that caused great anxiety. Luckily for Assam, the views expressed by the inspection Committee deputed by the University were fundamentally opposed to those of the critics. ... The Inspector of Colleges, Dr. Harendra Coomar Mukharjee (afterwards Governor of West Bengal), proved to be a friend in need; and to his sympathy and good will as much as anything else was due the quick recognition of the college by the University. I still cherish the memories of his delightful visits to the college in the subsequent years more as an esteemed guest than as an official mentor until his retirement from the University. The farsighted policy of Calcutta University was no doubt the prime factor in founding the first non-government college of Assam despite the unfriendly if not positively hostile attitude of the provincial Government."(*JBG* 2).

The Founding Fathers of JB College

Jorhat, in those days, housed many enormously wealthy tea-planters, many rich businessmen and many wealthy government officials of high rank. However, nobody other than Murulidhar Barooah came forward to help the college build a worthwhile fund. Devaprasad Sarbadhikari, the other inspector accompanying Mr. Mukherjee, made a fervent appeal on behalf of the college at a public reception accorded to him in Chandra Kanta Hall. His appeal fell on deaf ears. It was, therefore, not surprising that Calcutta University had no alternative but to bind the founding teachers to work without remuneration for four years. From this single fact, one can understand the attitude of the wealthy Jorhat residents towards higher education and their lack of sympathy for the poor students who were languishing in the towns and villages of Upper Assam after passing the College Entrance Examination. Many of the rich folks did not even hesitate to ridicule and tease those "college-makers" with comments like:

> "These unemployed graduates do not like to take employment away from home – we will see what kind of college they build."
>
> "They are collecting money on the pretext of starting a college. You will see, later they will spend it partying or on theatre."
>
> "This shows what tricks half-starved people will play just to suck a few rupees from (us)."

One reason why the rich people did not come forward to help the college was the fact that most of these people were loyal to the British Government, and the Assam Government was opposed to the college. As a matter of fact, Mr. Small, the then Director of Public Education in Assam, termed the college "a threat" and the Assam Government formally requested Calcutta University not to give affiliation to the college. Many rich and influential people of upper Assam who were or who needed to be loyal to the Assam Government, expressed their opposition to the college playing the same tune as the Government officials. This was a matter of concern to the founding teachers. However, many concerned and sympathetic citizens lent their voice of support to the college by writing letters to the Government and the members of the Council, urging them to do whatever necessary to see that the college gets affiliation. A copy of such a letter written by several prominent citizens of Sibsagar is still available in Jorhat College.

The inspectors from Calcutta University were so moved by the efforts of the teachers that Mr. Mukherjee termed it, "second only to Nalanda" in spirit and dedication. However, "the Assam Government vehemently opposed granting one affiliation on several grounds, the chief being political. Those were the days of the notorious Cunningham Circulars. The institutions growing in the wake of the popular movement were looked upon as harbors for rebels."(*JBG* 43).

Luckily, however, Mr. Shyama Prasad Mukherjee, then a member of the Calcutta University syndicate and later Vice-Chancellor, had boldly asserted that the affiliation would be granted in spite of the opposition by the Assam Government.

The students of Jorhat College were allowed to sit in the Intermediate Examination of Calcutta University in 1933. Calcutta University, however, instructed the college to dissolve the Jorhat Council of Education that was formed at the suggestion of K. K. Handique, and replace it with a Governing Body. The University expressed the opinion that it would not be possible for an independent body to run a college in India. Accordingly, a Governing body was formed with some influential residents of Jorhat as members.

The college did get the affiliation and its students performed well in the Calcutta University Examination right from the first year. Jorhat College became a reality and as suggested by the University, its administration was transferred to the Governing body.

From Jorhat College to JB College

We have earlier indicated that English education has consistently reinforced a class system in India. This can also be inferred from the difficulties that Phanidhar Datta faced to get an education. Education in India has always been very difficult, if not impossible, for the poor. The upper class in India saw English education as a privilege to them and jumped to take advantage of English education. The privileged class tried to keep the poor mass off from getting its benefits. If any of the common folk managed to get an education, people in the upper echelon tried their best to obstruct his path for success.

The inherent defect of the English education system popped its head again in case of Jorhat College as well. The very guide for selecting members of the Governing Body were wealth, power and influence upon whom the ruler could exert influence. This could be seen in the formation of the Governing body. The members of the Governing body were: Chandradhar Barooah, (tea planter), Murulidhar Barooah (tea planter), Maulavi Faizuddin Ahmed (Retired Government officer, an E.A.C), Principal, Tulashi Narayan Sharma.

A rift was opened between the teachers and Governing Body. The Governing Body made it a rule to take anybody as its member if he or she would donate two thousand rupees. This opened the door to the rich folks, who soon dominated the running of the college. The interests of the teachers and the teachers themselves began to be ignored. The governing body appointed some new teachers. Those newcomers were paid more than what the founding teachers were given as salaries. The founding teachers started feeling insecure in the college. After a lot of conflicts, five of the teachers filed a petition to the Governing Body on January 12, 1938.

> But we are really sorry to find that the Governing Body fails to appreciate our act of collecting funds from door to door ... our hardships of so many years, our promises to serve without remuneration put in writing in registered documents and recognized by the University as a substantial part of the funds in the college and our spending the best part of our lives without any care for our future – all these are beyond valuation.
>
> ... We therefore pray that we the undersigned professors and Professor T. N. Sharma be included in the Governing Body as Life Members in consideration of our sacrifices and other things mentioned above and for the purpose of making our positions secure in the college which is of our own making.

Phanidhar Datta, Gunagovinda Datta, Prafullapran Changkakati, Padmeswar Gogoi and Jogneswar Sharma signed the petition.

The Governing Body passed several resolutions at its meeting on June 25, 1938 rejecting the requests of the teachers and found more ways to alienate the teachers. The proceedings of the meeting contain such terse statements as, "read a letter signed by certain members of the staff," "The gentlemen, if they wish to be connected with the college as paid members of the staff, should give up the practice of law. This, however, should not prevent them from serving the college in an honorary capacity."

After that, those teachers felt very insecure about their future in the college they had started, in the college where they gave the best years of their lives, in the college they served without remuneration for several years. They all decided to find jobs that could provide some security for the future. Jogneswar Sharma went to Nowgong where he took charge of a new college there. Changkakati, Gogoi and Datta went to Cotton College, Gauhati. Only Gunagobinda Datta stayed back as he had no other alternative. The Governing Body was glad to see the founding professors go because in 1938, it was easy to find qualified persons who were more than willing to accept a teaching job at the college. The takeover was complete – The Governing Body was more than happy to enjoy and eat the cake that others had baked. According to Jogneswar Sharma, "The rich tolerated the teachers but did not want to help them; they reluctantly gave us the benefit of doubt. They, however, received our services without any qualms. This is the custom in our society." [Prantik, January 16-31, 1984].

In the same year, 1938, the Governing Body changed the name of the College after the tea-planter Jagannath Barua, who, as we mentioned, had a good sense of history. However, it is an irony of history that Mr. Barua's name should be associated with the college because in his lifetime he had vigorously opposed the idea of starting a college in Jorhat or Assam. It is ironical that the college he opposed bears his name. The changing of name reflects the narrowing of outlook: From the name of a region (Upper Assam), to the name of a town (Jorhat) and finally to the name of a rich man. The college that was started by the blood, sweat and toil of some dedicated young men, the college that was originally funded mostly by the donations of poor people, the college that was started to serve the cause of education among the poor folks of Upper Assam became the proud possession of the rich folks of Jorhat who needed it to serve their selfish ends.

It must be pointed out that rupee for rupee the value of the free services of the teachers was much more than the value of the JB property at that time. This is not an effort to undermine the contribution of Murulidhar Barua but just an attempt to point out that the contributions of the founding teachers were equal, if not more, to the contributions of Barua both in terms of cash value and spirit. So, it was unfortunate that the Governing Body so chose to kick out the founding teachers. This should not be construed to mean that I am suggesting a name change of JB College—I am merely telling an historical anecdote.

Later, the Assam Government also changed its attitude and sanctioned a financial grant to the college. So, the opportunity came for the people with vested interest to use the college as a power base or as a tool to serve their own interests. Once the college became able to support itself, the Governing Body completely ignored the founding professors. Phanidhar

Datta stayed at Jorhat College till 1938, when he received an invitation from his mentor and teacher Harsha Nath Sen to join Cotton College. This time he accepted the offer because he was having a hard time making ends meet as he had more mouths to feed (including the present author).

From the beginning, Phanidhar Datta and his colleagues followed Principal Sudmersen as their mentor and tried to do for Jorhat College what Sudmersen had done for Cotton College. They tried to build an institution with integrity that would impart education with character. They tried not only to bring higher education within reach of everybody in the region but also to produce educated young men who would have the same spirit of devotion to the people of the country as envisioned by Sir Henry Cotton. From the beginning Phanidhar Datta took upon himself the task of establishing the principles of Principal Sudmersen both inside and outside the classroom. In particular, he took charge of the games and sports and tried to create a healthy environment for learning through physical education.

We give here another anecdote to describe how the upper class tries to secure for itself what it tries to deny to the poor.

Girls' Section at JB College

It may be worthwhile to mention that the Governing Body of JB College started another project whose sole purpose was to serve the interest of the rich.

In those days it became customary among the elite to have their daughters acquire a college education. However, the rich folks of Jorhat did not like to send their daughters to Calcutta or to Gauhati. So, with the college at Jorhat, they saw good opportunities for their daughters' education. There was one problem—most of the students of JB College were boys from poor families or poor farmers. The rich folks of Jorhat could not bear the thought of their "sophisticated daughters" sitting in the same classroom with those poor uncouth lads from the villages. So, the members of the Governing Body and many influential rich men of Jorhat put pressure to start a Girls' section in the college.

At that time, many rich people came forward to raise a substantial fund for the girls' section. The widow of JB donated five thousand rupees for that purpose and many came forward with donations of more than one thousand rupees. It is needless to add that those people had not shown the same generosity when the college was started. If they had shown half as much generosity, then the founding teachers' job would have been much easier.

In any case, with a strong fund, a separate girl's section was started in 1946. At that time the college had 228 male students and 20 female students. The Governing Body made sure that all the resources of the college were used to serve the interest of the girls' section. Of course, most of the girls were daughters of rich people. For example, the girls' section met in the morning and the boys' section met in the afternoon. In other words, the teachers came fresh and energetic in the morning to teach the girls and came back tired and exhausted to teach the boys in the afternoon. JB College completely deviated from that goal with which Upper Assam College was established,. As a result, the education of the male students (most of whom came from poor families) suffered immensely.

Resentment started brewing and soon it resulted in an all out class war in Jorhat. On one hand were the rich, determined to keep their daughters away from the poor village boys, and inclining to give their daughters the best at all costs. On the other hand were the aspirations of the boys to get a good education, and get a fair share of what was meant for them. The ill feelings trickled to the female and male students of the college as well, and in many cases it took the appearance of a battle of the sexes. Many incidents, some funny, some unbelievable and some sad, took place. It is not my intention to describe them here. However, I will describe two incidents as examples.

Since the rich controlled the Governing Body and the female students were mostly from their or their friends' families, the girls were given the best of everything. Even in holding cultural or religious activities, the girls were asked to organize separately. The girls not only received more attention but also equal, if not more financial assistance even though the girl to boy ratio was 1:10. That kind of unfair treatment so infuriated the boys that one year they destroyed all the food prepared as prasadam by the girls, while celebrating the death anniversary of the Assamese Saint Sankardev. I do not know of any such disgraceful act committed by the Assamese in the name of their revered saint.

The other incident happened during a cultural evening organized by the girl students. Of course, they were allotted the prime time and the boys started making some noise and started disturbing the girls' function. So, some member of the Governing Body called the police. Hearing that the police were coming, the boys started plundering everything – breaking and throwing everything before the police arrived. As a result, the audience, consisting mainly of the rich and the elite of the town, ran away by the back door of the hall. By the time the police came, it was too late to prevent the show or to catch the culprits red-handed.

The college could not withstand the revolt by the boys for long and in 1954, the girls' section was closed. Since the college had come under Gauhati University and two of the founding professors were at the helm of affairs of Gauhati University, the Governing Body had no choice but to follow their advice of closing the girls' section. This act so infuriated the rich folks of Jorhat that they started a separate girls' college almost overnight. Those who took the initiative to start the girls college included Heramba Prasad Barua, a tea planter, Radhanath Phukan, a former high official of the British Government, and Kuladhar Chaliha, a member of legislative assembly and a flourishing lawyer of Jorhat. Mr. Chaliha had opposed the idea of establishing a University in Assam and a college at Jorhat. Mr. Phukan did not do a single thing to help Jorhat College even though he had both power and wealth at the time of its inception.

11
Indians Preserve the Integrity of Cotton College

To keep the continuity of the historical order of our tales, we go back to Cotton College again. Let us recall that Cotton College sparked a zeal for education in Assam that is truly exemplary. After the departure of Principal Sudmersen in 1926, Cotton College continued to flourish because of the dedicated services of the teachers whom Sudmersen himself had trained and for whom he was the role model. Soon the job of the Principal also fell upon Indians who had worked with Principal Sudmersen. His successors also provided the leadership that he had inspired. It continued to produce generations of intellectuals who molded the development and culture of the entire Northeastern India in more ways than originally envisioned. All this was possible because of Principal Sudmersen's unstinted leadership and commitment.

Yet the history of Cotton College has not always been rosy. But every time there were troubles, the native teachers and administrators labored to keep it alive with the same zeal with which it was established by the Englishman Sir Henry Cotton and the inspiring educator Sudmersen who molded it into shape. Here is an account of how the college was saved during the war years.

In 1937, the responsibility of the Principalship fell on Harsha Nath Sen, a mathematics teacher. Professor Sen was also present when Principal Sudmersen was giving his farewell address. After becoming the Principal, Professor Sen set his heart on getting the services of his favorite student Phanidhar as a Math teacher of the college. At his urging Phanidhar Datta joined Cotton College on September 22, 1938, on a temporary basis. Soon the second world war started and during the uncertain war torn years, Phanidhar lost that job. Meanwhile, he lost his license to practice law as well. He was no longer welcome at Jorhat College. So, he had to take up farming again. He joined Cotton College on January 25, 1942 as a Math Lecturer. Since that was a tenured position (permanent job), he moved his whole family to Gauhati hoping to live there happily for the remainder of his life.

The Second World War

Japan occupied Singapore on February 15, 1942 and the British Lion got frightened that the Japanese would come and invade India through its Northeast frontier. So, serious preparation started for a war with Japan on Assam's border. Thousands of allied troops, thousands of army vehicles of all kinds, and all kinds of war material poured into Assam. Gauhati became the base of all allied preparations. The war machinery filled all empty spaces of Gauhati and occupied all government buildings. The troops occupied or set camps on all school and college buildings including those of Cotton College.

On April 29, 1942, the British Government decided to move out of Burma (now known as Myanmar). Allied troops moved into the Cotton College hostels on May 31. All the hostel superintendents were ordered to move out of their residences by July 1. By that date, the army occupied all the buildings of Cotton College except the Physics and Chemistry laboratories. Cotton College was just about dead and a tempest blew over Assam's academic life. Mr. S C. Ray, the then Director of Public Instruction of Assam, directed to move the arts departments of the college to Barpeta, Nalbari, etc, and to move the science departments to Sylhet. Most of the professors found it a good opportunity to break up the college and move their own departments to their own towns, or according to their own self-interests.

In those troubled times, Harsha Nath Sen the Principal of Cotton College kept his cool and tried to find some ways to save the college. He called an urgent meeting of the faculty. The meeting bore no fruit because the news came that Burma, and the Assam border had already become a battleground. To make matters worse, Japanese aerial bombing reached as close as Calcutta.

Because of that uncertainty, and because of the fear that the family might have to face difficulties in Gauhati, Phanidhar Datta packed his baggage and moved his family back to Jorhat. Before his departure, principal Sen urged Phanidhar, "Phani, please come back immediately after putting your family safely in Jorhat. We have to do something to save Cotton College. We cannot allow Principal Sudmersen's college to disintegrate like this. We owe it to him and to our future generations to save the college." It should be mentioned that Principal Sen was earlier a math professor at Cotton College and Phanidhar was his favorite student whom he helped in every possible way. Sen used to comment, "There will never be a math student like Phani." So, Phanidhar wanted to do anything that he could for Sen out of gratitude and also for the merit of the project. Phanidhar came back to Gauhati after putting his family in the safe care of his brother and his sister-in-law.

Principal Sen told Phanidhar that if the teachers could arrange some living quarters for the students, then he could keep the college running in the Physics and the Chemistry labs. Immediately, Phanidhar Datta and Birinchi Kumar Barua proposed to rent a few houses in the Uzanbazar area to house the students. Many of the senior teachers of the college laughed at the proposal as totally absurd. But Sen, Datta and Barua started roaming all over Gauhati looking for houses to rent.

There were many empty houses because Gauhati was then almost a deserted town. The owners were reluctant to rent them to college students because they thought the youths might be rowdy. So people thought that they would wreck the houses and create havoc for the neighbors. However, the poetess Nalinibala Debi and a few others came forward to rent their houses.

Few houses were rented. Principal Sen engaged two teachers (Dandeswar Gogoi and Abdul Hye) to buy some used beds, desks and chairs. By the time the students returned from summer vacation, their living quarters were ready. Professors Datta, Barua and Gogoi each took care of two houses, and Abdul Hye took charge of a Muslim hostel. Cotton College kept running.

Then came another disturbance. Gandhi launched the "Quit India" movement on August 8, 1942, and all of India was engulfed in turmoil, which in some areas took violent turns. Many of the Cotton College students deserted the college, and many left their hostels without paying their dues and rents. Principal Sen and the four teachers had to pay part of the rent from their own pockets, and had to endure verbal abuse from the owners. Hoping that things would improve soon, Principal Sen urged the teachers to keep holding on to a few of the houses. That time, nobody except Phanidhar Datta and Dandeswar Gogoi heeded Principal Sen's request. Things did become quite normal towards the end of the year and many students returned and wanted to resume their studies. Datta and Gogoi again went around looking for houses and organized as many as 13 Hindu hostels and 5 Muslim hostels. Meanwhile, Principal Sen became the Director of Public Instruction and he helped Datta, Gogoi and Hye in every possible way. He also declared that any teacher who would organize a hostel for 50 students would be made a superintendent. Then Chandra Kanta Das organized a hostel in 1944. After that every returning student was accommodated, and Cotton College kept running in full swing through the ingenious makeshift arrangement of Principal Sen.

At first, there were no arrangements for the girl students except a missionary hostel run by the Baptist mission at Chatribari. Then a high government official Mrs. B. C. Lais, urged Datta and Gogoi to make some arrangements for girls as well. They organized a girls' hostel on the bank of Dighali tank and put a lady teacher Kamala Roy in charge.

That was how Cotton College survived during those turbulent war years. We should not forget that Principal Harshanath Sen saved the college from falling to pieces by his able and wise leadership. In this task his favorite student Phanidhar and Dandeswar Gogoi immensely helped him. True it is that a positive relationship between a teacher and a student remains productive and fruitful for ages. After the college started functioning properly, several of the senior teachers conspired to remove Datta, Gogoi, Das and Hye as the professors in-charge of the hostels that they laboriously had established. The senior teachers argued that since they were more experienced in running hostels, and since they were the ones who were kicked out of their official positions as superintendent of hostels, they should be put in charge of the makeshift hostels. However, Harshanath Sen firmly declared, "I have been able to do a very worthy deed in my lifetime and that is saving Cotton College during the war years. But that would not have been possible if Phani Datta, Dandeswar Gogoi, Abdul Hye and Chandra Das had not come forward to help me. I can never forget this." Principal Sen, in his capacity as the Director of Public Instruction, also arranged that if the army ever vacated the college dormitories, then Datta, Gogoi, Hye , and Das would be made the superintendents.

The army vacated the college in June of 1946. Sen retired before the army handed those hostels back to the college authority. What happened after that was described well by Gogoi:

> Then Rohini Choudhuri was the education minister. His brother Haren Choudhuri was also a former superintendent. So, all the former superintendents told Haren Choudhuri, 'We were all thrown out of our superintendent's quarters by the army–now that the army has returned those quarters, we are the ones who should receive those quarters.' They wrote a petition and submitted it to the education minister. During the time they sent the petition, Principal Thomas helped us. He discussed with DPI Lais that the old superintendents did not help the college in any way. All these days, we kept the college running

by arranging these makeshift hostels through great difficulties, they never helped us. So, Principal Thomas and DPI Lais made us the superintendents before anything else could happen.

Principal Thomas gave immediate orders making Phanidhar Datta the superintendent of mess no. 3, Gogoi that of mess no. 2, Das that of mess no. 1, and Hye that of the Muslim hostel before the education minister could take any action otherwise. Of course, to satisfy the interest of the education minister, his brother was put in charge of the remaining hostel. Principal Thomas urged the newly appointed superintendent to occupy their quarters immediately. So, on July 9 of 1946 they moved almost overnight to occupy the respective quarters.

It must be mentioned that a superintendent of the college not only got a spacious house in the heart of the college, but also enjoyed many other privileges. One fringe benefit is to the children. They get to live very close to their schools or colleges. In addition, they get to enjoy all the college facilities for extra-curricular activities like sports, gymnasium, communication etc. In any case, it was only after moving to the superintendent quarters in July, 1946 that Phanidhar Datta's family became settled comfortably.

Dandeswar Gogoi later retired as the School Inspector of Assam. In an interview with this author, Gogoi describes the services of Phanidhar Datta to Cotton College in the following manner:

> Datta played a very responsible role in Cotton College. He was the only person whom the Principal could trust to do every job. At that time, he did all the administrative work for the college. From starting the examinations to admitting freshmen, he did all the work on behalf of the Principal. That is why after he left the college in 1948, Bani Babu came to me soon after taking charge as Principal and said, 'One thing, we have lost Datta, he used to do so many things that now there is a problem, now you have to help.' I said O.K., I would try. Datta always came forward to do whatever was necessary. He never got agitated about anything. He was a very calm and stable person.
>
> I always consulted with him. It is like this or it is like that, what should I do now. So I remember all those things and I will always remember that many good things happened to me because he showed me the right path—you know how I opened hostels with him and how I became a hostel superintendent.

12
Assam Builds Its First University: Gauhati University

The Movement For a University in Assam

We have mentioned before that the British Government was not interested in establishing universities and technical institutes in India. The few universities that British India had were established more or less by the efforts of enterprising educated Indians. So, it happened that in Assam, a state bigger than the size of Great Britain did not have a university, a medical college or an engineering college. Assam also did not get a benevolent Governor or Chief Commissioner like Henry Cotton again. So, some educated Assamese took it upon themselves to start a movement for a university in Assam. There is evidence that some educated Assamese dreamt about having a university in Assam since the early part of the twentieth century. However, nothing substantive was done for a long time. In 1915, Sir Ashutosh Mukherjee, the Great Tiger of Bengal, came to visit Assam. His host, Nabin Chandra Bordoloi, asked Sir Mukherjee about the necessity of establishing a university in Assam. In reply, Sir Ashutosh inquired of Mr. Bordoloi whether he would like to have an official university with the Superintendent of Police as its Vice Chancellor. This incident is narrated by Gopinath Bordoloi in his article, "A Case for a University in Assam".[18] The establishment of the college at Jorhat brought new hopes that a university in Assam could be a reality.

The last western Principal of Cotton College was David Edwards Roberts, who retired in 1937. By then Cotton College had produced

[18] I do not know if this article was published anywhere, Bordoloi's daughter and my very dear friend Lily Mazindar Barua, who passed away a few years ago, gave me a copy of the article before she had handed the Bordoloi papers to the National Archive.

hundreds of well educated persons who started building colleges in other parts of northeastern India. We had seen this in the establishment of JB College in 1930. Since then several other colleges were started elsewhere—all of them resulted from the toil and sweat of Cottonians. So, when Roberts retired in 1937, there were not only many natives who were able to maintain the glories of Cotton College but were also ready to start a university in Assam. The university movement started earlier but it took a concrete shape after 1935, when the Assam Council appointed Richard Cunningham, a retired DPI of Assam as the Special Officer to prepare a proposal for a university in Assam. Following the method of Sir Henry Cotton, Cunningham prepared a set of questions for opinions to gather public opinion on the matter. However, unlike Cotton, Cunningham adopted a proposal that was contrary to public opinion. So, everybody revolted against his proposal.

Fast forward to 1940, the Saadulla ministry of Assam introduced a University Bill in the Assam assembly. We understand from Bordoloi's article that the University Bill did not specify a site for the university and it talked about minority representation at the university. Certain sections of the leaders from Sylhet[19] opposed the creation of a university in Assam. It is to oppose that bill and to criticize the Sylhet leaders that Bordoloi wrote the article while lingering in Jorhat jail.

After that the educated young men of Assam decided to take matters in their own hands and take positive steps to build a university on their own. It is needless to say that most of these young men were Cottonians, who had the courage, character and devotion to the people that Principal Sudmersen had instilled in them.

After getting out of jail, Bordoloi took the leadership of the university movement. He also started a fund to build a university. The educated people of Assam under the leadership of Gopinath Bordoloi and the untiring efforts of Sarat Goswami moved ahead to organize a convention at Gauhati on December 29 and 30 of 1944. Sarat Goswami, whom we have mentioned earlier, was the convenor of that convention. While making the arrangements for that convention, Goswami died on December 19 after suffering a massive stroke two days earlier. In his absence, the

---

[19] Sylhet was a town in southern Assam during the British rule. Now, it is a town in Bangladesh.

responsibilities of the convention fell upon Phanidhar Datta and a few other Cottonians. At the convention, a University Trust Board was formed with Gopinath Bordoloi as the President. They then launched a massive Fund Drive to collect money to build a University. To collect money for the fund, they sought just one anna (like a penny) from each donor and not more. The idea was to get more people involved, and to make even the poorest of the poor able to make a contribution to the university fund. Bordoloi actually refused to accept some huge donations by some rich persons. His idea was to build the university as a national institution. In any case, till India's independence, a university in Assam was nothing but a dream.

The Birth of Gauhati University

Fortunately for Assam, Gopinath Bordoloi was elected the Chief Minister (then called the Prime Minister) of Assam in 1946. Soon after that India became independent on August 15, 1947. Bordoloi wasted no time, and passed the Gauhati University Act on September 12, 1947 in the state assembly. The stage was set for the birth of Gauhati University.

All that remained was to find some trustworthy persons to start the university. Rumors and speculations started flying in Assam as to who would start the university, who would be its Vice Chancellor, its Registrar, etc.. Since nothing came out of the lips of Mr. Bordoloi, many thought that he himself was interested in becoming its Vice Chancellor.

When Gopinath Bordoloi had to open the Gauhati Convention in 1944, without his trusted friend Sarat Goswami, he had lamented, "All the plans I have been making to serve my motherland with the help of Mr. Goswami seems to have become dreams only. I have become disheartened looking for a true worker to complete this noble University Yajnya; it is needless to say that I cannot find any one capable of replacing him." So saying he broke down in tears. Bordoloi's eyes fell on Phanidhar Datta, who was taking an active role in the convention to complete the job his mentor Sarat Goswami had undertaken.

Dr. S. K. Bhuyan was then acting as a special officer of the University Committee. In November, 1947, Bordoloi advised Dr. Bhuyan to go to Calcutta and have discussions with Calcutta University regarding how Gauhati University might be able to take complete charge of all examinations in Assam. That was no surprise because Mr. Bordoloi had announced publicly that the target date of starting the university was January, 1948, and Dr. Bhuyan was also the DPI of Assam. What was surprising was the fact that a few days before Dr. Bhuyan was to leave for Calcutta, the Under Secretary of Education came down to Gauhati in person and hand-delivered copies of a letter of instruction that Phanidhar Datta, then a lecturer of Cotton College, accompany Dr. Bhuyan. The two went to Calcutta and Dr. Bhuyan assigned to Phanidhar Datta the task of finding out the nitty-gritty details of running the three college examinations: Matriculation, Intermediate, and Degree. After their return, Mr. Bordoloi asked Phanidhar, "Phani, do you think you would be able to conduct the examinations the next year?"

"Why not, we can definitely do it," replied Phanidhar. Bordoloi then instructed Phanidhar and Bhuyan to look for a house to start the University. Even then there was no clue as to who would be appointed in what capacity.

The announcement came a few weeks later on December 26. That day, a friendly cricket match was organized at Judge's Field, Gauhati between the Prime Minister's XI and the Governor's XI. Mr. Bordoloi started the game by delivering the first ball. Many high dignitaries including the Governor Akbar Haidari, came to watch the game. At the end of the game, Pulin Das and Kironmoy Lahiri (who later became the Chief Justice of Assam High Court) were awarded one cricket bat each for their performances. I also remember the beautiful and playful daughter of Governor Haidari. I remember that hundreds of college students, who came to watch the game, instead spent their time vainly watching the movements of the Governor's daughter. I also remember that the personal bodyguard of Haidari, a very handsome and young army officer, was busy keeping his eyes on the Governor's daughter rather than on the Governor. I do not know what those young college students did later, but I do know that the young army officer later married the Governor's daughter.

The Birthplace of Gauhati University

From the playground, Mr. Bordoloi sent the Education Secretary, S. L. Mehta to Phanidhar Datta. Mr. Mehta came running to the Superintendent's house. Huffing and puffing, Mr. Mehta told Phanidhar in great excitement, "Brother, you will have to start Gauhati University. Have you found a house? Come, hurry up , the Prime Minister has sent me to fetch you." Phanidhar Datta informed Mr. Mehta that there was a military go-down near the hostel that was lying unused. The building was strong, so examination papers could be safely stored there.

At the judge's field after distributing the prizes to Pulin Das and Kironmoy Lahiri, Mr. Bordoloi announced that he had chosen Phanidhar Datta to start the University of Gauhati. He would become its first Registrar and start functioning in that capacity from January 1, 1948. After that Mr. Bordoloi, Governor Haidari and many other high dignitaries walked with Phanidhar to look at the military go-down. They thought that the place was suitable. They ordered to start the university there. He told the education secretary to do everything necessary to release Phanidhar Datta from Cotton College. He instructed Phanidhar Datta to make all arrangements to hold the matriculation examination in 1948.

Nothing else was done. There was no mention of money and no other instructions. Feeling a little lost, Phanidhar Datta went to the Principal of Cotton College and told him what happened. The Principal, who was a very religious person, said a little prayer and after blessing Phanidhar, told him not to worry about formalities but to start working for the establishment of the University.

Lawyers' Book Stall

The next morning Phanidhar went to the Lawyer's Book Stall and broke the news to its proprietor and his high school buddy, Bichitra Narayan Dattabarua. Mr. Dattabarua listened to everything quietly, then taking a few quick puffs on his hooka, he shouted to one of his salesman in his characteristic commanding tone, "Bring two quires of paper, an inkpot, pens and whatever we got, the professor has to start the University. You see, Phani if Bordoloi says, you must understand, it has started." Holding onto those gifts from Mr. Dattabarua, Mr. Datta felt very inspired because they were the first concrete materials to fall in his hands towards starting Gauhati University. It is needless to add that Mr. Dattabarua supplied stationery for the university office free of charge for a long time. The event was publicized quite a bit, and it was announced on the radio.

The Bengali Carpenter

In this connection, another interesting anecdote is that the chair that Mr. Datta sat on, the first chair that the university owned was donated by a Bengali carpenter who had a shop near Bijulee Cinema Hall, a movie house in the heart of Gauhati. He came one day with that beautiful chair and told Mr. Datta, "I heard on the radio that Bordoloi Dangoria has started a university and you are the Registrar. Sir, I have been making this beautiful chair and after I finished it I was thinking to whom should I sell this? But when I heard the news, I decided to donate it to the university. I love Bordoloi Dangoria so much and I want to do something good. Sir please bless me by accepting this. I have really built this with a lot of love." Mr. Datta offered to pay him for it but there was no way that the poor Bengali carpenter would accept anything. I'm sure that many of the soulless modern scholars would portray this as a good marketing strategy, a good strategy to hook a promising customer. All I can say is that the present society and thinking have become so materialistic, so barren spiritually, that they cannot even recognize 'the noble' souls of the past.

With the furniture and stationery, Phanidhar Datta started the University of Gauhati on January 1, 1948 without any fanfare. He however, had many visitors, mostly colleagues from Cotton College.

Appointment of Krishna Kanta Handique

There was some delay in appointing a Vice Chancellor, for which Bordoloi had discussions even with Gandhi and Kaka Kalelkar. Mr. Bordoloi finally decided to seek a genuine Assamese scholar. Mr. Datta rather light heartedly told him that there were only two genuine bookworms in Assam, and they were Bani Kanta Kakoti and Krishna Kanta Handique. He also mentioned that it would be quite a task to persuade Mr. Handique to come to Gauhati but if he became the Vice Chancellor, then it would be a real blessing.

Mr. Bordoloi decided on Mr. Handique again because of the leadership and commitment he had shown in establishing and running JB College. In addition, he was also receiving a lot of admiration as a dedicated scholar. So, he took the challenge of persuading M. Handique to come to Gauhati. Mr. Bordoloi was exceedingly happy when Mr. Handique agreed to become the Vice Chancellor as we know from an entry in his diary. A few days later Mr. Bordoloi stopped by to see what Mr. Datta was doing. Mr. Datta then asked Mr. Bordoloi:

"Who is going to be the Vice Chancellor?"

"Why? Krishna Kanta Handique! I have sent a letter to him. I was thinking a lot about this university while I was in Jorhat jail. At that time I had decided that if I ever got the chance to start the first university in Assam, I would invite those people who started the first private college of Assam at Jorhat."

The Founding Fathers of Gauhati University

Eminent and trustworthy people like Jogneswar Sharma of Nowgong pointed, and rightly so, to three persons whom we should remember and to whom we should be grateful for the wonderful center of learning Gauhati University. The three persons are Gopinath Bordoloi, the first chief minister of independent Assam, Phanidhar Datta, the first Registrar upon whom Bordoloi entrusted the responsibility of building the University's foundation, and Krishna Kanta Handique the first Vice Chancellor of the University. I wish to discuss what role these three played in building this University, why we should remember them, and how we can guide the destiny of this great institution by following their example.

Before I do so, I must thank all those dedicated and remarkable people who for nearly two decades before the birth of this university were leading a vigorous movement to establish a university in Assam. Without their efforts, the University of Gauhati would not have been born on January 1, 1948. That's another story. Here, I would like to give a brief review of the three personalities.

Gopinath Bordoloi was a great leader of Assam. He was a true Gandhian with a very clear vision of a glorious Assam. He was truly secular, and he had a special kindness for the poor and the downtrodden. He had tremendous affection for the Hills people of Assam and Manipur. He wanted to build a colorful and distinctive society in Assam where people would live in harmony, loving and respecting the ethnic diversities of this land. As the Chief Minister, he organized the Hills and Plains festival the like of which later leaders did not even care to think of.

To give an example of Mr. Bordoloi's secular spirit, I must mention how he offered to resign rather than drop his Muslim friend, Toiyabulla, from his ministry as demanded by none other than the central home minister, Vallab Bhai Patel. Nowadays, secularism has different kinds of anecdotes, like somebody is included in ministry because he is a Muslim, but one never hears of somebody putting up a fight for someone saying, "I did not take him because he is a Muslim but because he is the right man. I would rather resign myself than ask Mr. Toiyabulla to resign." In any case, to build a golden Assam he needed a university that would bring education and higher education within reach of every person living in northeast India. Mr.Bordoloi wrote,

> It is also true that education today, hardly affects the villages, and if it at all does so, indirectly it creates more harm than good. The educated man instead of keeping in touch with and improving the village, has left it to indulge in the comforts of the town. The whole outlook of the so-called educated man has been one of self-indulgence and self-aggrandizement, with neglect of and oftentimes at the cost of the villagers. . . . To me, however, it is quite possible to bring into our society a new outlook—an outlook of service and duty to our fellow men, with a properly constituted educational center.

That educational center was the University of Gauhati. So, when the time came to select the persons to start the university, he looked for an educated young man who demonstrated an outlook of service and duty to fellow men. His first choice was Phanidhar Datta, who had spurned government service after getting his MA and BL degrees and had gone back to his village. Phanidhar Datta also worked very hard at immense personal sacrifice to establish the first private college in Assam, JB College at Jorhat, with the other founders of the college.

Phanidhar Datta was an educated youth who did not forget his village connection. In the words of Jogneswar Sharma, "Datta took an active part in all the activities of village life including farming, congregational chanting, staging traditional plays and so on. I know how he used to come to school after working in the field the whole morning. Even when he was a college student he worked in the field—and never tried to hide that fact like many did." Mr. Sharma gives another reason why Bordoloi selected Phanidhar to start the first university in Assam.

> Datta joined Cotton College during the war years. At that time, since the army took over the college hostels, there were a lot of problems in providing living quarters for the boys. But Datta so cleverly arranged hostels in the town for the boys and made arrangements to run them, that the Government started having trust in him. At that time, Gopinath Bordoloi and the top officials of the education department started having a very high opinion of Mr. Datta. He brought such an order to the chaotic situation of the student's problems that his dexterity expressed itself. Then in those days, nobody except Mr. Datta took care of all the exams. Because of those two reasons, when the University act specified that the government would appoint the first Registrar of the University, the government looked towards Datta as its choice. Actually, there were many who were coveting that post and many of them started feeling jealous of Mr. Datta – I know that for a fact. Jealousy is in human nature. Many of them disliked him very much, I won't name them. The government made it very convenient for him by letting him stay at the College Superintendent's quarters and working for the university.

The letter confirming the appointment of Phanidhar Datta as the Registrar, at a monthly salary of 500 rupee, came on January 7, 1948. After exactly 20 days, his salary was raised to 550 rupees a month. After drawing his plans for the matriculation examination, Mr. Datta went to Calcutta to finalize the take over of the responsibility from Calcutta University. At that time Mr. R. N. Bannerjee, the Registrar of Calcutta University and who was also a teacher of Mr. Datta, told the latter, "Phani, if you can conduct the examinations for the University of Gauhati in such a short time, I'll garland you." When Phanidhar Datta achieved that in 1948, Mr. Bannerjee followed through on his promise.

We have already given an account of the very humble background that Phanidhar Datta came from and how he had to struggle to get a higher education, he had to struggle to pay for his education. So, after finishing his master's degree in mathematics, he decided to dedicate his life to helping the poor and the destitute like him to get higher education. He spurned all efforts for government offices, went back to his village and started working vigorously to establish a college at Jorhat, and the first private college of Assam was born. In the beginning he worked for the college without any remuneration. He was happy working in the fields to feed himself and his family.

Mr. Handique was a rich man, being the son of a tea-planter, so all the luxuries in life were within his reach; nevertheless he chose a life of scholarship. He was a true scholar in constant pursuit of knowledge, and a man well versed in French, German, English, Bengali, Assamese, and Sanskrit. So vast was his scholarship, that he had mastered the great literary works of each of these languages. But it was the literary works in Sanskrit that he pursued with a passion. He lived a simple life drinking black tea with lemon and sugar, and reading—reading about 15 hours a day. He believed in pursuit of knowledge, and his idea of a university was a center of learning where people would take to learning with the passion and the zeal of a sadhu, wanting little but without any pressure from within or outside. He had received a great deal of his education in the west, notably in the United Kingdom and Germany. In addition, he also studied in Cotton College under Principal Sudmersen. He was a true believer of academic freedom. He did not want any interference from politicians, administrators, or students, in running the university. He expected a spirit of dedication from the students and the teachers to learning. At the university he wanted them to learn and develop that inner urge or that extra spark for knowledge. He was not willing to make any compromise academically. As the Vice Chancellor, he was determined to give that leadership to make the university a center for learning.

It is creditable that Mr. Bordoloi could single out a person like Mr. Handique to become the first Vice Chancellor of the new university. Even if we forget about everything that Bordoloi did for Gauhati University, his choice of the first Registrar and the first Vice Chancellor is enough to secure a place for him in the annals of Gauhati University.

In spite of these diverse differences in their personalities, the three founding fathers of Gauhati University had many things in common. First of all, they were all very simple; simple in their tastes, in their dress and in their manners. They were all great persons possessing honesty and integrity, and they could rise above and beyond their personal interest and needs for a cause. Let me illustrate this with some anecdotes.

The Vice Chancellor refuses to meet the Chief Minister

Mr. Gopinath Bordoloi came to meet Mr. Handique soon after Handique joined as the Vice Chancellor. Mr. Bordoloi came in his sky blue official car. The car stopped in front of Handique's gate and Mr. Bordoloi sent his peon to inform Mr. Handique. Mr. Bordoloi perhaps expected Mr. Handique to come running and greet him right there. But the peon came back with the message that Mr. Handique refused to see Mr. Bordoloi—that perhaps might have been the biggest surprise and disappointment that Gopinath Bordoloi met in his life. Seeing the Chief Minister's car waiting in front of the Vice Chancellor's residence, Mr. Datta rushed to meet Mr. Bordoloi and cordially brought the Chief Minister to his house. That was not all. A few days later when the Governor of Assam asked the Vice Chancellor to come and meet him at the Circuit house for some discussion, Mr. Handique sent a tart reply that he had nothing to discuss with the Governor, so he was not going to the Circuit house. The Governor took it as an insult and relayed his indignation to Bordoloi. That time Bordoloi was furious because he knew that the university he was so much interested in, the dream child of Assam that he had helped to make a reality, would give him no say in its running or its development. He let Mr. Datta know his mind, and asked Mr. Datta to convey his dissatisfaction to Mr. Handique. He wrote about all these in his diary from which it is clear that his displeasure knew no bounds. But did he take it personally? Did he try to get Handique fired? Did he try to pass an ordinance restricting the Vice Chancellors power or to cut off funds to the University? No, none of these—unlike many of our present day leaders, Bordoloi could rise above and beyond his self.

When Mr. Datta communicated Bordoloi's displeasure to Handique, Mr. Handique gave the short reply that Mr. Bordoloi should know because, "when I accepted the post, he promised me that no politician, no MLA (Member of Legislative Assembly) or government officers will be allowed to set foot in the university." When Bordoloi was told of Mr. Handique's reply, Mr. Bordoloi just smiled and said, "Yes, that is true, but I did not think that he included me among the MLA's." After that he did not try to meet Mr. Handique or come to visit the University. He realized that Mr. Handique wanted the University to be completely autonomous, and that Mr. Handique was trying to establish academic freedom of the highest order. Bordoloi knew it well because he himself wrote, while criticizing the Saadula's proposal of a university act, "There is no question of forcing the University Authority of whom the Chancellor also is one, to adopt a line of action determined by the Government of the day. I cannot think of a worse interference into the administration of a self-governing institution than that provided in clause 8 of the bill." Mr. Bordoloi knew well that Handique was keen on establishing a kind of university that Mr. Bordoloi himself was dreaming about, and that his don Sir Ashutush Mukherjee had so vehemently advocated in an open letter to Lord Lytton (Mr. Bordoloi refers to this letter in his article.) One can appreciate the magnanimity of Gopinath Bordoloi.

Phanidhar Datta with Prime Minister Nehru on the Inauguration day (29 August, 1955) of the Science Buildingof GU

The Vice Chancellor refuses to serve in the University Development Committee

After the site for the university was selected, the Assam Government passed an amendment to the Gauhati University Act in 1949, specifying the formation of a Development Committee to take the responsibility of the construction of buildings for the University. The Education minister was to be the Chairman of this Committee, and the Education Secretary was to act as its Secretary. The Registrar of the University was not included as its member. But when the Committee met for the first time on May 5, 1949, Mr. Handique refused to attend the meeting and asked Mr. Datta to attend the meeting in his place. Later, Mr. Handique made it clear that he was never going to serve in the University Development Committee and that he would have nothing to do with the constructions. So, the Education minister Gopinath Bordoloi held the meeting without the Vice Chancellor.

Making Gauhati University truly secular

Gopinath Bordoloi, however, could not stay away from the running of the University, so he would very often call Mr. Datta to the Circuit house to discuss things. Once or twice he even came to Mr. Datta's house. So, what did Bordoloi tell Mr. Datta? He would tell Mr. Datta something like, "Phani everything depends upon you. I have faith in you. You must see that nobody is able to buy degrees at this university, and nobody passes an exam by paying money. You must see that education reaches everybody, the Nagas, the Manipuris, the Khasis and all the tribal people." In addition, Mr. Bordoloi insisted that there be no consideration for caste, religion, or class. The university must be above all these. His guiding principles were clear: the university should be a completely secular institution; an institution that would bring socio-academic enlightenment to the people of Assam. It should be free of petty politics and petty considerations. Mr. Datta revered Gopinath Bordoloi. He looked upon Bordoloi as his leader and regarded himself as the chosen servant who had to carry out his wishes. Datta followed every word of Bordoloi's instructions.

Another very important thing is that both Bordoloi and Phanidhar Datta admired Calcutta University and admired the Bengalis for their achievements in the field of education. In partial support of these, let me again quote from Bordoloi's article, "Sacrificing leadership is as much necessary for the service of the masses as it is necessary to feed and clothe them. It is very necessary that our educated young men should be men with the full knowledge of the needs and necessities of the masses and of the means to satisfy them. They should be the fountainhead of the basic culture of communal unity and should represent a common meeting ground where all communal differences have found their settlement. They should be able to breathe freedom and exhibit character in all that they would feel, think and will. We can expect such young men to lead us and guide us, and any institution that would train them should receive our support. . . . It may undoubtedly be argued that the University bill must necessarily contemplate only a form and that such a contemplation will be possible only by the character of the people working it. I have only to say in reply that Calcutta University has that form and, I believe, is worked by eminent men of character and learning." He especially instructed Mr. Datta to go and learn from Calcutta University and to invite Bengali professors and scholars.

When the time came to hire professors for the university and Dibrugarh medical college, Bordoloi's instruction was to try to get the best men from wherever possible, not Assamese, not Bengali, not Hindu, not Muslim, but the best man. That's what Mr. Datta tried to do. Then Bordoloi created some foreign scholarships. His strategy was to send the best students from Assam to get higher training abroad, so that they could come back and give shape to this university and the medical college. Bordoloi saw Assam as a nation at its infancy and he wanted to guide its destiny to build it from within as a truly secular, non-violent and casteless society where the diverse ethnic groups would live in harmony burying the age-old rivalry and stereotyping. He wanted the university to give the nation both its character and develop its leaders. The very fact that Bordoloi chose Phanidhar Datta to start the first university in Assam showed his respect for the personality of Phanidhar Datta.

Born privileged but made destitute by fate, Phanidhar Datta inherited from his father an extra thirst for knowledge. As a poor boy, he faced immense obstacles to get an education and to quench his thirst for knowledge. As a person, Phanidhar Datta was very much like Henry Cotton. Like Cotton, he felt a deep devotion to the common mass and tried to make education more available to them. Like Cotton, he was very secular and democratic in his outlook. Like Cotton, he also had to fight against the reactionary forces of the ruling and the privileged class and paid dearly for it. Like Cotton, he always had a mentor whose ideals he tried to emulate sincerely.

A respectable secular institute that would bring enlightenment to every citizen of Assam be he poor, from a scheduled caste or scheduled tribe, was the dream of Bordoloi. Mr. Handique was determined to lay the foundation for a seat of learning where academic pursuit was the main goal of teacher and student alike, a seat of learning where academic freedom prevailed without any interference from politicians and self-seekers. Phanidhar Datta with his determined efforts succeeded in shaping that university. Phanidhar Datta saw Gauhati University as a large extension of Cotton College that would, among other things, maintain academic integrity, and establish a very fair, efficient, and honest examination system that everybody would be able to trust.

The three founders declared the goal of the university was to build men and women of character and integrity who would bring enlightenment to this small corner of the world. Yes, the university wanted to produce men of character—no education can be worth anything if it is not accompanied by strength of character. If dedication to learning, a desire to live honestly, and an inner urge to uplift the masses do not enter into the personalities of its degree holders, then the university will produce merely degree holders who do more harm than good to society. A lesson Phanidhar Datta learned well in Sudmersen's Cotton College.

Nowadays, people talk about role models. The University of Gauhati is very fortunate that every one of its three founders is a great role model—an honest, and hardworking person who dedicated his services to the cause of education, a true scholar who was committed to creating a free and congenial environment of learning, and a true secular leader who sought to uplift the masses. The University of Gauhati must set as its goal the production of people like these role models. These are the kind of people that this university needs badly now, and these are the kinds of people that Assam needs now more than ever. We must tell there stories so that the present and future students can easily find role models to emulate.

After some preliminary inquiries, Jalukbari (present Gopinath Bordoloi Nagar) was selected as the site for the University. The task of preliminary work like surveying, ascertaining the total land to be acquired, and how many people would be displaced, fell upon Phanidhar Datta. This was not an easy task because many villagers were unwilling to give up their land. Some even threatened to attack him if he ever set foot on their land. He needed to use all his persuasive powers to convince the villagers that the University would be for their benefit. Three things helped him to win the villagers to his side. First, the generous plan that he chalked out with the government for their resettlement. Second, the lenient attitude he took by allowing them to continue cultivating the land where construction was not started. Above all, he gave them his own example by stating that with the university on their own courtyard, their children would also have the opportunity to get a higher education.

Gauhati University Development Committee

We have mentioned earlier how Mr. Handique refused to attend the organizational meeting of the Gauhati Uninversity Development Committee. Mr. Handique asked Mr. Datta to attend the meeting. In addition to Datta, others present at that meeting were Education minister Gopinath Bordoloi, the Education Secretary, the Chief Engineer of Assam Government, the Deputy Commissioner of Kamrup, Executive Engineer Sarbeswar Das and Dr. Bhubaneswar Barua. Each one of the members was assigned a responsibility. After a few months, it became apparent that none of them had any interest to work wholeheartedly for the construction. Soon, Phanidhar Datta was not only made the Secretary of the Development Committee, but one by one he was given all the responsibilities of supervising the constructions of the buildings. He was to be assisted by Executive Engineer Sarbeswar Das.

Phanidhar Datta had to do virtually everything, including hiring architects, approving plans, hiring contractors, procuring controlled materials like cement, iron rod, etc. He had to devote his energies to the constructions as well. In addition to setting up the examination machinery, his services as the secretary of the Development Committee is the most admirable. Under his supervision and by 1957, Dalmiya Company built five buildings (Chemistry building, Physics building, and the No. 1 Hostel), and Gannon Dunkerly Company built three buildings (University Hospital, Girls' Hostel and No. 2 Hostel).

In addition, Phanidhar Datta hired local contractors to build 65 professor's quarters and 50 quarters for employees. To have all these ready in such a short time is not a small accomplishment. His honesty and his decisive personality were the main motive force behind those successful completions. Because of his honesty, all the contractors and the companies tried to complete everything on time and without any defects. One of the richest men of India, at that time and the Director of one of the companies, Mr. Dalmiya himself said,

"We have had business dealing in many parts of India, but nowhere we have found the same satisfaction as in working for Gauhati University. Mr. Datta is such an honest and saintly person that we find special satisfaction working for him. Always the bills are paid on time and very honestly. That's why I am taking the job of building Gauhati University as my own work. We are not keeping any eye on profit, and we are using the best of materials because we know that we do not have to bribe anybody, so we will profit by building the University well."

Dalmiya did take a personal interest in the construction, and he himself came to inspect the work more than once. In any case, people with knowledge of engineering do testify that all the buildings and houses constructed under the supervision of Phanidhar Datta are built better than the ones constructed later, and that, too, at a cheaper rate.

At first Mr. Datta did not even want to take the responsibility of the constructions, but people holding the helm of affairs and the leaders like Gopinath Bordoloi, and Krishna Kanta Handique kept putting that responsibility on his shoulder. Because of the trust and cooperation of those leaders, Datta took those duties cheerfully and was proud when India's President Dr. Rajendra Prasad (while inaugurating the Physics building on 21 February, 1954), Prime Minister Jawaharlal Nehru (while inaugurating the chemistry building on 29 August 1955) and others praised the building program of the University. Even then, because of the ever increasing examination burdens and his deteriorating health, Mr. Datta more than once tried to give up the position of the Secretary of the Development Committee, but Vice Chancellor Handique would no way let him do that. Mr. Handique's blunt assertion, "Where am I going to find a trustworthy person to take care of the buildings involving lakhs[20] of rupees?"

The immediate goals of the University soon after its establishment may be summed as:

*To conduct matriculation, intermediate and degree examinations for the schools and colleges of Assam.

* To build permanent buildings for the University after selecting a suitable location.

* To start post-graduate academic programs.

* To initiate plans and programs for medical and technical education in Assam.

Mr. Gopinath Bordoloi, the Chief Minister himself took the initiative to start the medical college at Dibrugarh and the Agriculture College at Jorhat in the same year, 1948. To put everything in first gear, Mr. Bordoloi himself took charge of the education portfolio. Because of his leadership, people of Assam also did not remain idle. Many enterprising and dedicated

[20] 1 lakh = hundred thousand is a popular unit in India.

people took the initiative to start private schools and colleges in different parts of the state. Because of their efforts, several noteworthy colleges came into being in the region. Perhaps each private college of Assam is the result of dedicated services and sacrifices of some noble souls–Jorhat College is a good example. The new University, especially its Vice Chancellor and the Registrar who were two of the stalwarts of the college at Jorhat, did provide expertise, encouragement and all possible help in establishing colleges in different parts of the region.

It is really creditable that some dedicated and educated young men were able to start these colleges with donations from concerned citizens. Almost every private college of Assam is a living monument to the dedicated services and generosity of some of Assam's noblest sons and daughters. It is simply because the Assamese by nature often fail to appreciate noble deeds.

The University of Gauhati started post-graduate classes from 1949 with Sri Sarat Kumar Datta as its Secretary. Later, Mr. Handique showed good leadership by separating the functions of the University and putting three dedicated persons in charge of each. Dr. Birinchi Kumar Barua was put in charge of post-graduate classes, Phanidhar Datta was assigned the duties of controller of Examinations, and the general administration of the office was put on the shoulder of Cidananda Das as the Deputy Registrar.

The Early Years

So, in the early years, work on Gauhati University had to progress in three directions:

*construction of permanent buildings at Jalukbari,

*setting up the examination machinery and

*developing its academic programs.

Krishna Kanta Handique entrusted the responsibility of the first two activities to Phanidhar Datta while Dr. Birinchi Kumar Barua was entrusted with the responsibility of building the academic programs. For the benefit of future generations, we give here an overview of Phanidhar Datta's contributions in these areas and his modus operandi. Dandeswar Gogoi, a former professor of Cotton College, a neighbor of Datta, and one who always offered a helping hand to Datta, told us:

> In case of the new University, a lot had to be done before establishing it at Jalukbari. If those things were not properly done, we would not have had such a fine university there today. At that time, all the

planning, all the leadership that was needed and making sure that what was being done was done properly at the direction of our Datta. We have seen by our own eyes that everything was accomplished in a disciplined manner because of him. Gauhati University soon got established as a very good university. Even though it followed the model of Calcutta University, it was reckoned as equal to Calcutta University.

What Mr. Gogoi saw is described vividly by Dambarudhar Pathak, a former Chief Justice Assam High Court,:

On 2nd of July 1958, I joined the Gauhati University Law College as a part-time lecturer. At that time the administrative complex of the University was housed in a block of buildings belonging to Cotton College at Panbazar. On many occasions during that period I had to come to the administrative office of the University for some urgent works. There I came in close contact with two dedicated officers of the University who were reputed to be the king-pins of the administration due to their sincere and unstinted devotion to their duties. One of them was Prof. Phanidhar Datta who was Registrar of the University and who also functioned as a Controller of Examinations. Incidentally Prof. Datta had been my teacher in Mathematics at the time I was a student in Cotton College. The other was Shri Chidananda Das who was at that time a Deputy Registrar of the University. Now I recall that both the officers were loved and respected by all concerned for their amiable behavior and also for their persuasive way of getting the works done for the administration.

Very often I was sent for by Prof. Datta for some urgent works, and I had to be closeted in his chamber for hours together with him till the works were completed. I was surprised to see Prof. Datta working for such long hours. In the midst of the works, after about two hours he would casually tell me to be engaged till he returned within a few minutes after taking an insulin injection. In retrospect, in the background of the present day lack-luster work culture of the officers and staff in all spheres, I like to reminisce with high degree of appreciation the selfless hard work rendered by Prof. Datta and his colleagues for setting a good name and tradition for the University.

[Abhinandan Grantha Sri Chidananda Das, hereafter referred to as AGC]

Because of able leadership of Mr. Handique and the hard work of Mr. Datta, the fame of Gauhati University as a prestigious university spread all over the country within a very short period of time after its establishment, That was mainly because of the leadership of Mr. Handique and because of the selfless work by Phanidhar Datta and a trusted band of dedicated people that he gathered to run the university. There might have been some minor omissions or mistakes here and there. But everything was taken care of, maintaining the reputation of the university, which was always soaring higher and higher. So, within a few years, Gauhati University earned a reputation that was far beyond anybody's dream. The main architect of all these was Phanidhar Datta. Handique provided the leadership, Bordoloi planted the seeds of purpose and dedication, and both of them (even though he never got a chance to sit together after the university was born), provided the strong support and help that was needed.

Phanidhar Datta established the honest and efficient machinery that was needed to set the university on a firm footing. As Professor Jogneswar Sharma has said, Phanidhar Datta built the university literally brick by brick. Many others like Professor Nilima Datta, Nanda Talukdar (in the biography of Dr. S.K. Bhuyan), Abdus Sattar (in the biography of K.K. Handique), Dr. Venkata Rao, have gone on record to say that nobody worked so hard to maintain the honesty and the integrity of the university as did Phanidhar Datta.

All the employees of the University from peons and security men to the top officials, were inspired by Phani Datta's devotion to duty and tireless efforts to work with a sense of devotion and unselfishness. Phanidhar Datta had to work so hard for the University that he had no time to think about his family, and he even neglected his own health. He sacrificed everything for the University and devoted all his energies for its well-being. His main motivation was to remove all the obstacles of higher education (that he himself had to face in his pursuit of higher education) for the future generations of Assam and the neighboring areas. The spark that was lit in a slate-house of Sadiya started burning one hundred years later on the fields of Jalukbari, and he felt that he was carrying that spark through his father and grandfather. That full fire supplied him with all the energies. The fire was nurtured by the trust and confidence the elders of the society such as Gopinath Bordoloi, Dr. Bhubaneswar Barua, Omeo Kumar Das and Krishnakanta Handique, etc.. Phanidhar Datta served as the Registrar for fourteen years and in recognition of his services, he was elected as the Vice Chancellor before finally retiring in 1962. Many now refer to him as an architect of modern Assam.

An architect of modern Assam—yet he was the product of western education that India adopted. Could that have been possible if William

Griffith had not sparked a zeal for knowledge in his grandfather's mind? Could that have been possible if Nathan and Eliza Brown had not taken upon themselves the task of teaching the Assamese to read and write? Could Phanidhar Datta and his colleagues have succeeded in establishing a college if Henry Cotton and William Sudmersen had not set the stage for higher education in Assam? Perhaps yes, perhaps no, who knows? It might have happened otherwise, but that is the way it happened in Assam. It may be true that 'East is east, West is west and never the two shall meet', but it is true that the West can inspire good karma in the east and the East can inspire good karma in the west. After all it is good karma that keeps Creation alive and mankind soaring higher and higher as time rolls by.

Phanidhar Datta leading the academic procession of the first convocation of Gauhati University in 1953.

Epilogue

The present education system in India is essentially British in character. As told by Henry Cotton.

> We owe to Lord William Bentinck, under the inspiration of Macaulay, the foundation of an educational system which has revolutionized India. The establishment of Medical Colleges is due to William Bentinck and to Lord Auckland. . . . To Lord Dalhousie we owe the initiation of a policy for developing the resources of the country which is now bearing fruit. His name is also associated with the establishment of Universities in India. [*IHM* 195-196]

Even though many criticize the system introduced by the British as deficient in many respects, independent India has not been able to change or improve it during the last fifty-six years. In any case, the Indian education system still remains the backbone of India's continual progress.

The Governor-Generals or the Viceroys of the British Government merely gave the legislative framework for the system, but the actual work was carried on by the foot soldiers like Cotton, Sudmersen and the native educators they inspired. We who are closely connected with the education system in India do clearly see the fruitful interplay of western ideas and Indian karma in the development of the system.

We have tried to give an interesting perspective of this fusion by telling a few tales about the birth and development of JB College, Cotton College and Gauhati University in northeastern India as seen through the life and good karma of my father Phanidhar Datta, who is regarded as an architect of Modern Assam. He started as a very poor lad always struggling to get an education. After getting his education, he spent his whole life trying to make education more available to others. Almost by his own design, he died a poor man. At the time of his death, he had no bank account, no house of his own, and no valuable possession. He used to say that his only valuable property was his children whom he had educated in the institutions and the education system he worked hard to establish.

Mr. Datta was able to cross the barrier of poverty during his lifetime but he remained a true servant of the poor community on the other side. From this side of well-to-do's, he never forgot the have-nots on the other side. He took birth among the poorest of the poor, but he was able to get an education, and place himself among the elite of the society – even then he always remained humble, simple and free of greed for money and earthly possessions. Instead, he always tried to secure for the poor an avenue for upliftment through education. In this regard, he was very different from many educated Assamese of that time.

He never gave up the honesty and the gentle nature of a farmer. Corruption, greed or lust for power could never touch him. On the other hand, embracing Karma (duty) as his dharma (way of fulfillment) he fought his whole life against some evil forces of society. In the words of Suren Bharali of Jorhat who knew him closely since his schooldays, "Phani was always honest. His whole life was truly noble and free of blemishes. He lived a life without luxuries."

Jogneswar Sarma, a founder professor of Jorhat College, a dedicated educationist and a close friend of Phanidhar Datta since his school days had this to say, "Only people who are always very honest and who could engage themselves persistently to their work can acquire a personality. One can acquire a personality only through honest and diligent work. Phanidhar Datta had both those qualities." Even then Phanidhar Datta's last few years at the university were not very happy because the changing political climate and the misdeeds of some self-seeking individuals flung the university into a state of turmoil, a turmoil from which it is yet to recover. Ever since the departure in 1957 of Vice Chancellor Handique, politicians and the ruling class in their attempt to gain control of the university started a campaign of false accusations, exaggerated failures and character assassination. That is a long story that we do not intend to go into now. He resigned as the Vice Chancellor of the university in 1962.

Phanidhar Datta passed away on October 29, 1963, barely a month after seeing his son (the present author) go to England for higher studies with a fellowship from the British Government. At that time Phanidhar Datta expressed his three last wishes. They were:

(1) Do not waste any money on my funeral services or any sraddha ceremony for me.

(2) Do not try to marry off my daughters without letting them complete the education they seek.

(3) See if you can do something for the cause of education in my village.

His first wish was really because of our financial condition at that time. But with the host of friends and relatives who loved and admired him dearly, it was not possible to let him slip away so quietly. So, with everybody's help, we performed a very simple but meaningful sraddha ceremony. Even with that, every day since his death has been a sraddha day for us because we never pass a day without remembering him and paying homage to his noble personality.

About the daughters, our two elder sisters Lalita Bora (wife of Late Kumud Chandra Bora of Ottawa, Canada) and Shanta Phukan (wife of Sri Dimbeswar Phukan of Beltola) both had finished their master's degrees while father was still alive.

It should be mentioned that in Indian tradition, when the head of a household dies, the responsibility of looking after the family falls on the shoulder of the adult males. It often happens that to reduce the burden, they try to get rid of the girls by getting the girls married as quickly as possible. So it was that the responsibility of educating the remaining four daughters fell upon my elder brother and myself. Both my brother Sri Pradip Datta and myself regarded our younger sisters as nothing but sources of love and cheer, and tried to provide for whatever education they sought to have. Gita Deb (wife of late Arabindra Deb) and Pranita Barua (at present Head, Department of Mathematics, Handique Girls' College and wife of Prof. Chandra Barua of Senduri Ali) both obtained master's degree from Gauhati University before getting married. Rita Rajkhowa (at present Principal, Girls' Polytechnique, Gauhati and wife of Sri Jyoti Rajkhowa, a member of the Indian Administrative Service) was the first Assamese female to join the Assam Engineering College and did complete her BE degree before getting married. Rita took advantage of her husband's assignment in Delhi to obtain the ME from Delhi University a few years back, just about the same time as her son finished his bachelor's degree. Our youngest sister Anita Khaund (wife of Dhurjjuty Prasad Khaund, BE) is at present the Senior Architect, PWD, Assam. She also finished her B.Arch (Baroda) and M.L.Arch (Delhi) before getting married. Thus my father's second and the most important last wishes have been honored by our sisters.

Phanidhar Datta's grandchildren are now scattered all over the world and all of them have learned from their parents to value education. It is hoped that the emphasis on education which has become part of the family tradition will always be maintained by their descendents as well.

Coming to Phanidhar Datta's third wish about doing something for the betterment of education in his village Gayangaon on the outskirts of Jorhat, it must be added that the whole village had rejoiced my father's success in the matriculation examination and the villagers had all contributed whatever little they could to help him get his college education. Even though he made immense contribution to founding JB College at Jorhat and in building the University of Gauhati, deep in his heart he hoped to spend his last days after retirement helping the children of Gayangaon get a decent education. Since fate took him before he could do anything in that direction, I took upon myself the task of starting an elementary school in Gayangaon. I tried for nearly fifteen years to do so, but I faced so many obstacles that I virtually gave up all hopes of ever accomplishing that goal.

Remembering what my father and my grandfather had done to fulfill the wishes of their respective father, I was inspired to keep trying. Finally, the following institutions are taking shape in and near Gayangaon, where my father had spent his early life. (1) A school complex in Gayangaon (Phanidhar Datta Shiksha Prakalpa), (2) A free elementary school (Ratneswari Datta Aamaar Porahsali) for poor children in nearby Goal Gaon and (3) a High School (Phanidhar Datta Bidyapith) in Chuladhara.

JB College is now a premier college of Assam. For nearly seventy-five years, JB College has served the cause of education in Upper Assam far beyond the wildest dreams of its founding fathers. It is planning to celebrate its diamond jubilee in 2005.

In 2001, Cotton College celebrated its centenary and its alumni came literally from every part of the world. Nowadays its alumni are serving as teachers, professors, engineers, scientists, doctors and the like not only in every part of India but in such far off countries as Australia, the United States, Japan, Saudi Arabia, Russia, etc. The present author, a professor of mathematics at the University of Rhode Island, USA, is also a product of Cotton College. Gauhati University is now a sprawling campus near the capital of Assam (on the eastern part of the big city Guwahati). The two institutions still bask in their old glory and continue to serv the cause of education in eastern India admirably. Looking back we do owe their establishment and survival to the westerners like Henry Cotton and William Sudmersen. However, these institutions have survived through the good karma (dedicated services) of natives who were the product of western style education that were brought directly or inspired by great visionaries like William Griffith, Nathan and Eliza Brown, Sir Henry Cotton, Principal Sudmersen. Principal Harshanath Sen.

Justice B.N. Sharma inaugurating the Birth Centenary celebration of Phanidhar Datta at Gauhati

Coincidentally, Phanidhar Datta was also born the same year as the Cotton College. People and various organizations in the state also celebrated his birth centenary in 2001 and 2002. We owe to Phanidhar Datta and his colleagues not only the survival of Cotton College during the war years but also the establishment of JB College in Jorhat and Gauhati University in Assam. Dr. Hiren Gohain, a former Dean of Faculty of Arts, Gauhati University, has described it eloquently in his article, 'An Architect of Modern Assam':

> It is a great relief to many considerate and thoughtful people that the people of the state have, after a grave lapse of memory for many decades, rallied to pay a belated tribute to Phanidhar Datta, outstanding educationist and one of the builders of higher education of Assam. The spontaneity and warmth of the tribute in different places of Assam suggest that people have felt deeply the injustice under which the memory of his services has languished so long. After all, no nation which can boast of even a flickering conscious life, can afford to be so ungrateful.

Dr. Radhakrishnan (with turban) on way to deliver the first convocation address of Gauhati University. Mr. K.K. Handique is on his left. Phanidhar Datta can be seen between the two scholars.

Phanidhar Datta is recalled by devoted subordinates who had worked under him as an outstanding administrator and organizer. An eminent teacher of the premier college for undergraduate education of the state, he abandoned his teaching career at the call of Gopinath Bardoloi, to serve as the first Registrar of Gauhati University. At that time Gauhati University had no campus of its own. Land has been purchased, but it was still a wilderness of wooded hills, swamps and paddy fields. But the university had come up as a result of a popular movement that had swept through the state reaching even the grass roots. Its work could not be kept pending. Classes were started in a number of barrack-like rooms. What was lacking in facilities and infrastructure was made up by the devotion of the staff and the enthusiasm of the students.

Among the staff, distinguished by outstanding human qualities, Phanidhar Datta earned a position of eminence with his phenomenal capacity for hard work, his ability to inspire loyalty and devotion among his subordinates, and his enterprise and initiative. He laid down the basis of the administration of the university, organized the secretarial staff into efficient teams, and evolved the guidelines for work to be done on routine lines. At the same time he met single handed many of the practical challenges without disturbing the reclusive scholar Vice chancellor. He would work till late into night and inspired the staff under him to work uncomplainingly for long hours. His interest in the weal and woe made them devoted to him, and Gauhati University soon rose from its infancy into a vibrant institution.

Phanidhar Datta, it may be recalled at this point, had no precedents to guide him, no tradition of higher education in the state to help him. His personality, an interesting mixture of grit and tact, kindness and sternness, helped him. But what must have been of greater help was his deep, unspoken love for Assam and her people. He had himself come from sturdy peasant stock, the backbone of the Assamese nationality and had learnt in early childhood both the capacity and skill for unwearying physical exertion and the values bequeathed by our great Vaishnava traditions, clouded but not yet extinct. A meritorious student he had been forced to interrupt his studies now and then for lack of financial support. He must have keenly felt the obstacles to education faced by the poor people of the state, and this appears to have fired his zeal to turn Gauhati University into a vigorous centre of higher learning at the shortest possible time. Unlike the case with some institutions today there was no question of sacrificing standards in his mind, or in the mind of his eminent contemporaries."

[A Tribute on the occasion of the Birth Centenary of Phanidhar Datta by Dr. Hiren Gohain, The North East Times, Guwahati, January 8, 2002. Dr. Hiren Gohain is a leading intellectual of Assam. He was a Professor of English at Gauhati University and retired as the Dean of Faculty of Arts. Dr. Gohain is an author of reputation and has published numerous books and original papers both in English and in Assamese. He is currently the Editor of the English daily The North East Times, Guwahati.]

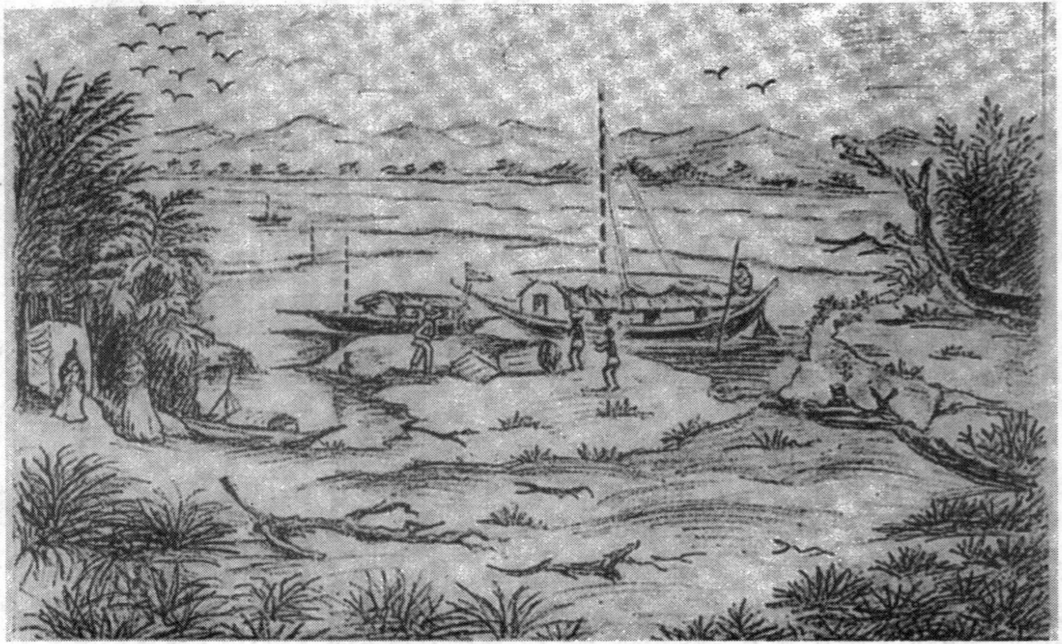

Moored To A Brahmaputra Sandbank

On the spot drawing by Nathan Brown some time in 1840's. Redrawn by Sukanya Basu

Courtesy: *The Whole World Kin*

Appendix

A. William Griffith

[The following obituary note appeared in the *Proceedings of the of the Linnaen Society*, No. xxv, 1845]

William Griffith, Esq., the youngest son of the late Thomas Griffith, was born on the 4th of March 1810, at his father's residence at Ham common, near Kingston-upon-Thames, in the county of Surrey.

He was educated for the Medical profession, and completed his studies at the London University, where he became a pupil of Prof. Lindley, under whose able instructions, assisted by the zealous friendship of Mr. R.H. Solly, and in conjunction with two fellow pupils of great scientific promise, Mr. Slack and Mr. Valentine, he made rapid progress in the acquisition of botanical knowledge. The first public proofs that he gave of his abilities are contained in a microscopic delineation of the structure of the wood and an analysis of the flower of *Phytocrene gigantea*, in the third volume of Dr. Wallich's *'Plantae Asiaticae Rariores'*; and in a note on the development and structure of *Targionia hypophylla*, appended to M. de Mirbel's Dissertation on *Marchantia polymorpha*, both published in 1832. So highly were his talents as an observer appreciated at this early period, that Dr. Wallich speaks of him as one "whose extraordinary talents and knowledge as a botanist, entitle him to the respect of all lovers of the science;" and M. de Mirbel characterizes him as "jeune Anglois, très instruit, très zélé et fort bon observatuer."

His note on *Targionia* is dated Paris, April 2nd, 1832, and in the month of May of the same year, having finished his studies at the London University with great distinction, he sailed from England for India, which was destined to be the scene of his future labors. He arrived at Madras on the 24th of September, and immediately received his appointment as Assistant-Surgeon in the service of the East India Company.

His first appointment in India was to the coast of Tenasserim; but in the year 1835 he was attached to the Bengal Presidency, and was selected to form one of a deputation, consisting of Dr. Wallich and himself as botanists, and Mr. MacClelland as geologist, to visit and inspect the Tea-forests (as they were called) of Assam, and to make researches in the natural history of that almost unexplored district.

This mission was for Mr. Griffith the commencement of a series of journeys in pursuit of botanical knowledge, embracing nearly the whole extent of the East India Company's extra-peninsular possessions, and adding large collections, in every branch of natural history, but especially botany, to those which, under the auspices of the Indian Government, had previously been formed. He next, under the directions of Capt. Jenkins, the commissioner, pushed his investigations to the utmost eastern limit of the company's territory, traversing the hitherto unexplored tracts in the neighborhood of the Mishmee Mountains, which lie between Suddiya and Ava. Of the splendid collection of insects formed during this part of his tour some account has been given by Mr. Hope in the Transactions of the Entomological society and in the eighteenth volume of our own Transactions.

His collection of plants was also largely increased on his remarkable journey, which was followed by a still more perilous expedition, commenced in February of the following year, from Assam through the Burmese dominions to Ava, and down the Irrawadi to Rangoon, in the course of which he was reported to have been assassinated. The hardships through which he passed during the journey and his excessive application produced, soon after his arrival in Calcutta, a severe attack of fever; on his recovery from which he was appointed Surgeon to the Embassy to Bootan, then about to depart under the charge of the late Major Pemberton. He took this opportunity of revisiting the Khasiya Hills, among which he formed a most extensive collection; and having joined Major Pemberton at Goalpara, traversed with him 400 miles of Bootan country, from which he returned to Calcutta about the end of June 1839. In November of the same year he joined the army of the Indus in a scientific capacity, and penetrated, after the subjugation of Cabool, beyond the Hindoo Khoosh into Khorassan, from whence, as well as from Afghanistan, he brought collections of great value and extent. During these arduous journeys his health had several times suffered most severely, and he was more than once reduced by fever to a state of extreme exhaustion; but up to this time the strength of his constitution enabled him to triumph over the attacks of disease, and the energy of his mind was so great, that the first days of convalescence found him again as actively employed as ever.

On his return to Calcutta in August 1841, after visiting Simla and the Nerbudda, he was appointed to the medical duties at Malacca: but Dr. Wallich having proceeded to the Cape for the re-establishment of his health, Mr. Griffith was recalled in August 1842 to take, during his absence, the superintendence of the Botanic Garden near Calcutta, in conjunction with which he also discharged the duties of Botanical Professor in the Medical College to the great advantage of the students. Towards the end of 1844 Dr. Wallich resumed his functions at the Botanic Garden. In September Mr. Griffith married Miss Henderson, the sister of the wife of his brother, Captain Griffith, and on the 11th of December he quitted Calcutta to return to Malacca, where he arrived on the 9th of January in the present year. On the 31st of the same month he was attacked by hepatitis, and notwithstanding every attention on the part of the medical officer who had officiated during his absence, and who fortunately still remained, he gradually sunk under the attack, which terminated fatally on the 9th of February.

[Courtesy: M'Clelland, John, *Journals of Travels in Assam, Burma, Bootan, Afghanistan and the neighboring Countries*, arranged by Bishop's College Press, Calcutta, 1847, Reprinted by Ch'eng Wen Publishing Company, Taipei, 1971*]*.

B. Eliza Whitney Brown

Eliza Whitney Brown (1807 - 1871) may be regarded as the mother of modern education in Assam. She was not only the first to start a school in Assam but also the author of several elementary texts in the Assamese language. They were the earliest printed texts in the language and were the only available texts for more than two decades. Her contributions to the introduction of formal schooling and scientific education among the Assamese are second to none. Even though her texts are not original work but mostly translation or adaptation of English or Bengali books, her originality lies in the fact that she had mastered the Assamese language and was bold enough to show how to write scientific knowledge in the Assamese language. It is said that Mrs. Eliza Brown spoke Assamese like a native and wrote it better than any native could in those days. She wrote the first Assamese book on Modern arithmetic and the first Assamese text on geography. Her texts were used in schools for more than two decades. She also published a juvenile series of twelve tracts These included African Prince, Eagle's Nest, The Story of Ramgoti, The Story of an Orphan Girl, The Story of Science. These were the first ever published

Assamese storybooks for children. In addition to these texts, she wrote regularly in the Assamese news magazine Orunudoi, edited by her husband Nathan Brown. It was because of her example that later Assamese were able to start writing Assamese texts for schools in Assam.

Eliza Brown did all those pioneering work for the Assamese language and education in Assam through immense hardships and personal suffering. Misfortunes came to Eliza one after the other, but this brave lady did never give up. Her life and works have been beautifully described by Rev. E.H. Gray in a memorable sermon preached at her funeral. The sermon was later printed in the form of a pamphlet, titled *Songs in the Night*. The following brief note about her life and works is based on Gray's pamphlet.

Eliza was born Eliza Whitney Ballard at Charlemont, Mass, USA on April 12, 1807, where she grew up and had her education. She started teaching in a seminary in nearby Benington when she was twenty-one years old. Nathan Brown joined the same seminary soon afterwards. Here, the two got drawn to each other and to missionary work. The two got married on May 6, 1830 and later moved to Brandon, Vermont, where Nathan became the Editor of the Vermont Baptist Telegraph. On December 22, 1832 the Brown couple and their first child Dorothy Sophia sailed for Burma.

They reached Maulmain, Burma in May, 1833, after a voyage lasting more than four months. They stayed in Burma till August, 1835. That year Major Jenkins, the British officer in charge of Assam, offered the American Baptist Mission a sum of one thousand rupees to establish a mission in Sadiya. The American Baptist Mission accepted the offer and selected the Brown couple to start the mission. Sorrow and bereavement came to Eliza and her husband right from the day they started their journey for that assignment.

The Browns booked their passage to Calcutta, but their second child was seized with brain disease and died the very morning they were to leave. They had the funeral services the same afternoon, graced by Dr. Judson who preached a touching sermon. The same evening they set sail for their new appointment. They arrived in Calcutta on September 2, 1835 and immediately embarked on their arduous journey up the river Brahmaputra in a native boat. It took them four months to reach their destination. They arrived in Sadiya on March 2, 1936. What they did in Sadiya and their misfortunes there are described in chapter 2 of this book. In Sadiya, Eliza gave birth to two more children. After the Khamti raid, the Browns moved to Jaipur, where they were comfortably placed but the climate there proved very unhealthy and her children had to endure physical ailment of one kind or another. To give them medical attention Eliza once made a perilous journey to Calcutta alone with her two little children only to be told that her son's disease was incurable. The little child succumbed to the disease after returning to Jaipur. Finally, the Brown family moved to Sibsagar.

The climate in Sibsagar seemed more favorable and the Browns were able to engage in productive activities both in missionary work and in running schools. As the Assam Mission was able to set up a press in Sibsagar, Eliza , like her husband, started writing texts for use in the schools they were establishing. In the beginning, Eliza was planning to keep her children with her and to educate them at home and in her school. She, however, had to abandon that idea after her husband narrowly escaped death from an attack of cholera and her daughter came near death with fever.

After losing three children in a foreign land, she tried to find an answer to the question, should a mother stand by and see her remaining children die in a country where malaria, cholera and black-disease kill thousands each year. Eliza Brown also knew that it was impossible for her husband to leave missionary work that finally looked promising. The fortitude and energy of Eliza Brown rose to the occasion, she decided on a course that was later adopted by missionaries who followed the Browns. She decided to take her children back to America and look for suitable family or families who would be willing to adopt and raise them. The arrangement would be made so that the children would maintain their ties with their biological parents but would be loyal to their adopted parents. It was not to be a formal arrangement with legal papers but an arrangement based on mutual love and respect. With that idea in mind in September 1846, the brave lady started a homeward voyage with her two little children—one may appreciate her courage when one thinks about the realities of a sea voyage from Calcutta to Boston in a sailing boat across the oceans and around the cape of Good Hope lasting more than four months. Eliza Brown made it safely to America. In America, Eliza Brown not only secured for the children the best homes possible, but also found ways to save the Assam Mission. While in America, Eliza Brown discovered that the Assam Mission which her husband had so laboriously established was facing abandonment because of the lack of public support in the churches and in the Board. So, the energetic Eliza Brown led a vigorous campaign to arouse attention and interest to the Assam Mission. Her campaign was successful and it resulted in the appointment of two additional missionaries for Assam.

Mission accomplished, she again headed to Assam to join her husband.

It should be pointed out that Eliza Brown's solution to the problem of raising and educating children whom the parents may not be able to provide a healthy environment, seems to be a very humane solution. Most of the missionary children who were raised in that manner did prove to be very capable and fruitful persons. One shining example is Eliza Brown's daughter Elizabeth Whitney Brown. Elizabeth was born a day after the death of Dorothy Sophia and she was the baby that Eliza had in her arms while fleeing the Khamti raid, and she is the author of *The Whole World Kin,*[21] a major source of this book. Following Eliza's example, Miles Bronson, another famous missionary to Assam, had later placed his children at homes in America. Among them, Sophie Bronson Titterington established herself as a very successful author, especially of children's book, and Harriet Bronson Gunn wrote the memorable book *In a Far Country.*

In 1849, Eliza Brown rejoined her husband in Assam, and started her most productive work in the Assamese language. Nathan and Eliza Brown left Assam in 1855. Back in the States, the Browns gave up missionary work for a while. Eliza Brown's last years of life were marked by constant suffering with frequent and long-continued illness, brought on by the hardships of twenty-three years of hard life in Assam. In 1869, she was injured from a fall, from which she never recovered. Rev. Gray tells us that Mrs. Brown cherished in her heart a desire to return to Assam almost till her death in 1871. She lies buried in a family graveyard in East Charlemont, Mass, next to her children where friends and relatives constructed a monument honoring the Brown family.

C. Life and Works of Nathan Brown

Born: June 22, 1807 in New Ipswich, New Hampshire, USA.
Died: Jan 1, 1886 in Yokohama, Japan.
Resident of:: Whitingham, Vermont
Married: (1) Miss Eliza Whitney Ballard of East Charlemont, Massachusetts (May 6, 1830)

[21] Many Assamese sources mistakenly refer to Brown's wife as the author of *The Whole World Kin.* This is perhaps because of the similarity between the two names, Eliza and Elizabeth.

(2) Mrs. Charlotte A. (Worth) Marlit of Jersey City, New Jersey (July 24, 1872).

Education

Williams College, Williamsburgh, Mass (Class of 1827)

Andover Newton Theological School, Newton, Mass (1832)

Awarded the degree of Doctor of Divinity by Williams College in 1854.

Professional Career

Teacher, Bennington Seminary (1827 – 1830).

Editor, Vermont Telegraph (1831 – 1832).

Missionary to Burma (December 1832 – later half of 1835).

Missionary to Assam (September 1835 – 1855)[Arrived Sadiya, Assam on March 22, 1936]

Editor, Orunudoi (first newsmagazine in Assamese) 1846 – 1855.[22]

Editor, American Baptist, (1857 –1871).

Founder President, The American Philological Society, (1863 – 1871)

Editor, The American Philological Magazine (1863 – 1871).

Missionary to Japan (1872 till death)

Publications

ASSAMESE

1. *Sarup Ashroy*, (The True Refuge), 1835
2. *Amar Trankarta Prabhu Yishu Christar Natun Niyam* (Translation of the New Testament), 1847
3. *Christar Bibaron Aru Subhabarta* (The Life and Gospel of Christ), 1854
4. *Jatrir Jatra* (with Nidhi Levi) [Translation of Pilgrim's Progress],
5. *Josephor Kahini* (The story of Joseph), 1851.

[22] The complete set of *Orunudoi* produced under the editorship of Brown has been published by the Publication Board, Government of Assam,1983.

BURMESE

6. *Arithmetic in Burman language*, 1835
7. *Hymns in Burman Language*, 1835

ENGLISH

8. *Spelling Book in English, Asamese, and Shyam or Tai,* American Baptist Mission Press, 1836.
9. *Proposal for forming a comparative vocabulary of all the Indo-Chinese Languages,* Baptist Missionary Magazine, 1836, Vol. XVI, 203 – 207.
10. *Comparison of Indo-Chinese Languages,* Journal of Asiatic Society of Bengal, Vol. VI, 1837, 17.
11. *Alphabets of the Tai Language,* Journal of Asiatic Society of Bengal, Vol. VI, 1837, 1023-1038.
12. *Specimens of Eastern Languages, illustration of a plan for forming a comparative vocabulary of all the Indo-Chinese Languages,* Baptist Missionary Magazine, 1839, Vol.XIX, an eight-page insertion.
13. *Specimens of the Naga languages of Asam,* Journal of the American Oriental Society, 1851, Vol. II, 156 – 165.
14. *Grammatical Notices of the Assamese Language,* 1848.[23]
15. *Zyx and His Fairy or The Soul in Search of Peace*, Brown and Duer Publishers, New York, 1866
16. (Published under the assumed name: Kristofur Kadmus) *The History of Magnus Maharba and the Black Dragon,* New York, 1867
17. *A Missionary's Daughter*
18. *Comparative vocabulary of the Sgau and Pwo Karen dialects,* Journal of the American Oriental Society, Vol. IV, 319-326. Perhaps reprinted by American Philological Society, New York, 1867.
19. *The Saxon Language—Its Eclipse and Relumination,* American Philological Society, New York, 1867.

[23] The fourth edition (1983), Asam Sahitya Sabha, Jorhat, Assam

Brown Bibliography

1. Barpujari, H.K., *American misonarisokal aru Unobingsha Satikar Asom*, Asom Sahitya Sabha, Jorhat, 1983.

2. Bennett, A.A., *A biographical sketch of Nathan Brown, D.D.*, The Yokohama Seishi Bunsha, Japan, 1895.

3. Brown, Elizabeth W., *The Whole World Kin: A Pioneer Experience Among Remote Tribes, and Other Labors of Nathan Brown,* Hubbard Brothers Publishers, Philadelphia, 1890

4. Gillespie, George, *Missionaries and Dictionaries: An annotated bibliography of linguistic works prepared by American Baptist missionaries in Northeast India*, Indian Church History Review, Vol. XI, No.1, 1977.

5. Gray, Rev. E.H., *Songs in The Night: A Sermon, preached at the Funeral of Mrs. Eliza Whitney Brown*, Thomas Holman Printer, New York, 1871.

6. Gunn, Harriette, *In a Far Country: A Story of Christian Heroism and Achievement,* American Baptist Publication Society, Philadelphia, 1912.

7. Hewitt, John, *Williams College and Missions*, The Pilgrims Press, Boston, 1914.

8. Max Müller, F., *The Science of Language,* Vols. I & II, Charles Scribner's and Sons, New York, 1891

9. Neog, Maheswar (Ed.), *The Orunudoi: 1846 – 1854, edited by Reverend Dr. Nathan Brown*, Publication Board, Assam Government, 1983.

10. Parsons, Rev. E.B., *Williams Obituary Record*, Williams College, 1895.

11. Sarma, Banikanta*, Asomiya Bhasa Sahityaloi Misonarisokolar Abadan*, Asom Sahitya Sabha, Jorhat, 1984

12. Titterington, Sophie Bronson, *A Century of Baptist Foreign Missions, an Outline Sketch*, American Baptist Publication Society, Philadelphia, 1891.

13. Whitney, William Dwight, *Language and Study of Language*, Charles Scribner & Company, New York, 1867

Some Documented Tributes

Rev. Nathan Brown was a well-known intellectual of his time. His interest in language studies, his energy and interest, his unflinching adherence to his convictions and his noble visions had profound influence on culture, science of language and people of his time. Below are some documented tributes to Nathan Brown.

> In 1855, after twenty-two years of toil and sufferings, both returned to America, where Dr. Brown was pronounced 'a wreck in body and mind.' After a rest of two years and a partial recovery of health he became editor of the American Baptist, a position which he held for fifteen yeas. The term of his editorship was a most important period in the history of the nation, and his editorials discussed the affairs of a government in a vigorous way. His pronounced anti-slavery principles, sometimes, occasioned him personal danger. On account of his prominence in such discussions he was selected as one of the committee of three to wait on President Lincoln before the issuing of the Emancipation Proclamation. (Hewitt, John, *Williams College and Mission,* hereafter referred to as *WCM, 138).*

> His scholarly and literary impulses were powerful enough, had he aspired to the prizes of worldly ambition, to have assured him a distinguished worldly career. Fifteen years after his graduation at college the tradition of his attainments was living there. He was permitted to render a protracted service in what was to him the highest of human callings and he rests well. [Rev. Dr. L.E. Smith in the editorial column of the *Watchman* (quoted here from *Williams Obituary Record* 6)].

> He has left an untarnished record, extending over three score years and ten; and has set a noble example of ceaseless industry, and of self-sacrificing, unflinching adherence to what he believed to be right. (American Baptist magazine, July, 1986, 182).

> Teeming with information, felicitous in language, independent in thought, vigorously combining logic and rhetoric to strengthen his points, and connected and consistent in all the minutiæ of his discourse, he possesses abilities which render him one of the ablest preachers whom we have heard on this course. (*WCM* 138-139).

Professor F. Max Müller, one of the founders of modern Philology, was a great admirer of Nathan Brown both as a pioneer in the field of Comparative Philology and as a philosopher. He has quoted Nathan Brown in his famous books *The Science of Language,* Vols. I & II, Professor Max Müller writes:

> Thus Brown says: 'To be without language, spoken or written, is *almost* to be without thought.' But he qualifies this *almost* by what follows: 'That man can reason without language of any kind, and consequently without general terms—though the opposite opinion is maintained by many very eminent philosophers. (Max Müller, F., *The Science of Language,* Vols. I, Charles Scribner's and Sons, New York, 1891, 78)
>
> Among modern philosophers, Brown dwells most strongly on the same subject: 'How much the mere materialism of our language has itself operated in darkening our conceptions of the nature of the mind, and of its various phenomena, is a question which is, obviously beyond our power to solve, since the solution of it would imply that the mind of the solver was itself free from the influence which he traced and described. (Max Müller, F., *The Science of Language,* Vols. II, Charles Scribner's and Sons, New York, 1891, 702)

In *The Whole World Kin: A Pioneer Experience Among Remote Tribes, and Other Labors of Nathan Brown,* we also find the following quotes of a letter that Prof. Max Müller wrote to Sir Charles Trevelyan, Oxford, Oct. 25, 1854.

> I return Mr. Brown's letter with many thanks—it is a very interesting letter—it has turned a name with which I have been familiar for many years, into a real man, and what a man! ... I should like to write to Mr. Brown, and send to him my book on the Turanian Languages, where I have had to quote him so many times. He is one of the few men whose opinion I should like to have on the classification of these dialects on the borders of India and China, which I have attempted there for the first time. (*WWK*, 602)

Unfortunately the theory of Turanian Language put forward by Max Müller and Nathan Brown did not find support from latter scholars. So, Brown's contributions to Philology got obscured by the later Theory of Indo-European Languages. Brown's work just became a footnote in the history of Philology. Thus, William Dwight Whitney, Professor of Sanskrit and Modern Languages in Yale college, and an exponent of the modern classification of Languages while mentioning the difficulties of learning about 'the exceedingly numerous and not less discordant dialects which crowd the mountain valleys on either sides of the great range of the Himalayas,' acknowledged the distinguished service rendered by Brown as one of the enterprising collectors in a footnote:

> Among these, Rev N. Brown and Mr. B.H. Hodgson have especially distinguished themselves. (*Language and Study of Language*, Charles Scribner & Company, New York, 1867, 22)

D. Nathan Brown's Death Centenary At Williams College

On September 28, 1986 the American-Assamese gathered at Williams College to celebrate the death centenary of Nathan Brown. I reproduce here a report of the event as published in the local newspaper *The Berkshire Eagle* on Monday, September 30, 1985.

Williams graduate honored for work in Assam in 1800s

By Julie Sell

WILLIAMSTOWN -- The life of a Vermont farmboy and Williams College graduate who went on to become a missionary and revered figure in the Indian state of Assam was remembered during a series of events at Williams this weekend.

The occasion was the 100th anniversary of Nathan Brown's death, and some 40 people came from around the Northeast — a few even traveled from Assam — to honor this man and recall his contributions to Assamese life in the 19th century. A larger turnout had been expected, but Friday's nasty weather deterred some from making the journey.

The weekend commemoration was organized by the Assam Association of North America and the Assamese Literary Society in India.

Association President Dilip Datta, a mathematics professor at the University of Rhode Island, said he conceived the idea for such a gathering when "it dawned on me that, since some of us have been here 15 or 20 years now, we should find our connection with this land."

Datta said Brown is widely known in Assam not only for his work as a missionary, but also for his efforts to preserve the Assamese language, which had practically died out in the last century. The professor likened

Brown to Henry David Thoreau in this country, a man known both for his contributions to language and to society at large.

Assam, a 47,000-square mile state in northeast India that borders on Bhutan and Bangladesh, is linked to the main body of India only by the narrow state of Sikkim. Assam has a population of 11.8 million people.

A panel discussion in Thompson Memorial Chapel on Saturday Afternoon afforded the weekend visitors an opportunity to hear about Brown's life and work.

Gifts for panelists

Among the crowd were a half-dozen women in flowing mekhalas, traditional two-piece outfits, consisting of a wrapped scarf that reaches from the waist to the ground, and a half top. Following Assamese custom, the women presented each of the panelists and honored guests with a red and white gamocha, an intricately decorated, hand-woven cotton cloth that is a symbol of respect and love.

John M. Hyde, professor of history at Williams, related the details of Brown's early life and college years. He painted a picture of a precious youth who was born in 1807, grew up in Whitingham, Vt. and started teaching school in 1815, while younger than many of his students. In 1824, at age 27, Brown was admitted to Williams with sophomore standing.

Hyde's research revealed that Brown was greatly influenced by the late Rev. Edward D. Griffin, president of the college during Brown's undergraduate years and a great believer in the missionary movement. Brown "distinguished himself as a leading scholar of the class of 1827," showed a particular interest in mathematics and astronomy, and graduated as valedictorian.

Immersed in Society

The Rev. George Gillespie, a noted scholar of the Assamese language and former missionary to Assam, said the Assamese people have a broader and more correct view of a missionary's work than do Americans. His remarks focused on Brown's immersion in the society he was aiding — he was in Assam from 1835 through 1855 — and the missionary's wide range of interest.

As publisher of Orunudoi, the first news magazine in Assamese, Brown covered not only Christian teaching, but also local and foreign news, information on tribal people, science, mythology, history and social issues. He also collected old Assamese manuscripts and did considerable work in linguistics, through the publication of language lists, dictionaries and alphabets.

Professor H. Barpujari, an author and former history professor in Assam, went so far as to call Brown "the savior of the Assamese language."

After recounting the history of Western missionaries in Assam — Brown was the first American to come to the state— Barpujari told the crowd about the schools that Brown set up and his insistence that children learn their native language as well as English. At the time, the Bengali language was becoming much more common in the area.

President Abraham Lincoln was said to have been a great admirer of Brown, with whom he shared strong views opposing slavery in this country. Brown was also editor of the American Baptist, and did missionary work in Burma and Japan.

Other events over the weekend included the dedication of the Nathan Brown Memorial Collection in the college library, a worship service and a wreath-laying ceremony yesterday at Brown's grave in East Charlemont.

[Courtesy: The Berkshire Eagle and Julie Sell]

E. Frederick William Sudmersen

Fredrick William Sudmersen holds a unique place in the history of modern Assam. As the Principal of the first college in India's northeast region, he made outstanding contribution in uplifting the people of that region. Sudmersen thought that to build a nation one must shape the character of the people, and the character of the people can be molded only through education. According to him, education is the panacea for all social evils. He sought to remedy the death-like inertia that had taken hold of the Assamese people under the Burmese occupation with the help of education. The guiding principles of the education he tried to impart were clear:

Avoid all narrowness of thought or class or creed.

Work hard to learn more about every sphere of human activities.

Learn how you can be of greater service to mankind.

Realizing that the students who came to Cotton College were the cream of the crop, he sought to make each one of them an educated man of character who would be able to guide the destiny of the people. He set very high standards for learning and never compromised with what is to be learned. He sought to instill in the young minds an urge for learning that would take them higher and higher. To give the students mental tenacity, he demanded hard work in their studies. Principal Sudmersen taught the students manners, behavior and discipline that he regarded as an integral part of education. He did succeed in so shaping his students that most of his graduates in later life left their mark. Yet very little is known about the personal life or the personality of Principal Sudmersen except what we can gather from his former students, who perhaps could never get close to the family or into the inner circle of the reclusive Englishman.

Fredrick William Sudmersen was born on December 30, 1870 in England. After graduating from college, he entered the Indian Education Service. In those days many English youths prepared to serve British India by taking competitive examinations held in England. Of course, the Administrative Services or the Armed Forces Services were more lucrative and more popular than the Education Services. The very fact that Fredrick William Sudmersen chose the Indian Education Services shows that he must have been a dedicated educator and perhaps came from a family with ties with the academic world. We have described how he first joined Bareilly College and then later came to start Cotton College.

Principal Sudmersen served the College long enough to see the fruits of his labor. He had Cotton College graduates coming back with higher degrees and taking up teaching jobs at the College as early as 1917. Then many others took responsible jobs in the education department of the state. He was made a C.I.E. (Companion of Indian Empire) in 1926 and he retired the same year. After retiring, he moved to Sussex, England and lived in a farm with his son Eric. He lived with Eric till the early forties. With advancing age he started having problems hearing and became quite deaf. As a result, to his grandchildren, he became a remote figure, quiet and withdrawn. Sudmersen's wife died in the Spring of 1940. After Eric's marriage, Principal Sudmersen moved to Eastbourne (about 30 miles away). He died in Eastborne on Sunday, February 8, 1953. The Sudmersens were both buried in their Parish Church at Fletching. But there is no memorial there as they didn't want one.

Besides Eric, Sudmersen had two daughters Ida and Viola. Unlike other Europeans, Sudmersens kept their children with them and educated them in Gauhati. They were all very much attached to Cotton College and they all visited Gauhati and Cotton College later. Eric moved to New Zealand in early 70's and died there on 13th May, 2000, a few months after posting a letter to the Cotton College Centenary Celebration Committee on November 3, 1999. Part of his letter read:

> .... it was so unexpected and such a deep honor to my father's memory to be thought of after so many years, he would be so proud and happy to know that Cotton College is to celebrate its centenary with such great success.
>
> I have an elder brother who is buried in Guwahati, and two sisters who have died. My eldest sister has no children. My other sister has one boy and two girls all living in England.
>
> My thoughts have so often turned to the 10 years I spent in Guwahati now some 80 years ago. I can picture it as it was then, with Cotton College and our bungalow alongside. I can remember the Church Maidan, Digley poukery(?) and the gates. I just cannot imagine how it could all look now. On the 15th November, the New Zealand cricketers will play a one day match at Guwahati. I shall be watching it closely for any views. (*Cotton College Centenary Volume*, 2001, hereafter referred to as *CCC* 100).

A Story

Sudmersen's eldest daughter Ida had no children and Viola lived in North London. Miss Meryl Gover, the eldest daughter of Viola, sent the following story that she had heard from her grandmother:

Our grandfather never told us anything about his life in India—perhaps we were too young to ask him about it. I do remember one story which my mother told me—I am not sure about the details, but perhaps someone else may be able to correct them. It shows, I think, the respect in which my grandfather and the College were held by someone outside the College.

There was one occasion when the students were protesting about something and had announced that as part of the protest they would boycott the examinations. My grandfather gave an ultimatum that any one not turning up for the exam would be expelled from the College.

Unknown to him, the students had telegraphed the authorities (I do not know who this would have been at the time). A telegram was sent back saying that he must withdraw the ultimatum and that under no circumstances was any student to be expelled.

This was received at the telegraph office early on the morning of the examination concerned. The clerk who received the telegram realised that if my grandfather received it, he would have to obey and would therefore have no option but to resign as Principal since his authority would have been destroyed. Unknown to anyone else, he kept the telegram secret at the telegraph office for several hours until well after the examination was due to start.

Knowing that my grandfather would keep his word, the students all turned up on time for their examination, and the protest was broken though I believe the problem, whatever it was, was subsequently sorted out. (*CCC*,100-101).

I give here few more anecdotes about Principal Sudmersen that I had heard from a venerable old employee of Cotton College—perhaps one with a record years of service to the College. His name was Jahormol, a well-known person of Assam in the last century.

'The Vice Principal'

Sudmersen had appointed the uneducated young man Jahormol as a personal peon of the Principal. Though uneducated, Jahormol was a very capable person. He made the rounds with Principal Sudmersen and saw how the Principal looked after the College. Jahormol and Principal Sudmersen were almost inseparable. Later on, Jahormol used to look after all the necessary things like making sure the classrooms were clean, the benches and desks were in place, the supplies were there, the drinking water jar was duly filled and so on. The same way, he went to the hostels. Even after Principal Sudmersen retired, Jahormol continued to work in the college and broadened his sphere of activities to teachers and students alike. If a teacher came late to class, Jahormol would go and tell, "How can you teach if you come late like this?" If he found some students loitering in the streets after dark, Jahormol would go and tell them, "What are you doing here, your parents are spending all these money for your education, how can you waste time and money like this? Go back to the hostel right now and study." Everybody respected Jahormol because they knew that he was simply trying to remind them of certain things that Principal Sudmersen liked to establish in Cotton College. In any case, for his dexterity Jahormol earned the nick name 'Vice Principal'.

Jahormol refused to accept retirement and continued to make his rounds in Cotton College till one day in 1958, he died in his ripe old age just after returning home from the College. As a child, we still remember how Jahormol used to walk every morning from his residence, more than a mile away from the College, and make his rounds in the College making sure everything was in order and everybody was fulfilling his or her duty. Anytime he talked about something he would always bring in Sudmersen Sahib (as he used to respectfully call Principal Sudmersen). He used to come and visit my father very often and used to tell us many stories about Principal Sudmersen. In those days, I never paid any attention to them. But somehow a few of them stuck in my memory.

A Dog on The Roof

Jahormol as well as Principal Sudmersen used to be quite superstitious. In addition, Principal Sudmersen used to be very respectful of local customs and beliefs. Knowing that one early morning a few students took a little puppy and put him on the roof of Cotton College. The poor little dog could not get down and kept barking loud and long enough to draw the attention of Principal Sudmersen, who immediately sent for Jahormol to find what was the matter and what to do. Jahormol was frightened because according to the Assamese, a dog on the roof of a house is a very ill omen. He told Sudmersen that something very bad might happen to the College so an offering must be made to the Hindu God Narayana and prasadam ought to be served to the participants. Of course, a good many of the students were ready to do that—enjoy the prasadam. Later on, Jahormol did realize that it was a trick played by the students, but he kept quiet and the students got to eat some good prasadam.

Who won?

Once three of the students of Cotton College had a fight with two Englishmen somewhere outside the College Campus. The students were infuriated because the Englishmen were really telling them off calling them 'dirty Natives', 'savages', 'dumbheads', etc.. One of the students, Parasuram Datta was a big strong man with very low boiling point, and he did not want to take it quietly. So, the two parties came to blows and the fight was quite nasty. After taking the beating, the Englishmen ran to the Police and the students ran to their hostel. The students knew the Englishmen's next move—come with a platoon of police and raid the hostel. So, the students ran to Principal Sudmersen and told him what happened. Sudmersen listened to the details of the fight and asked, "Who won?" The students did not know what to say because if they said 'we won' that would mean admitting they beat up Sudmersen's fellow country men, and if they said 'the English won' that would mean admitting defeat. They did not know what Principal Sudmersen would like to hear. As the students were looking at each other figuring out what to say, Principal

Sudmersen was getting impatient and repeated several time "tell me , who won". Finally, Parasuram said, "To tell you the truth Sir, we won,". To their surprise, Sudmersen was happy to hear that. "Good. If you won, then don't worry, I will take care of everything. In future try to avoid fighting but if you fight make sure you win." In those days, the Police never dared to enter the Cotton College campus. The Police authority sent the Englishmen to get permission from Principal Sudmersen to enter the College. The Englishmen did come to Principal Sudmersen and asked permission to find and arrest the culprits. They had to go away disappointed because Principal Sudmersen asserted that his students would never pick a fight without a good reason.

Sudmersen's Pea Cultivation

Principal Sudmersen used to be very fond of having a vegetable garden. This went well with the Assamese residents of Gauhati because the Assamese people, living in Gauhati those days, were also in the habit of growing vegetables at home —that healthy habit was perhaps because most of them had moved there from their villages. However, Principal Sudmersen differed from the Assamese in one respect. Every year he would grow some pea plants and tend them with the utmost of care. His pea plants would produce abundant jolly green giant type of peas but Principal Sudmersen would never harvest the peas or eat them. He would let them wilt and rot on the plant or on the ground. He would not pick a single one. Principal Sudmersen never told anybody why he did so, nor did anybody dare to ask him about it.

One year a senior student could not resist the temptation of picking Sudmersen's peas. He persuaded some of his friends to go with him at night and they picked one and all the peas from Sudmersen's garden. The next morning, when Principal Sudmersen found out what happened to his peas, he was dumbfounded. He went to the College looking very grim and mad. He sat in his office for hours without talking or saying anything to anybody. Soon the words got around among the teachers and the students as to what had happened. Nobody knew who did it and what to do about it. Finally, seeing the agony of Principal Sudmersen, the leader of the culprits, Mahendranath Deka Phukan, went to the Principal's office and apologetically but boldly told him, "Sir, I am the person who stole the peas from your garden. I know that every year you grow peas but do not harvest them. That's why this year I persuaded some of my friends to go with me and we picked the peas so that they would not just rot away." Principal Sudmersen looked in his eyes and said, "What did you say?" The student repeated what he had said. Principal Sudmersen asked the student to leave and wait outside.

The student waited and waited for a long one hour. When he was called in, he saw that Principal Sudmersen was leaning with his elbows on the table, his head resting on the palms of his hands, and tears were rolling down his cheeks uncontrollably. Perhaps the Principal was crying all the while the student was waiting outside. Asking the student to sit down, Principal Sudmersen told him in a soft voice, "You are really a brave young man. You know, we had a son who died in an accident here. He was a wonderful little boy and we loved him dearly. He used to be very fond of eating fresh peas on the pod. That is why, every year we plant peas in his memory. We never touch or eat those peas. Nobody ever touched them. This year you picked them. I am glad that you had the courage to come and tell me. Perhaps, my son would have done the same thing. What is more, if my son was alive, by now he would have been a young man like you." The student felt very sad and with tears down his eyes touched the venerable Principal's feet as was the Assamese custom of asking forgiveness from an older person. Principal Sudmersen raised him and embraced him like his own son and the two parted happily.

Like Principal Sudmersen, Mr. Mahendranath Deka Phukan carved for himself a place in the annals of Cotton College by designing the beautiful Cotton College emblem in 1933.

We conclude this section with the message that Principal Sudmersen had sent to the Cotton College Golden Jubilee Celebration Committee from Sussex on May 26, 1951.

> The principles which guided its past must guide its future. Avoiding all narrowness of thought or class or creed with charity towards all, let students and staff remember that education is only of value as it leads to greater service to mankind, that narrowly pursued it produces but Dead sea fruit of disappointment and embitterment. (*CCC*, 16).

Even though Principal Sudmersen sent that message to the staff and students of Cotton College, the noble motto that *education is only of value if it leads to greater service to mankind* has a message for teachers, students and parents all over the world. It is with such noble ideals that Principal Sudmersen had succeeded in welding the students of northeastern India, who were of mixed descent—Assamese, Bengalis, Manipuri, Nagas, Khasis and many other groups from the hills and plains of Assam—into a well-disciplined but happy family.

To learn what is ailing this happy family now, we refer the reader to

Sanjib Baruah, *India Against Itself: Assam and the Politics of Nationality*, University of Pennsylvania Press, Philadelphia, 1991.

F. The Non-Cooperation Movement

Indians in general and, Indian soldiers in particular, rendered invaluable service to the British empire during the First World War (1914 - 1918). In return and when the war ended, the Indians were expecting some concessions towards self-rule. The British concessions came in the form of the Government of India Act of 1919, which came into operation early in 1921. Though the Act provided for elected legislative assembly and some role in the Government, the provisions of the act fell far short of Indian expectations. Indian leaders also doubted the sincerity of the British Government because in the same year (1919), the Government also passed the Rowlatt Act, which sought to perpetuate the extraordinary repressive powers of the Government given during the war. The repressive measures included the power to do away with ordinary legal procedures, the power to imprison without trial, and the power to use other coercive measures.

The intentions of the British Government expressed itself also in the Jalinwalla Bagh massacre. On April 13, 1919 a British General killed 379 and wounded 1,200 unarmed Indians including a large number of women and children who were holding a meeting. What is more, the firing came without any warning as graphically portrayed in the award winning movie 'Gandhi'. There was a big outcry all over the country. The Government restored order by applying the Rowlatt Act in full force with a heavy hand. There was a short lull and the British Government thought that they had saved India from revolution, but in reality it succeeded in hastening the end of the British rule in India. It thrust Gandhi, who had returned from South Africa, as the leader of the Indians and gave birth to the Non-cooperation movement.

The Congress Party held a special session in Calcutta in September 1920 to discuss those Acts of 1919. During that session and under the leadership of Gandhi, the Congress party adopted the famous resolution of Non-cooperation movement. The Non-Cooperation movement called for: (i) renunciation of government titles, (ii) boycotting of the legislatures, law-courts and government educational institutions., and (iii) non-payment of taxes. The Indian National Congress also redefined its goal as 'the attainment of self-rule within the Empire, if possible, without, if necessary.'

Swami Vivekananda in Chicago, 1893

Courtesy: Advaita Ashram, Calcutta

The Non-cooperation movement received overwhelming support from the Indian masses and two-thirds of the voters abstained from taking part in the election to the legislative councils held in November 1920. Emboldened the Congress Party formally adopted the Non co-operation resolution at its annual session at Nagpur in December, 1920. So, since 1921 the Non-cooperation movement became the main tool in India's struggle for freedom. A large number of students came out of schools and colleges, many lawyers gave up their practices, and many teachers and government employees gave up their posts. A mighty wave of mass demonstrations, strikes, unrest and rioting rocked every corner of India. Again, the British government tried to suppress the movement with a heavy hand and in some places mobs resorted to violence.

Disturbed by the violence, Gandhi temporarily suspended the movement for a while. But, in a self-destructive act, the British Government arrested Gandhi and sentenced him to six years' imprisonment (he was released after two years in 1924). The Non-cooperation movement continued in some form or other till India gained independence in 1947.

G. Swami Vivekananda's Meeting with Sir Henry Cotton

On April 5, 1901 Swami Vivekananda, accompanied by his mother and few of his disciple went to visit the Kamakhya temple at Gauhati. They came there from Chittagong and on their way spent a few days at Goalpara.

> "Both at Dacca and at Kamakhya, Swami's health went from bad to worse. He decided to go to the delightful hill-station of Shillong, where the air is drier. It was thought that his health might improve there. Shillong was then the seat of the Assam Government, and the late Sir Henry Cotton, a champion of the cause of India , was the Chief Commissioner. He had heard much of Swami Vivekananda and was anxious to meet him. At his request Swami delivered a lecture before the resident English officials and a large gathering of Indians. Later, Sir Henry Cotton, who had very much liked the Swami's speech, visited the latter, exchanged greetings with him, and spent some time discussing India and her national problems. Seeing that the Swami was ill, he instructed the Civil Surgeon to render him all possible medical aid. Throughout the Swami's stay, the Chief Commissioner daily made enquiries about his health. The Swami spoke of him as a man who understood India's needs and aspirations, was working nobly for her cause, and deserved the love of the Indian people."
>
> Speaking about his Shillong visit to Sharatchandra Chakravarty, the Swami said: "The Shillong hills are very beautiful. There, I met

Sir Henry Cotton, the Chief Commissioner of Assam. He asked me, 'Swamiji, after travelling through Europe and America, what have you come to see here in these distant hills?' Such a good and kind-hearted man, such as Sir Henry Cotton, is rarely found. Hearing of my illness, he sent the Civil Surgeon and inquired about my health mornings and evenings. I could not do much lecturing there, because my health was very bad. On the way, Nitai served and looked after me nicely." [LSV]

According to Swami Vivekananda, Henry Cotton was a man who understood India's needs and aspirations. Swami Vivekananda also emphasized that Henry Cotton deserved the love of the Indian people. Swami Vivekananda breathed his last in Calcutta on July 4, 1902, a few months after his return from Assam. This glowing tribute by a great personality like Swami Vivekananda tells more about Sir Henry Cotton than any body can describe.

Glossary

Abor (or Adi): name of a tribe in northeastern India. Since this was a name given by the Assamese which the tribe did not like, they are now called Adi.

Advaita (Non-duality): A school of Vedanta philosophy which advocates that in the Absolute Reality there is not the slightest touch of dualism. The Oneness of All Beings is central to Advaita philosophy. In the words of Vivekanada, "In whom is the Universe, Who is in the Universe, Who is the Universe; in whom is the Soul, Who is in the Soul, Who is the Soul of man; knowing Him, and therefore the Universe, as our Soul, alone extinguishes all fear, brings an end to misery and leads to infinite freedom."

Ahom: A section of the Shan tribe who entered Assam in the thirteenth century and ruled Assam till the advent of the British in the early part of the nineteenth century.

Angad: Son of Bali and Tara.

Anna: One sixteenth of the British Indian currency rupee. It has now been replaced by naya paisa.

Arjuna: The third of the five brothers of the Pandava clan, The epic *Mahabharata* narrates the lives and struggles of the Pandavas. Lord Krishna first narrated the Bhagavad Gita to Arjuna.

Avatar: A descent or incarnation of Lord Vishnu. Since mortals have to be the judges of who is an avatar and who is not, there are many avatars depending upon whom you ask or trust.

Ayah: A female servant.

Baba: Baba literally means 'father', the word is perhaps of Mideastern origin. Indians have the habit of addressing their baby as a father (Baba) that is why there is a mistaken belief that the word comes from the English word 'baby'.

Babu (or Baboo): A term one applies to one's superiors. So, they apply the term babu to anybody who can serve them as a babu. It is added to the name of a person as a mark of respect, thus Dondi babu. The British used it to mean a native clerk or to a man employed by them to do work other than menial work.

Bacshish: In a way it means tip, but with a big difference—in America, one expects a tip for a service rendered. However in India, some people expect bacshish for anything like standing near you or looking at you.

Bahatia: Laborer.

Baisakh: The first month of Indian calendar. Usually begins on the 14th of April.

Bali: Powerful king of Kishkindha, whose heroics are described in the *Ramayana.* Bali was killed by Rama.

Bazar (or Bazaar): A market. A Street lined with shops, stalls or vendors. A fair at which miscellaneous items are sold.

Bhagavatam *(or Srimad Bhagavatam):* A popular Hindu scripture that tells the stories of all the incarnations of Lord Vishnu. ISKCON publishes a complete set of the Bhagavatam with translations in English and many other languages.

Bhagadatta: Powerful king of Kamrupa (which embraced present Assam) mentioned in the *Mahabharata.*

Bhaji: Spiced vegetable medley.

Bhamo: A town in Burma where a large number of Assamese, taken prisoners by the Burmese in the early part of the nineteenth century, had settled.

Bharat: The ancient name of India, name of an Aryan tribe, the name of a prince mentioned in Kalidas's immortal play *Abhigyanam Shakuntola,* the name of a brother of Rama. As told in the epic *Ramayana* , Rama and Bharata were both sons of king Dasaratha but from different mothers. Bharata's mother was able to persuade Dasaratha to name Bharata as his successor instead of the elder brother Rama whom the king had to exile for fourteen years. After Rama set out to carry on his father's wishes, king Dasaratha died. All these things happened while Bharata was away from the capital. When Bharata returned, he was furious that his mother would make such an unjust arrangement. Bharata refused to sit on the throne. Instead, he went to persuade Rama to come back and be the king. Rama refused since he could not disobey his father's orders. Disheartened, Bharata brought a pair of Rama's wooden sandal, set it on the throne, and ruled the kingdom as an emissary of Rama. Rama returned after fourteen years and Bharata set Rama as the king.

Bhisma: The name of a famous bachelor prince of ancient India and a central figure in the epic *Mahabharata.* The word bhisma means one who undertakes a difficult vow and fulfils it. To assure a maiden that if she married his father then her son would be the king instead of him, prince Bhisma had taken the vow, "I shall never marry and I dedicate myself to a life of unbroken chastity". Bhisma, though admired, is not accepted as a role model by Indian youths.

Bhismak: A king of the ancient kingdom of Videha. It is believed that Videha was situated in what is now Assam. In any case, Bhismak's daughter Rukmini was one of the favorite wives of Lord Krishna.

Bihari: A person who hails from the Indian state of Bihar.

Bisa: Name of a village in the mountains of northeastern India.

Bootan (or Bhutan): An independent kingdom on the foothills of the Himalayan mountain. It is on the north western side of Assam.

Brahma: Hindu God of Creation.

Brahmin: A man belonging to the priest class of Hindus.

BT : Bachelor of Teaching.

Burha Gohain: The chief minister of a Ahom king.

Coolie: A person who earns his livelihood by doing menial work. The word perhaps originated from the Kols. When the Kols were deprived of their natural habitat and their nomadic way of living, they had no choice but to live by performing menial work. The British rounded up the Kols and other poor people whenever they needed unskilled laborers. That was also the case when the British Government started the tea-industry in Assam. However, all coolies are not Kols. The term is often used in a derogatory manner. Thus, many Englishmen referred to Mahatma Gandhi as the 'Coolie Barrister' and Sir Henry Cotton as a 'Protector of Dumb Coolies'. Civil tongues do not use the term 'coolie' but take help of such terms as tea-garden laborer, porter, etc.

Chira: Cereal made of a certain kind of rice.

DPI : Director of Public Instruction

DSP: Deputy Superintendent of Police.

Dangars: A tribe from central India.

Dharma (Dhamma): means righteous duty that one must perform to find ultimate union with the Great Soul. Of course, Hindu scripture lays out some rules about an individual's dharma. Originally, when the Hindu society was divided into four major castes, Dharma was laid out for each caste. In the modern society that kind of dharma is not pertinent. However, the basic principle remains—whatever you do must be rightful according to the laws of the land and according to the ethics of the profession one chooses; no matter what profession one adopts it is one's righteous duty (dharma) to render one's services with heart and soul. Dharma is to do what is beneficial to the individual, to the family, to the society and to the world as a whole. This way one can make one's life spiritual. This doctrine of dharma is very much against the capitalist idea of 'profit' or 'money'. Of course, many say that with money you can do good to others and the world—but, how many can transform that 'profit motive' or 'greed for money' to a love for services to benefit others?

Dheki: A huge hammer like device used by the Assamese to thatch rice from its husk. In old days, usually girls or younger women operated the dheki because it was supposed to make their back and legs strong. The movement required to operate a dheki is very much like what is needed to exercise on the modern mechanical device known as a stepper. The dheki has virtually disappeared from Assamese villages because of the modern rice mills, where people can easily thatch their rice. This has proved beneficial to the doctors because constant back ache together with painful child-births have become rampant among the Assamese ladies.

Dhekia: The green vegetable known as fiddle-head. It grows by itself all over Assam and is easily available everywhere. It is not necessary to buy them since one can walk outside and pick it. In towns and cities, villagers bring and sell them very cheap. So, in Assam it is considered a poor man's food but in the west, where it is difficult to find, fiddle-head is very expensive and is considered a delicacy that only the rich can afford. In any case, it is a very healthy green with many beneficial ingredients that are not found in other vegetables.

Dhekia khoa Namghar: Literally means the village prayer-house where (he) ate dhekia—'he' here refers to saint Madhabdev, the chief disciple of Sankardev, who had a meal here of rice and dhekia after he was released by the Ahom king.

Dhoti: Loose loin cloth worn by Indian male, very comfortable in hot climate but not as comfortable as a short. However, it hides anything ugly on one's legs better than a short.

Digaru: A tribe of northeast India; the name of a river and of a town in Assam.

Dravidian: A large family of languages including Tamil, Telegu, Malayalam and Kanarese spoken mainly in southern India, Singapore and northern Ceylon—these languages are very different from the Sanskritic languages; a member of any of the peoples that speak one of the Dravidian languages. It is believed that Dravidian people lived all over India before the advent of the Aryans. Dravidians have physical features that are different from other Indians. They also have social and cultural traits that are different from those of other Indians. In spite of these differences in modern times the Dravidians seem to have the same propensity for corruption as those possessed by other Indians. Nowadays, power or wealth seem to corrupt all Indians, Dravidians and Aryans alike.

Eri: A strong and durable raw silk produced in Assam. Eri is regarded as the second best silk in the world. The eri threads and clothes made of eri silk are very durable. Shawls made with eri clothes are very popular in Assam because of their warmth and durability.

Eri kapur: Shawl made of eri silk.

Gamocha: Cloth to wipe one's body, so an Assamese towel made of thin cotton, usually hand oven .

Ghat: A river dockyard for boats.

Goot (or got): *see paik*

Gurkha: An ethnic group predominant in Nepal. They are known to make good soldiers and very faithful security guards.

Guwahati (or Gauhati or Gowahatty): Biggest city in Assam. Dispur, the capital of Assam, is actually a part of Gauhati.

Havildar: A police or army Sergent.

Hindustani: A language of northern India that is a mixture of Hindi and Urdu. Hindi is the national language of India, and Urdu is the national language of Pakistan.

Hirimba: A wife of the Pandava prince Bhima.

Hironyakashipu: An atheist monarch of ancient India, slain by the Lion-man (Narasingha) incarnation of Vishnu.

Hironyakshya: A brother of Hironyakashipu slain by the Boar (Baraha) incarnation of Vishnu.

Hooka: An Assamese smoking pipe designed with a wooden or bamboo pipe set on a coconut shell containing water which cools the smoke and absorbs some of its bad gases.

Howri (or Hori): A name of Lord Krishna.

Jingsha: A village near Sadiya.

Kakoti: The Ahom kings used to appoint learned people as clerks or writers and conferred upon them the title of Kakoti. After the dissolution of the Ahom rule, it became a surname that one inherited from ones father. So a Kakoti nowadays is not necessarily learned.

Kalita: A surname in Assamese. Many claim that Kalita was a distinct ethnic group who once had a separate kingdom that was destroyed by a great flood. Kalitas, like many other Assamese groups, think they are superior to the others.

Kamrupa: An old kingdom containing a large chunk of India's northeast. Nowadays, it is the name of a small district of Assam.

Karma: Action or work. Karma means a deed performed according to some guiding principle. The guiding principle may differ according to one's religion, personal beliefs or convictions but in the Hindu context, the guiding principle comes from the common premises of Hindu philosophy. The following premises are very important:

1) Every living being is an indestructible soul which guides the body (including the subtle body called mind) to perform karma.

2) A soul by itself cannot perform any karma, only the body can do so—the soul like the charioteer of Arjuna in the battlefield of Kurukshetra can simply provide the guiding principle.

3) The soul needs to link with the Great Soul, the reservoir of all things both material and spiritual. The Great Soul exists in a state of ultimate goodness,

supreme consciousness and in eternal tranquility (this is called Sat-cit-anand in Sanskrit). Hindus do not know how or why the individual souls separated from the Great Soul but they accept the fact that each individual soul needs to get back and ultimately find union with its source the Great Soul.

4) Yoga literally means 'linking', linking with the Great Soul. That linking is possible among others through pursuit of knowledge (Jnan-yoga), through devotional activity (Bhakti-yoga) and through good karma (Karma-yoga).

5) A karma is good if its goal is spiritual (meaning the goal is to link with the Great Soul) and it does not seek any physical or material gain. A good karma is therefore, unselfish, non-violent and beneficial to others. Simply speaking, a good karma helps the soul that guides it to link with the Great Soul. A bad karma is just the opposite — it moves the soul that is dwelling in the body away from its ultimate union. A bad karma is marked by selfishness, hatred, violence and harm to others. A good karma inspires others to do good karma.

As a matter of fact, William Griffith, Nathan and Eliza Brown, Henry Cotton, Frederick Sudmersen, Silmon and Ward all performed good karma even though they were not Hindus. Their good karma inspired others, especially native Hindus, to perform good karma. Above all they showed to the people who came in contact with them some avenues of good karma which were not known or were not shown by the Hindu pundits.

Kayastha: A caste in Assam. Many Kayasthas, like the Kalitas, think they are superior to the others. Other Assamese believe neither the Kayasthas nor the Kalitas.

Khamti: A tribe of northeast India. Before the advent of the British, they occupied a large number of hills at the head of the Assam valley. The word Khamti perhaps came from Kamtai, which suggests their connection with tai's or the Shans.

Khasiyah (or Khasi): A tribe of Meghalaya in northeast India. It is believed that the Khasis are a remnant of the first Mongolian overflow into the northeast. Their language is very different and they still maintain a matriarchal type of society—property is inherited by the female and after marriage the husband goes and lives in his bride's house, if she has one. This, of course, gives the wife a right to kick out her husband when she wants— many women of modern India wish they had this set up.

Khirododhi: Sea of milk. The ancient Indians believed that there were seven seas in the world and one of them was the sea of milk. It was perhaps a wishful thought because milk was not easily available in ancient India—why it was so, please take a look at an Indian cow.

Kirtana: Assamese prayer book composed by Sankardev. Each prayer of the Kirtana narrates a story from the incarnations of Lord Vishnu based mostly on *Srimad Bhagavatam*, but composed in beautiful concise form making them very suitable for congregational chanting.

Koch: A caste in Assam, member of the Koch caste. Koches are a mixture of Aryan and non-Aryan tribes.

Kochari: A non-Aryan tribe of northeast India. It is believed that the Kocharis were the earliest known inhabitants of Assam. They are closely allied to Koches, Bodos, Chutiyahs, Lalungs, Morans and many other tribes of Assam. It seems probable that at one time the major part of Assam was part of a great Kochari (or some closely allied tribe) kingdom. It is also probable that in modern times, it will be difficult to find an Assamese without any trace of Kochari blood.

Kokilamukh: A small village near Jorhat.

Kols: A primitive but non-Aryan and non-Dravidian tribe living in the hills and the jungles of central India. A large number of them were brought to Assam to work in the tea-plantations.

Krishna: Perhaps the most popular incarnation of Vishnu.

Lama: A Tibetan word meaning a superior person, so a Buddhist monk or teacher.

Lakshmi: The goddess of wealth and well-being.

Luci: Deep fried (usually in purified butter fat, called ghee) rolled white flour bread—it is usually regarded as excellent if it is round and puffy. It is called a poorie if the dough is made of wheat flour and fried in inexpensive oil. Whole wheat flour and oil being cheaper, poorie is used to be the poor man's choice. However, the word poorie has nothing to do with the English word 'poor'.

Mahabharata: One of the two great epics of the Hindus. The Mahabharata describes the fight between two ruling clans of ancient India. It is a great source for ancient character, religion and culture.

Makum: A town in northeast India.

Manu: The name of an ancient Hindu sage who prepared the code of conduct for the Hindus. The word literally means 'man'.

Marwari: A person who hails from Marwar, a district in the central Indian state of Rajasthan.

Matak: An Ahom word meaning strong, an adjective applied to strong subjects of the Ahom kingdom; it also referred to the region controlled by the Bor Senapati during the later part of the Ahom rule because the invading forces, including the British, found the army of this region hard to defeat.

Mauzadar(or Mouzahdar)**:** Mauza means a county or a small area of a district and a mauzadar is a person assigned to collect taxes. A mauzadar is not usually a paid officer of the government but keeps a certain percent of the taxes collected.

Mekhala: The bottom portion of an Assamese woman's three piece dress. Assamese women usually wear a three piece dress. A blouse, a mekhala both of which are partially covered by a light weight chadar. The chadar is much narrower and much shorter than a sari. The chadar is usually made of cotton but for formal occasion, the females usually wear a chadar made of silk, The mekhala is usually made of a durable golden Assamese silk called muga silk. Mekhalas made of heavier cotton with solid colors are also popular.

Mem Sahib: Lady, from 'madam sahib'.

Meru mountain: A mountain around which the Sun was supposed to revolve.

Miri (or Mising): A tribe of northeastern India, a large number of them live in Assam. Members of this tribe also do not like the name Miri which was given by the Assamese. So, they identify themselves as Mising.

Mishimi: A tribe of northeastern India.

Mizho: A tribe of northeastern India. Now there is a separate state called Mizoram.

Moffassil: Places remote from the head-quarters, up country, the provinces.

Mogoung: A region bordering Assam and Burma.

Mohan Bagan: A soccer team of Calcutta.

Moonsif: Judge of a district court.

Munshi: Interpreter or language teacher, especially of the Persian or the Arabic language.

Muri: Rice crispy.

Nabob (Nawab): A ruler of a province under the Muslim emperors of India.

Naga: The collective designation given by the Assamese to the people of Nagaland. The Nagas belong to a diversity of tribes of Mongolian descent. Each Naga tribe speaks its own language and identifies itself with a distinctive name.

Nalanda: A town in South Bihar, famous for its Buddhist university that was flourishing during the Gupta period (320 – 495 A.D.).

Namghar: A house for chanting; in addition to congregational chanting, a Namghar is the center of community activities in an Assamese village.

Narasingha (Man-lion or Lion-man): An incarnation of Vishnu as half-man and half-lion. He assumed this form to slay Hiranyakashipu.

Narayana: A name of Lord Vishnu.

Orunudoi: First Assamese news magazine. The American Baptist Missionaries started publishing it in 1846. The first editor, except for a few copies in the beginning, was Nathan Brown, who edited it for ten years.

Paik: During the Ahom rule, the whole male population between the ages of fifteen and fifty were liable to render service to the State. They were known as paiks, or foot soldiers, a term which was formerly very common in Bengal where, for instance, it was applied to the guards who surrounded the palace of the independent Mohammedan kings. The paiks were organized into small groups called 'goots'. A goot originally contained four paiks, but in the reign of Rajeswar Singh the number was reduced to three in Upper Assam; one member of each goot was obliged to be present, in rotation for such work as might be required of him, and, during his absence from home, the other members were expected to cultivate his land and keep him supplied with food. In times of peace, it was the custom to employ the paiks on public works. That is how the enormous tanks and the high embanked roads of Upper Assam came into existence. When war broke out, two members of a 'goot,' or even three might be called on to attend at the same time. The nobles, priests and persons of high caste and their slaves were exempt from that service.

Pragjyotish: The ancient name of Guwahati.

Prasadam: Food offered to the Gods. Hindus offer food to their deity before any ritual of worship or congregational prayer. Of course, at the end those who pray eat the prasadam.

Pukhuri: Man-made tank or reservoir for water.

Puranas: are ancient Hindu scriptures containing stories and legends of Gods, kings, sages and heroes of yonder years. There are six puranas devoted to Lord Vishnu, six devoted to Lord Brahma and six to Lord Shiva accounting for eighteen major puranas. Of these the Bhagavat purana describing the glories of Lord Vishnu and his avatars is perhaps the most prolific. It is believed that the puranas were developed to explain the teachings of the Vedas

Ram (or Rama): King of Ayodha in north India, an incarnation of Vishnu.

Ram-Bol-Howrie: Assamese Hindu prayer intoning God Ram.

Ram-Krishna-Prabhu: Assamese Hindu prayer intoning God Ram and Krishna.

Ramakrishna Poromhonsa (1836-1888): was a self realized ascetic who had realized the Truth about God. Swami Vivekananda accepted Swami Ramakrishna's guidance and help. After Ramakrishna's death Swami Vivekananda set out to spread the teachings of his master all over the world.

Ramāyana: The great Indian epic describing the life story of Ram, who was an incarnation of Vishnu born as a king. A great epic that beautifully brings out what is noble in the world.

Ronga: A common name of Assamese male. 'Ronga ' means red in Assamese.

Rungagara: A village in northeast India near Sadiya.

Rupee: Indian unit of currency.

Ryot: Tenant, a subject, a farmer because he is a tenant of the state and the land belongs to the state

Sadhu: Literally means one who seeks knowledge (or God) with dedication and right earnest. A holy man, a scholar of humble means and nature.

Sadiya: A town in northeast India.

Sahib: Sir, formerly applied to Europeans only, nowadays applied to anybody wearing a tie and a jacket, however dirty; also, affixed rank, thus 'Collector Sahib'

Sanaton Dharma: Another name for Hinduism, it literally means eternal righteousness.

Sandah: Cooked powdered rice, a favorite snack of Assamese villagers—town-folks avoid it because of its laxative power.

Sankardeva (1449-1569): A great Vaishnab leader of Assam. He was an all-round genius—a great scholar, a musical virtuoso, and a social organizer. His life and work made the Assamese what they are today and his impact is seen on every aspect of Assamese culture.

Sarai: An Assamese serving utensil made of brass or other alloy. The sarai is usually used to put offerings to a deity. It is also used to show deep respect to a deserving person. A sarai always carries a message of utmost respect that a person or a congregation can show.

Satyabrata: A pious king of ancient India.

Senapati: Commander-in-Chief.

Sepoy: The word means a soldier. For some reason, the British gave this name to native soldiers they trained to serve in the British army while every white soldier was given the rank of an officer. However, that was not the only reason why the sepoys rebelled against the British in 1857—the British called it the Sepoy Mutiny. The Indians like to call it a fight for Independence.

Shans: Shans form a group of Mongoloid tribes living in southern China, Thailand, Burma and parts of Assam.

Shan Sukapha: The chief of the Ahoms who first entered Assam and established the Ahom kingdom. Sukapha showed both dexterity and wisdom as a nation builder.

Sib (or Siba or Siva or Shiva): One of the Hindu Trinity of Brahma, Vishnu, and Siva, the destroyer of the universe.

Singpho: A tribe who once lived on the border tracts between Assam and Burma. They were very powerful in the early part of the nineteenth century and gave the British a lot of trouble. After subjugating them, the British offered them friendship by treating them with opium. The Singphos enjoyed British friendship and opium so much that after hundred years they just about became extinct.

Slate-house: The name given by Eliza Brown to the first school she set up in Assam to impress upon the students that they had to come there with their slates and clay pencils.

Sraddha: literally means an act to pay homage. It usually refers to the ceremony one performs to honor the dead. Sraddha is a common Hindu ceremony and every household performs an annual sraddha ceremony for each of the dead parent. Remembering and paying homage to one's forefathers is in the heart of Hindu culture and traditions.

Sudra: A name the Aryans gave to the original inhabitants of India.

Supahi: The petal of a flower, a popular female name in Assamese.

Swami: A religious or a spiritual perceptor of the highest order.

Swamiji: Respected Swami.

Sylhet: A town in old Assam but now part of Bangladesh.

Tara: Bali's wife. Tara remains one of the revered role models for Indian women.

Tingrai: A town in Northeast India.

Tortoise: An incarnation of Vishnu.

Upanisad: (See Vedas)

Upper Assam: The eastern part of Assam.

Vaishnab(or Vaishnav): One who believes in Vishnu as the Supreme Being. Vaishnabs worship Vishnu and his incarnations.

Vedas: are the sacred books of India. They are the earliest known literature of the human race. Veda means what is known, accordingly Vedas do not refer to particular book or books but the literature of a period extending over hundreds of years. This literature is classified into four different types from the point of age, language and subject matter. These four types are: Samhitas (or collection of verses), Brahmanas, Aranyakas and the Upanisads. There are four Samhitas: Rig Veda, Sama Veda, Yajur Veda and Atharva Veda. (In a limited sense, people refer to the four Samhitas as Vedas.) The Brahmanas are written in prose and explain the sacred significance of different rituals. The Aranyakas (or forest treatises) are meant for old people who retire to the forest and are unable to perform elaborate rituals. The Aranyakas are attached to the Brahmanas as appendices. The Upanisads develop the germs of all philosophic speculations of the Samhitas. The word upanisad means 'sitting near devotedly' and are perhaps the careful notes of pupil who learned the material sitting devotedly near the sages and original thinkers of ancient India. The Upanisads are attached as appendices to the Aranyakas. In any case, the upanisads are essentially the source of all Hindu thought.

Vedanta: means 'the concluding part of the Vedas' and as such it refers to the Upanisads. The Vedas dictated the path of karma. They contained commandments to perform certain actions and prohibitions against certain others (nisedha). The Upanisads dictate the path of knowledge (jnamarga: pronounced gyanamarga). It is believed that there were many Upanisads but only one hundred and eight survived. Of the surviving Upanisads the following are the most notable: Brhadaranyaka, Chandogya, Aitreya, Isha, Kena, Katha, Prasna, Mundaka, Mandukya, Taittriya, Kaivalya and Svetasvatara. Because of the diversities of the authors and the interpretors, the knowledge of the Upanisads are not organized in a systematic manner. Sankara (788 – 820 A.D.) is credited with giving a coherent and unified theory. Sankara's system is known as advaita (or non-dualism).

Other systems based on the Upanisads include Dvaita (dualism) of Madhava and Visishta-adaita (qualified monotheism) of Ramanuja. The term Vedanta philosophy is applied to mean any one of these systems of thought derived from the Upanisads.

Vishnu: One of the Hindu Trinity of Brahma, Vishnu, and Siva; the preserver of the universe.

Vivekananda (1863 - 1902): The greatest exponent of the Vedanta philosophy and the star of the Chicago Parliament of Religion of 1893, was perhaps one of the most influential persons of his time. During his brief life, Swami Vivekananda brought new wisdom and enlightenment to the world for all days to come. He was born on January 12, 1863 in Calcutta. His father Viswanath Datta was a successful lawyer. His mother Bhubaneswari Datta possessed a very sweet voice and rejoiced in singing the songs about Lord Krishna. After graduating from Calcutta University, he became a disciple of Swami Ramakrishna. After the death of Ramakrishna in 1888, Narendranath took the leadership to bring together all the disciples of the Master and to organize them so that they could spread the teachings of Swami Ramakrishna. That brought him to the USA where he started the Vedanta societies. The first Vedanta Society was formed by Swami Vivekananda in New York on November 4, 1894. Soon afterwards, his followers established branches of Vedanta Society in various parts of America.

Yajna: means a sacrifice, a devotional act that requires sacrifice. The sacrifice may be material, emotional or spiritual. Material sacrifice may be a donation of money, a cow, a plot of land and so on; emotional sacrifice may be crying, remembering, abstinence from sensual activities, and so on; spiritual sacrifice may be in the form of fasting, praying, worshipping and so on. The purpose of a yajna is not personal gain of any kind but an act that is for the good of others or for the good of whole mankind and the world we live in. Often people sacrifice an animal in the name of a yajna and then eat its meat as a blessed food called prasadam. Many Hindus still seek nirvana by performing this kind of ghastly acts of animal sacrifice—which in the true sense of the term is no sacrifice at all. This kind of violent rituals is one of the reasons that compelled Buddha to seek better avenues of nirvana.

Bibliography

1. Charles Allen, *A Mountain in Tibet*, Futura Publications, 1983, London [contains a lively account of the early British adventurers in the Northeast region of India] [AMT]

2. The American Baptist Missionary Union, The Assam Mission of The American Baptist Missionary Union: Papers and Discussions of the Jubilee Conference held in Nowgong, December 18 - 29, 1886. [ABM]

3. Sanjib Baruah, *India Against Itself: Assam and the Politics of Nationality*, University of Pennsylvania Press, Philadelphia, 1991.

4. S.K. Bhuyan, *Anglo-Assamese Relations*, Department of Historical and Antiquarian Studies in Assam, Gauhati(1949)] [AAR]

5. S.K. Bhuyan (Ed.), *Asomar Padya Buranj,* Department of Historical and Antiquarian Studies in Assam, Gauhati(1964)] [APB]

6. *Bronson Papers*, Andover Newton Theological College Library. [BP]

7. Elizabeth Brown, *The Whole World Kin*, Hubbard Brothers, Philadelphia, 1890 [WWK]

8. Nathan Brown, Grammatical Notices of the Assamese Language, 1848.[GNA]

9. Maj. John Butler, *Travels and Adventures in the Province of Assam* (1855), Reprinted by Vĭvek Publishing Company, Delhi, 1978.[TAA]

10. Sir Henry Cotton, *New India or India in Transition*, Kegan Paul, Trench, Trübner, & Co., London, 1907. [NIT]

11. Sir Henry Cotton, *Indian and Home Memories,* T. Fisher Unwin, London, 1911. [IHM]

12. Cotton College Centenary Celebration Committee, *Cotton College Centenary Volume*, 2001 [CCC]

13. K. S. Deka, *(ed.), Abhinandan Grantha Sri Chidananda Das*, published by Madhumita Das, Guwahati, 1999[AGC]

14. F.S. Downs, *The Mighty Works of God*, Christian Literature Centre, Gauhati, India, 1969.

15. H.B. Gunn, *In a Far Country: A Story of Christian Heroism and Achievement*, American Baptist Publication Society, Philadelphia, 1912.

16. E. Gait, *A History of Assam* (1902), Reprinted by LBS Publishers, Guwahati, 1981. [HA]

17. His Eastern and Western disciples, *The Life of Swami Vivekananda*, Revised and Enlarged Volume II, Advaita Ashrama, Calcutta, Fifth Edition, 1981. [LSV]

18. J.B. College, Golden Jubilee Commemorative Volume, 1982. [JBG]

19. Haren Kalita, *Guwahati Biswabidyalayar Samu Avas*, Gauhati University, 1958. [GB]

20. John M'Clelland, *Journals of Travels in Assam, Burma, Bootan, Afghanistan and the neighboring Countries*, arranged by Bishop's College Press, Calcutta, 1847, Reprinted by Ch'eng Wen Publishing Company, Taipei, 1971 [JTA]

21. Moffat Mills, A.J., *Report on the Province of Assam*, (1854), Publication Board, Assam Government, Guwahati, 1984[Mill's Report]

22. *Notice of William Griffith*, Proceedings of the Linnaen Society, No. xxv, 1845

23. Nanda Talukdar, *Surya Kumar Bhuyan*, Pragjyotish Granthamala, Gauhati, 1984. [SKB]

Index

About The Author

Dilip K. Datta, a professor of mathematics at University of Rhode Island, is an academician with varied interests. He is a native of Assam, in northeastern India, but his academic pursuits have taken him all over the world.

Prof. Datta is the author of the highly acclaimed *Math Education At Its Best: The Potsdam Model,* about which Professor Ken Ross, a former President of the Mathematical Association of America wrote to him, "Thanks for putting this book together. You've done us all a service." With the present book, Prof. Datta has done us all a service by bringing out some tales about the positive fusion of the East and the West. He has also authored several books in the Assamese language.